Best wishes

And sometimes, the dog was busy!

Careering around the lower leagues.

by
Fergus Moore & Roger Slater

Best Wishes

Roger Slater

This edition published by CAMS
This edition © copyright Fergus Moore & Roger Slater
Copyright © 2018 Fergus Moore & Roger Slater
First published September 2018 by CAMS

Printed in Great Britain by:
People for Print Ltd,
Unit 10 Riverside Park, Sheaf Gardens, Sheffield, S2 4BB UK

Edited by Roger Slater

ISBN 978-0-9566621-3-2

FOREWORD BY FRANK O'BRIEN

Leading up to the World Cup in Spain 1982, I along with Gordon Bartlett completed the Level Two Coaching award at Whitchurch Playing Fields in Stanmore. Deemed to be competent, my coaching journey began.

My first appointment was in Finchley for a club called St Phillips. The club had one ball, no cones and no bibs, but plenty of kids who wanted to play football. Amongst the group of players was a family of three brothers (who also had their dog with them). The youngest of the brothers and arguably the best player amongst the whole group was Fergus Moore, who stood out not only for his ability, but also his long shorts, not football shorts, just, well, shorts!

Even then, he showed an excellent attitude and determination towards his football. His love of the game was apparent and that has remained with him in all the years I have known him. Throughout the years we have kept in contact and we've often bumped into each other at a club or a game and we'll occasionally catch up on the phone, chatting about all levels of football and life, that same enthusiasm for the game to the fore.

I was delighted for him when he was offered an apprenticeship at Brentford and although that didn't work out, I have followed his subsequent non-league career with interest. He has not always found it easy and just as in those early days, he has had to deal with disappointment as well as success. To his credit, he has bounced back from each disappointment, always more determined to prove his critics wrong. He established himself as an uncompromising defender; tough, fiercely determined in everything he did and with a decent left foot. Whilst our football journeys have taken different routes, our paths have sometimes crossed as they did at Wealdstone FC where he had a number of spells with varied success...

Thirty-six years on from our first meeting, on a Bank Holiday Monday, I was driving through the streets of Borehamwood going to watch a local Senior Cup Final at Arkley. Not for the first time, I saw in the distance a young man pounding the streets. I drove on and as I got close, I recognised Ferg. I wound the window down and said *"Hello"*, he replied *"Where you going?"* *"A game of course, where are you going?"* I replied. *"A game!"*, he said with a smile. With that I gestured, he jumped in the car and off we went, talking football... It was no different as we sat in the stand watching that afternoon, all the while talking about the game unfolding in front of us, who was decent, who was less so, all mixed with our general conversation of 'the game' as a whole.

Over the years I have been fortunate to work and play with many players at various levels, who for sure were and are better and more memorable perhaps than Ferg, however, throughout my time I cannot think of one player who has been more committed in everything he tried to do on the football field. In training or in a game, his love and passion are there for all to see and his outlook and attitude remain infectious. They have never diminished.

Now in the early stages of what I am sure will be a long managerial career, those are traits that will help him (and his team) immensely. He has started out at Edgware Town and I've been pleased to assist him on a couple of occasions in his first season, running a couple of training sessions that I have thoroughly enjoyed. His natural enthusiasm lifts me never mind his players. There is a note of caution though; just as when he played, a problem Ferg will come across is that not all of his players will or will be able to match his enthusiasm and passion for the game.

I feel privileged to have known him as a young boy and to have seen him grow into the man he is, and I have also been privileged to see a kid give everything he had in his efforts to forge a career as a player. Now I look forward to seeing him develop a new career as he moves into management. It's a tough role, more so now than ever.

Finally, a note to his players and prospective players; If you are ever fortunate enough to play for one of his teams, all you will be required to do is match that enthusiasm and determination. If you can do that and add it to your natural playing ability, you will be a half decent player, and Ferg will have played a part in that.

Frank.

FERGUS MOORE

Like the picture on the back? You may remember Stuart Pearce in that pose – it's just one of several similarities between us....

both played left back,
both lived in North West London,
both played for Wealdstone,
both have a never say die attitude,
both known for passion and 100% commitment to the cause,
both captained a number of clubs that we played for,
both had careers spanning over twenty years in the game,
he was good enough to go on and captain England...

...but i'm not sure his Dad ever recorded a single!

I was a decent player as a kid, decent enough in fact to get into the youth system at Brentford where I started out on the ladder to professional superstardom. A first, initially tentative step towards the glitter, glamour and of course the money that being a professional footballer could provide. A few months later, just before my eighteenth birthday, the glitter stopped shining, the glamour looked decidedly drab and the money (about a hundred quid a week at the time) stopped. My professional football career had come to an end. No drama, no scene, no big bang as the manager's door shut behind me, it just sort of fizzled out half way through a training session when I was called to one side.

I suppose that I'd seen it coming as from Brentford Reserves I'd been shipped out on loan to Yeading FC, then playing in the Diadora (Isthmian) League Division One. I thought and hoped that it was part of my football education, that I'd do well and be welcomed back to Griffin Park for the next step of my career, but it wasn't to be. Eighteen, no professional contract and no club.

Yeading was an option – I'd got to know the club and Manager and it meant I'd be playing. I thought I'd be in the shop window, looking to get back into a pro side. They were based in West London albeit a bit nearer to Heathrow, and still a football club, but that was where the similarities ended.

From the comparative dream of being a contracted professional footballer (though I only ever played in the stiffs) to playing in front of a few men and the occasional dog, overnight. I became a part-timer, playing for fun and a few quid. The reality hit home with my next pay packet. I realised I also needed a job.

Twenty-eight years on, another season beckons. Twenty-seven seasons and eighteen clubs in twenty-odd spells (a couple of them had me back!) I've played for clubs that have won major competitions, the FA Vase and the FA Trophy at Wembley, non-league clubs that have made it to the second and third round of the FA Cup to face the might of Rotherham, Newcastle and such like.

And they all did it without me, either before I arrived or after I'd left. I've never made it through more than a couple of FA qualifying rounds, I've never had my five minutes of fame in a Football Focus or Match of the Day interview or made the sports pages of The Sun (or any other 'national' come to that). Thankfully my timing in a tackle is a bit better (more often than not), and at least I've been famed as the oldest player in the FA Cup for a couple of seasons!

Despite a lack of national glory, there are a batch of medals in the collection. A few leagues won and a cup final or two. There are a few Player of the Year awards as well, but most of all there are the memories and unlike the boots I shall eventually hang up, they will last forever.

Last season was a new challenge as I was appointed Co-Manager / Player Manager of my current club, Edgware Town FC. A step five club playing in the Spartan South Midland League Premier Division. At the very least, it brings a final chapter or two to end to this tome. Will it be the start of another twenty-odd year career? Who knows. I've survived the first year and looking back, it was a decent season in the main. New experiences and challenges and a view from the other side of the line.

I've learned a bit and maybe that will lead to something more but that will be another story...

I know it's a cliché, but none of what you will read here would have been possible without so many other people, good and not so good. Many, many people are mentioned within, but there are some that I want to say a personal *thank you* to:

Where could I start except with my Mum and Dad for bringing me into this world. My parents, Seamus and Helen may have only been to a handful of games, but I know it doesn't mean that they weren't interested, they have just let me make my own decisions. They've been there when I needed them, and they really have made me what I am today.

From an early age when I was a schoolboy at QPR they let me try and chase my dream of being a professional footballer. Indeed, when I got my YTS contract at Brentford there was no-one prouder than my parents.

While I was growing up chasing the dream they kept themselves busy running public houses in and around North London. The pub scene for the Irish community is a full-time job, it took up all their time and provided the income that supported my two brothers and me. There wasn't much time left, which is not a bad thing as I have seen many a parent, especially Dad's interfere too much with budding football careers.

We don't tell each other all the time, but we love each other and will always be there for one another. Thanks Mum and Dad and I love you both always xxx

My two brothers, Neil and Declan: I would like to thank for toughening me up somewhat when I was growing up! Being the youngest, I was always copping a 'little brother slap' now and then, and they've done me no harm later in life!

They too, have followed my career with great interest and they do try to get to as many games as they can. As we've aged, I think that they have become prouder of me in their big brother way. Many a time when I'm out someone will approach and say: *"your Neil (or Dec's) brother"*, letting me know that my brothers have been talking about me and my football career in a complimentary way. Thanks bros xx

Hayley and our three beautiful children deserve more thanks than I could ever give for putting up with me. I've said it many times and written it many times in this book, but it's still not enough, especially in making up for those times when I've not been myself after a bad performance or result. I know it's pathetic but that's the way I am. Please forgive me. I love you all and I am so blessed to be your husband and dad xxx

To all my teammates and managers (there's been a few): Thanks for putting up with my moods and tantrums and occasional outbursts. I hope you can see from this book that nothing was personal, it's just the passion and adrenaline of this game that at times has made my emotions spill over, whether winning or losing. Thank you for all the wins we've shared together and in defeat how we've come battling back. I've had a few run-ins with Managers and perhaps overstepped the line a little and for that I'll apologise, but to each and every one of you, I'd do it all again because you are all part of my football history.

To the teammates and managers in my later years, you have been with me when I have battled with my self-doubt and inner demons the most, but you've helped me pull through and restore the other 'happy' side. Thank you.

To all the opponents I have come up against, thanks for giving me that competitive streak and for helping me take my strengths (whatever they may be) to the next level. Thanks for the times you've wound me up in defeat and given me an extra incentive to come back and beat you the next time!

Many opponents have also gone on to become friends of mine, friendship built on a bond of mutual respect for which I am ever grateful. I genuinely thank you all xx.

Lastly to my co-writer Roger Slater for seeing some sort of story in me. (I hope you can to!) Roger is a supporter of Wealdstone who could 'see what I was about' enough to put up with all my random thoughts and missed deadlines as I struggled to put into words what my whole life has meant. Top man Roge!

To the readers, this book should have been a year in the making, I hope that you will think it's all been worthwhile, six years on!

Ferg.

SEASON BY SEASON

1989/90	Brentford FC.
1990/91	Brentford FC, Told I was being released in November and joined Yeading FC initially on loan.
1991/92	Yeading FC Joined Staines Town on loan then signed for them and got released!
1992/93	Uxbridge FC
1993/94	Uxbridge FC
1994/95	Uxbridge FC
1995/96	Wealdstone FC
1996/97	Wealdstone FC
1997/98	Wealdstone FC
1998/99	Wealdstone FC. Joined Chertsey Town FC in the New Year
1999/2000	Hemel Hempstead Town FC
2000/01	Hemel Hempstead Town FC
2001/02	Wealdstone FC
2002/03	Hemel Hempstead Town FC
2003/04	Hemel Hempstead Town FC Joined Boreham Wood FC early in the season
2004/05	Boreham Wood FC Joined Northwood FC early in the season
2005/06	Northwood FC
2006/07	Wealdstone FC
2007/08	Wealdstone FC Moved to AFC Hayes then onto Edgware Town
2008/09	Leyton FC Joined Berkhamsted Town FC on loan, then joined Bedfont Green FC
2009/10	Bedfont Green FC (who became Bedfont Town FC)
2010/11	Bedfont Town FC (Player/Assistant Manager)
2011/12	Windsor FC Joined Hanwell Town FC mid-season
2012/13	Cockfosters FC
2013/14	Cockfosters FC
2014/15	Cockfosters FC Moved to Edgware Town FC mid-season.
2015/16	Edgware Town FC
2016/17	Edgware Town FC, for the first time more on the bench than off
2017/18	Player, Co-Manager, Edgware Town FC
2018/19	Player Manager, Edgware Town FC

HONOURS

1989/90	Brentford YTS Player of the Year
1990/91	Yeading FC Middlesex Charity Cup Runners-up
1992/93	Uxbridge FC London Senior Cup Winners
1996/97	Wealdstone FC ICIS (Isthmian) League Division III Winners
1997/98	Wealdstone FC ICIS (Isthmian) League Division I Promoted
2009/10	Bedfont Green FC Combined Counties League Champions
2012/13	Cockfosters FC Spartan South Midland League Division 1 Champions
	Southern Floodlight League Cup Winners
	Spartan South Midland Division 1 Cup Winners
	Player of the Year
2013/14	Cockfosters FC Managers Player of the Year
	Chairman's Award – Clubman of the Year
2015/16	Edgware Town FC Spartan South Midland League Division 1 Champions
	Edgware Town FC Spartan South Midland League Division 1 Cup Finalists
2017/18	David Allbone Award – Clubman of the Year
	Didn't get sacked…

CONTENTS

I - The Player

Someone said I was so old I still get changed in black and white, and the first time I got booked, the referee used chalk and a slate to write my name down.

I think I'm a bit like the last bottle of a favourite wine, maturing with age, kept on show, never poured. It's unique after all...

FIRST IMPRESSIONS

I had only been out of the professional setup at Brentford for a few weeks. Even at youth level there were people who looked after us, sorted the kit and suchlike and now I was about to play my first game as a semi-pro player. Bag in hand, boots polished, a guy called Steve Newing (who was to become a good friend) was giving me a lift to my first game as a Yeading FC player in Diadora League Division 1, away to Dorking FC at the uninspiring Meadowbank Athletic Stadium.

I'd only trained with my new side a couple of times and didn't know many of the lads, but Steve and I arrived about half past one and made our way to the bar to meet up with the rest of the team, or at least those that had arrived. No coach travel to leafy Surrey at this level, players making their own way to most games, most cadging lifts but one or two on public transport, meant the arrival of the whole squad could be spread over an hour, even on a good day.

As we approached, I looked around at the small groups gathered in conversation. Some with a coffee, many with a cola or orange juice and finally, one at the bar with a partially-drunk pint of lager. And a cigarette. I watched the routine: Smoking fiercely as the cigarette was moved back and forth between mouth and ash tray, every second or third time, interspersed with a slug from the fast-emptying glass. Well, he won't be starting I thought...he must be on the bench.

We moved in and joined one of the small groups. More accurately, Steve moved in and joined one of the groups, I just tagged along as the new boy, but it didn't matter as I don't think anyone noticed! They were a tight-knit bunch of mainly older, experienced players who had won the FA Vase the previous season at Elland Road, Leeds, after a draw at Wembley. They weren't ready to accept an 18-year -old who'd peaked at an occasional start for Brentford Reserves before being cast out into the non-league world.

I stood there trying not to look to awkward and I tried to listen, even looking interested, occasionally catching an eye or two as Steve Croad, Earl Whiskey, Jon Denton, Stuart McKenzie, Paul Sweales and my driver for the day Steve

Newing – the inner circle - chatted away. All bar one completely unaware of the interloper in their midst.

As my interest waned, matched by their constant disinterest in me, I looked around and my eyes settled once again on the bar. The only change to the scene was that the previously emptying pint was now full again. A second beer just before 2pm? And almost with one movement he stubbed out his cigarette and immediately lit another while I watched! Not even on the bench, I reckoned. Must be injured...

I smiled inwardly as Gordon Bartlett (then Yeading FC Manager) appeared and called us down to the dressing room. Once everyone had settled and the banter (from which I was summarily excluded) had died down, the team was named. I was on the bench while the chain-smoking lager drinker was starting at centre forward! Vic Schwartz was a bit of a cult figure on the non-league circuit and a decent goal scorer throughout his career and that, I learned, was his pre-match ritual. A couple of pints and a ciggy or two to settle his nerves. I was to play alongside him at a few clubs over subsequent seasons and it was always the same - but on day one it took some understanding! Welcome to non-league, Fergie!

I watched from the bench almost in silence as the game started. Until you've been there, it's hard to realise quite how oppressive being the new boy in that environment can be - and if no-one is there to metaphorically (or literally) put their arm around you and include you in the banter, it can be a lonely place on a cold afternoon.

The game progressed, and I got on with about 25 minutes to go. I did OK or at least I think I did (no-one said so), but either my performance or injuries to others was enough to earn me a full debut at another uninspiring ground in the next match, away from home again on the massive pitch at Aveley. As it turned out, the desolate surroundings were surpassed by our performance in a 0 – 1 defeat but I'd done OK, the gaffer telling me that he was pleased with me at the end of the game. In the dressing room he dissected the match and what we could have done better (scoring would have been top of a long list) then he asked if anyone else had anything to say about the goal we'd conceded. Captain Steve Croad piped up *"yes "*.

Now I and no doubt a few of the other lads knew the goal was his fault, but he stood up and pointed straight at me. *"The goal was his fault"* he said. I thought he was winding me up, but he continued *"he missed his man completely. He got drawn across the box and let them get a cross in"*. That, even though we all knew that the guy he was marking had all the time in the world to pick his spot with a free header. It was a rude awakening to non-league cliques and attitudes. I thought to myself then that I was now among people who would say their piece, right or wrong. I was young and raw, and it was a good lesson and it has stood me in good stead since. From then on it was sink or swim and now I'm a bloody expert – crawl, breast stroke, butterfly, back stroke, I was a quick learner when it came to standing-up for myself!

You take it on the chin when you're wrong and you enjoy the plaudits when you are right, but you can't get carried away with the good stuff. One second in a game can change the whole outlook and turn it against you. In the last few years, approaching and now reaching my mid-forties, the criticisms dig a little deeper as with increasing age the bravado of youth is replaced with ever-increasing self-doubt. It's one part of my career I have no control over no matter what I try, think or do. The older I get, the more each error (and we all make them) makes me wonder if it's time to give up.

Each is another experience that I try to learn from, and I put it in the memory bank for future reference. In my eyes, the reaction to criticism will always be a pointer to the mental strength of a player. It's something I didn't have at Brentford and it killed me – and my career. I couldn't adapt from being a good youth team player taking that step up into the Reserves and playing against old pros and their tricks. I couldn't adjust and went into my shell. Thankfully, that afternoon at Aveley, I cottoned on. I had to.

More importantly, after that game I signed a contract. At all of £45 per week, I was now a fully-fledged semi-pro player, and I was at least earning a few quid for the foreseeable future. Few is the key word in that sentence. In the real world I still needed a job.

Brentford had sent me off with a few quid when I was released and once again 'few' is the well selected adjective. That first week at Yeading I was given a signing-on fee of around £150 plus the first week's money. For all of about half an hour, I was an eighteen-year-old and loaded!

Looking back the contract was a bit light and I was naïve. I knew nothing about contracts or what they really meant, and to this day I've never read one, nor signed one since! (Yes, a couple have been offered!). As a player, I've always told young players not to sign either. Not that it may not be worth their while, but if they find themselves out of the side, they can't just leave. You may be out of favour, but you can end up tied to the club and if all you want is to play, that's very hard. Fine I suppose if you are only there for the money, but that's not me. To me, playing is important and the money isn't the driver. It's why I've played on so long and believe me, it's been less than 'expenses only' for a few years now.

As a manager, I haven't (so far) had to worry about the money side. We haven't got any, we don't pay any, and no, we don't pay expenses either. If I move on and move up, who knows…. Eventually, I'll have to park my personal beliefs and for the good of the club and convince players to sign on the dotted line. With so little money in the lower levels of the game one decent player sold on can mean the survival of a club for a couple of years.

It's quite emotional looking back to those first few weeks. I remember exactly how I felt when Brentford let me go; I wasn't shocked as I felt I was nowhere near the first team as players such as Terry Evans, Keith Millen, Jamie Bates and Jason Cousins were all in front of me. As a kid I just didn't have the self-belief or confidence to think I could be a threat to any of them, but my release was still a bit of a blow when it happened. Even after my pay-off, I had no prospect of a job or an income and I had no real education or qualifications as all I ever wanted to be was a footballer.

Luckily my old youth team manager, Joe Gadstone, was still at Brentford and he had heard the news. Then after I'd been at Yeading a few weeks, he pointed me in the direction of some people he knew in the leisure industry. I got the chance to give that a whirl. Perhaps if I hadn't been so weak mentally I could have trialled at another pro club or two, but I really didn't come to terms with the rejection and I wallowed in self-pity for a few weeks. My lifetime dream of being a professional footballer had lasted barely 6 months.

I've seen it since as well, players that have come to the clubs I've been at, coming straight out of the pro game. Some come in like 'Billy Big Balls' and generally the banter will take them down a peg or two. After all, they've been dumped like me and many more before them and that's not really a qualification for lauding it is it? Others come in, knuckle down and try to get back into the pro game or give their all for the club they're at. If they do, they'll soon earn the respect of the older hands and in general (unless it's your place in the side the new kid is after) we'll help where we can too.

PRE-SEASON

We got over the blip at Yeading when I joined and having been near the bottom of the table in November, we finished sixth. I started almost every game and we got to my first Cup Final, of the Middlesex Senior Cup against former England International Peter Taylor's Enfield FC, played at Edgware Town's White Lion Ground. It was my first final played in front of a good bank holiday crowd. A young forward called Paul Furlong played for Enfield that day and scored the winner. I wonder what ever happened to him!

Over the summer, I did what I always did and still do, a bit of running and general fitness stuff, all to try and keep me in reasonable shape as the boot-camp of pre-season training looms large.

Pre-season training is an effort for some but in truth, it never has been for me, I love it. Sure, as I've got older it becomes a bit harder but there's something about getting back together in that atmosphere. Seeing the old faces from the previous season or seeing the trialists that inevitably turn up, even joining a new club, it's still special to be there and be involved. As I've grown older it has become a matter of honour. Invariably being the oldest participant, I convince myself that I must be at the front leading by example, not coasting along at the back like some I could name. (Actually, there's far too many to name: every club, every season, there's two or three...). It's more of a challenge now as the Manager because I want my side to be made up of players who all have that mentality and want to get to the front. Well, second anyway...

As a Diadora First Division club, effectively three promotions from the Football League at the time, pre-season was run professionally, and the first team squad didn't tend to see to many of the 'turn–ups' or even the invited trialists until the dross had been weeded out. There were a few that sneaked through, but Gordon Bartlett and Leo Morris (you'll get to know them a bit better in the pages that follow) would take the trialists and chancers out on their own for a couple of sessions and only the couple that might have had a chance would make it through the gaffer's filter into a full squad session. In fact, Gordon used to stitch Leo up at the trials as well; they'd discuss each player while a match was going on, pick a couple to invite back that 'GB' would generally have a word with, then he'd be off to let Leo get the contact details and (gently, Leo) shatter the dreams of the thirty or so others that weren't up to the grade. Among the cast-offs were the full kit wankers. In fact, the lower down the pyramid you go, the more there are. Imagine the scene: you have about thirty turn-ups, some invited by choice of the management, some that have written in and asked for a trial. You do a bit of background to see what they've done football-wise, but it's rarely fool-proof. There was one year a lad turned up, a goalkeeper, whose CV said that he'd been at Arsenal for five or six years. It raised an eyebrow or two, as to be with a side like that for five years as a youngster, you must have something about you. Ten minutes into a game set up between two sides of trialists, this lad (resplendent in a full Arsenal kit that should have been a warning in itself) had plenty about him. Plenty of forwards, defenders, mud and dirt. I think his only three touches were picking the ball out of the net. He'd been at Arsenal for five years all right: As a steward on matchdays!

Others have turned up with brand new boots, full kit and tracksuit from their favourite club and frankly wouldn't have been able to trap the ball at their feet if it had been stationary. It's only when you see some of these lads (who at least in their own minds are 'good enough' for whatever level) that you realise there probably is a market for a manufacturer brave enough to make pairs of two left (or right) boots.

Every non-league club at whatever level nationwide gets their fair share of turn-ups who can write better than they play; goalkeepers like Dracula who fear crosses; defenders that think they're Bobby Moore but play more like Patrick Moore; midfielders who think a great engine is enough, even though they can't get within twenty feet of the ball and can't tackle either; and forwards whose favourite position is offside. I've seen them all. One or two by some strange quirk of fate or with good luck and bullshit have made it onto the pitch in a real match. I'd love the chance to ask Graeme Souness or Ali Dia how that happened!

Twenty-five years on, I did a pre-season at Cockfosters of the Spartan South Midland League Division One. Just like that first year at Yeading, our last game had been a cup final in mid-May, although we ran out winners this time after a tough game against Stotfold. Winning, we celebrated in true non-league style in the bar. It's another memory banked and one I was lucky enough to share with my boys Aaron and Callum, both old enough to come along and understand a bit about the match and what it meant to their old man. Each moment is one to be treasured, and finals are extra special as they become rarer. I think back to that first one at Yeading and realise that I probably should have appreciated it more at the time, but I was young and raw, whatever you want to call it. I thought there would be at least one a year!

For me, win, lose or draw, the last match like the season it ends soon becomes a bit of a let-down as the buzz wears off. Even at forty-six, I'd happily keep training with the boys through the summer, (I keep up the running on my own) but then, I suppose I'd lose those personal challenges that pre-season brings.

That first night at Trent Park in my last season at Cockfosters there were 24 involved in the run that we call the Trent Park Triangle. (Every club has their own local version and now at Edgware it's Silver Jubilee Park where the ground is situated). I was sixth and well happy with that. It's about three quarters of a mile each circuit and we did it twice, but the last third is uphill and a killer for players old and new every year. To me, that's the psychology of the other lads. They don't like it, in fact a few hated it to such an extent it made it more painful and harder every time, almost as if they were running up there carrying extra weight. To me, no pain, no gain, so I got on with it, hopefully to reap my reward. At least coming sixth gave me bragging rights over a few of the youngsters then and I still want that now with 'my' squad.

You need that in a club, the banter. Between players, baiting and challenging each other. It's all a bit of willie-waving really but it does (assuming you're giving the stick and not taking it) help keep you and the session sharp. It's more difficult at a first session because, unlike me, so many of last season's squad will (*have a last-minute holiday / *get held up at work / *think its next week. *delete as applicable) do their best to style it out and miss the first couple or sessions. That, in tandem with the new faces that don't know who's who and what's what can make the early sessions a bit quiet sometimes.

Those early runs sort the wheat from the chaff too. At lower levels, some of the trialists won't be expecting anything more than a kick about and the run often becomes the up-chuck run as the sedentary bodies that have dreamed of stardom on Match of The Day get put through their paces. I love it too when a couple of kids come along. Off they'll go at full tilt for the first circuit (at Trent Park), up the hill and onto lap two. Then the legs or their lungs start to give in and the pack closes in. Most of the old hands will smile and in true non-league style offer friendly advice and the odd gesture (of support, of course) as we cruise past them.

By the second or third session, a few more of the previous season's squad will be around. It happens just the same whatever the club, and it shouldn't be a surprise as by then, the first pre-season friendly is homing into view. The lads that have been invisible for the previous fortnight suddenly appear with stories of how they ran on the beach every day and they feel sharp, or how they've been running daily through the summer to ensure they're ready. I must be missing a trick. I still do bloody run on the beach and every day at home throughout the summer.

Managers and Coaches have heard it all before, as players will try the exact same excuses and stories repeatedly. Now, I'm a Manager. One or two of the savvier (and I'll include me in this) will even shift sessions about in pre-season knowing that some players won't be around for the first couple, starting off with some ball work and circuits and such like, saving the runs for the third or fourth session when the match players (aka lazy bastards) will all suddenly appear.

So, there we are. Any year, any club and a couple of weeks later than the rest, true to form the missing players will return. The personal benefit is that it does make my aim for the top third of the run tougher and in general it makes the session sharper which can only be a good thing. Especially if you are coming off the back of a previous decent season as you want to build on that, to pick up where you've left off. Conversely, coming off a poor year any player worth their salt should want to prove themselves and do better.

That first session at Trent Park with Cockfosters sticks in my mind for several reasons. Firstly, once the session was over there was no chance of a pint as there isn't a clubhouse or bar in Trent Park, so it was a quick dash off home listening to the World Cup semi-final between Brazil and Germany. I got home at 1-0, had a quick shower and missed three goals! A hell of a drubbing, the final score was 7-1 and it could have been ten, but we've all been there. I've played in a few sides when we have had our pants pulled down and our arses collectively spanked. A couple of years ago, it was by London Colney, a match that ended with the same score line but thankfully that scene played out in front of about ten spectators. God only knows how Brazil will have felt in a packed stadium with millions watching on TV all over the world!

I had to smile. On a night where history was made, a then forty-two-year-old dinosaur non-league footballer was running his socks off around a park in North London in the peeing rain hoping he'd done enough to get the call on Saturday to start season number 25. Lovely!! Cue Greavsie, *"it's a funny old game"*.

I also remember as I was leaving home to go to the session that night, my two-year-old daughter Holly came up and asked where I was going. When I told her *"football training"* she said *"why?"* Then, as for many summers before and since, she'd been used to having me around in the evenings. Suddenly, I was not going to be there. That certainly does get harder as you get older as the football bug takes over, even at this level. Indeed, at my age it *has* to take over. Deep breath taken, off I went once again with a heavy heart and thankfully, a patient family.

Football has a habit of reminding you who's in charge as well. 10th July 2014 was my tenth and first 'significant' wedding anniversary. Hayley, my wife, is my rock and I love her tremendously but even she cannot get through this urge or force that is football. No romantic anniversary night out or a shared meal, as not for the first - and probably not for the last - time I went pre-season training. It was just another case of football upsetting the applecart. There have been countless landmark occasions missed but I just have to carry on, turning up selfishly at football to train or play, not wanting to miss out. It's my drug but at least it's a legal one.

There have been a few rows, but I think we both know eventually, no matter how unwillingly, she'll give in and off I'll go (well, at least until she reads this). I do know how much I owe her and one day I PROMISE she'll get everything she wants and deserves as I repay her faith and her patience. There, I've written it down. I must mean it.

I spent that tenth anniversary like so many others. Pushing myself up a bloody hill surrounded by sweaty blokes, some starting out with a bit to prove, some blowing out of their backsides as the cloggy ground and the incline took its toll and me, nearer the middle than I wanted. I may not have made the top third that night, but I almost got a personal best and then I went and showed some of the youngsters who was the daddy in the 'fives'. Pinging the ball back and forth my favourite move is to shout: *"don't move!"* or *"sorry!"* as I ping a ball through to the striker's foot. Cocky or what? I learned that off a former team-mate and a bloody goalkeeper at that! A real former Arsenal goalkeeper at youth level, Noel Imber. He was deadly accurate with most of his kicks from the ground or hand and definitely at his cockiest when a long strike hit the mark. Then, he made sure his teammates, the opposition and the fans knew how well he'd delivered the pass. Little victories. Every single one matters.

Anniversaries aside, there is the occasional concession to family life and at the very least a chance to collect a few well-earned brownie points. With one pre-season underway and a couple of games under the belt, I planned to take Hayley to Dublin for a belated 40th Birthday celebration. Sod's law, as the weekend of the trip approached we got beaten. It was only a pre-season friendly I know, but WE GOT BEATEN.

"And you won't be there for the next game" said the demons in my head.

What if someone does well and I lose my place, they said. I wished the lads well but honestly, as I went off for the break I wouldn't have minded at all if my replacement didn't shine. Paranoia or what?

So, roll on Dublin and a Saturday when during the afternoon and evening I built up a massive mobile phone bill as I started ringing everyone from about 4:45 onward. I wanted a full run down. From Rochey (the Manager) and most of the lads and for everyone that I spoke to that left a question in my mind, I rang two more. One person telling me was never going to be enough. I needed to know from five, six, eight, ten, all of them. They could all tell me the same thing, but I still need to hear it from as many different sources as I could, good or bad. Hayley and patience go hand in hand as I'm on the phone longer than the game lasted. Every call ends the same way: *"I'll be there Tuesday, though...."*

MOVING ON, CLUBS AND MANAGERS

That very first non-league pre-season at Yeading was a real eye opener for me. Despite becoming a regular in the side in my first season, an old pro turned up at the pre-season sessions and was playing in my place! Robbie Johnson it was. Lots of experience at a good level, he was good on the ball and as a side, they could make more of his ability and distribution than mine.

The season started with me as the defensive stopper at full back but if the opposition played narrow without wide men or wingers, Robbie came in and I was benched. As the season progressed, Robbie was keeping me out of the side more and more. I kept pulling the gaffer aside as I wanted to play. He kept telling me I was in the plans, but I still wasn't in the side. I knew Robbie wasn't going to be around forever, but I wanted games, tucked in at centre half or whatever, but when I got a game there it was only because Croady or John Denton were injured. That made it even tougher to be dropped when they returned especially when I'd been told how well I'd played.

Young, keen and (in my own mind at least) good enough, I wanted to play every game, then just before Christmas, I got an offer to join Staines Town on loan. They were struggling in the Premier Division, but I took the opportunity to go there and get some games in, initially for a month.

I did OK and played a part in a slight improvement in their results, but then I was called back for a Middlesex Cup game v Feltham. Perhaps naively, I thought I'd been called back because the gaffer wanted me to play. Nope. I was covering an injury and I was a sub. As I came out of the dressing room at kick off I noticed Steve Perryman, my former Brentford Manager stood by the stand. I'd always got on with him and so with the game kicking off in the background, I stopped for a chat.

Time flies! Fifteen minutes in and forward Hector Welch got injured. All I heard was the shout of: *"Fergie, Fergie"* from the bench. I thought they were winding me up – you don't bring on a left back when your centre forward is injured! I made my way round to the bench and lo and behold didn't get put on. In fact, I didn't get on all game and when the wage packet came around the next day mine was a bit light as I'd got a fine. I pulled Leo (who looked after the wages and administration stuff) to one side and asked why. He reckoned I was going to go on as sub but wasn't ready, so I got fined. I know it was the management showing me who was in charge (another lesson learned) but it pissed me off, on top of being back at the club and still not playing.

It was time to move on and Neil Price wanted me to join Staines. After a bit of to-ing and fro-ing between the clubs, Yeading finally released me from my contract and I was off. No contract but more money!

I enjoyed life in the Premier Division and was playing regularly which, I enjoyed more. Then results turned and though Pricey was Player Manager, his discipline wasn't great. In one game he got sent off, then his brother got sent off, then there was typical football 'handbags' in a couple of games which didn't go down well with the club.

After a run of discipline issues mainly on the field, Neil was sacked (another lesson) and a guy called Wayne Wanklyn took over. He and his number two brought in their own players and tried to run the rest of us out of the club. They tried to bully players, and it seemed me in particular. Anyone who had a bad game just got a mouthful: f-this, f-that, over and over. After one outburst aimed at yours truly I remember another senior player, Gerry Crawford telling me not to worry about it, but much as I tried to ignore it and dig in, it hurt being dug out for no reason.

My season and my time at Staines ended after an away match at Basingstoke Town. Pulled aside after the game, Wayne and his 'oppo' basically told me they didn't want me back. It was after the transfer deadline and with a month to go of my second season in non-league football I was without a club. It felt like in two years my game had gone from top to bottom.

Overall, the career has been more ups than downs, but attitudes and opinions change as do managers and coaches. Sometimes, you just don't fit in. Over the years, I've come across most types of management style. Some I'll take note from and I'll use some of the experiences as a manager myself. It's tough and probably tougher as I start as a player manager, but that's another challenge. As the body gets older (and I don't finish in the top third in pre-season) the playing will lessen, I'm sure. Just not yet. Maybe next year!

Over 20-odd seasons I think I've made a decent enough impression as a player and a person, as several managers have signed me more than once. Gordon Bartlett heads the list having taken me on at Yeading and signed me three times for Wealdstone. I was going to say 'so far' but now I'm 46, and he's been sacked at Wealdstone, it may be a bit late unless he takes over their walking football side...

I first came across him when he came into Brentford to do some coaching for the YTS scheme (2nd year). I was a bit of a big time Charlie playing well at South East Counties level and I had a bit of banter about me, a bubbly character who was on top of his game and I got Player of the Year that season.

When I got to Yeading he didn't actually do much coaching, there was always someone else around to do that, the likes of Willie Wordsworth, Frank O'Brien, Gilly (Mark Gill), Leo Morris and such like. He man-managed his squad and set the style and he was good to play for too. He doesn't bawl or shout though he can get a bit fierce occasionally. He has a nickname, 'Pencil Face' which was what we christened him at Wealdstone. When he got angry, he'd curl his lips up into a ball and fix you with a stare! A couple of former 'Stones: Lee 'Walks' Walker, Paul Lamb (Lambie) and I still get a laugh out of that when we meet up. Perhaps sometimes he should have dug people out, but I can't ever remember him doing it, he'd go the other way and get at the team or the work ethic.

He's always very patient with players and that is something I think I struggle with to be fair. Even the likes of goalkeeper Lee Carroll who went missing. He let us down a couple of times as he was having a hard time outside of the game, even failing to turn up on a couple of occasions, but Gordon always tried to help and give him a way back. On the downside, I think he could be a bit too patient with players who didn't look up to the grade sometimes. Nine times out of ten he was right though, despite what others said or thought. GB has that sixth sense and can see a player if there is one in there somewhere. Luckily, at Wealdstone for twenty-two plus years, he had a Board that gave him that time as well.

He'd also perfected the 'two o'clock tap' on the shoulder. I had it a few times and so did many others. Come two o'clock you feel the tap and it's: *"let's have a quick word...."* Never a name, just a tap or him catching your eye. After the first couple of times you didn't even have to hear what he said as it was always: *"leaving you out today, blah blah...."* No-one was ever happy about it, but that's right as well. You should be unhappy about not playing. For the rest of us? Someone else getting the tap always meant you had an hour or so to get focused on your game. To be honest, I'd have preferred to know the day before as I'd have prepared and settled into it much better, but that was his way, it's how he always worked.

GB would keep players that were right for him for three maybe four years, but he was not afraid to change things, always looking for players to improve a squad. Most of his sides would see a 50% or 60% change from the start to the end of a season, but there was the odd exception when his side were challenging at the top of the league for a couple years, there were still changes but maybe only 30%!

The best thing? Even now, he's someone I can ask for advice. I've said many times he's my football father figure. There aren't too many others who I call.

We did have one major falling out after my last spell at the 'Stones. I was out of the side (who were struggling) and I felt I could do a job, but he sent me out dual signed to AFC Hayes *'to get games'.* To me, that was out of sight out of mind. I got games, but I never heard from him nor, as far as I'm aware, did anyone else. No-one had asked how I was doing and I never went back. I felt I'd been let down and it soured a good relationship for a while. Previously, even after I'd left Yeading and the 'Stones the first couple of times, we'd still talk on the phone and share a beer after a game, but not that time. Nothing. It went on for a couple of years until we were put back in touch, but it did take a while to get the relationship back on track. Thankfully it remains good today and once my opportunity to take on the role at Edgware came to light, GB was right up there at the top of the list for a phone call and advice. In fact, the call went on for so long a few others never got a call at all. If you are reading this, Gord, rest assured I'll be back on the phone mate....and if you get a job, I might need a player or two on loan here and there. (No left sided defenders though!)

Close second on my Top Managers list is the late George Talbot, my manager a couple of years later at Uxbridge. Another person I was proud to call 'gaffer' at the club I grew up at and where I learned so much.

After the end of season debacle at Staines, I got a couple of calls including one from George, a former Staines player with a long and distinguished career behind him and who still knew people at the club, one of whom gave him my number.

I turned up for the 1992-93 pre-season and found his training methods were different to say the least. He'd join in and kick the hell out of players and he'd give you verbal from a distance if he didn't think you were putting in the effort. He'd also join in the running and then burst through a crowd of players, chest puffed up and shoulders flaring. If he didn't knock you out of the way and out of your stride, he'd try and trip you up! He had an old school coach there too – Micky Nicks, they made a great double act, George with his particular style and Micky who loved his drills and routines. It was all a bit of a shock to me. Looking back, I have to say that every session kept me interested, each was a real learning curve and a fantastic way to build a spirit in the squad. Lesson learned, George.

I've been lucky at most of my clubs (or should I say with most of my managers?) At Hemel and Wealdstone spirit was always important and it supplemented a lack of money, but at Uxbridge it was and remains to this day something special. It was perhaps the first time I'd really seen it to such great effect. George signed players like him. Decent ability, 110% effort, great characters. Jokes, one-liners, banter from the top down, all sorts and as if George wasn't enough, madmen Troy Birch and Lee Hanratty on the playing side would always be looking for a target. One big change was that 'newbies' were always taken in as friends even if they nicked your place, but that was George's way. All for one and one for all. We may not have had much, but we all had it. I signed after that first session.

A couple of months into the season I remember one Talbot rant in particular. He was addressing just about everyone in earshot, saying: *"look at this guy, his professional attitude…why aren't you all like that?"* It was me he was talking about. Back then, I still had that professional mindset: After the game a quick

ONE drink in the bar, then off home ready to come back for training or the next match. I hadn't got into the non-league culture of play the game, forget the result win or lose, go and get drunk in the bar. Seriously, it just wasn't me. I took the result home and sulked when we lost. Part of that was living in Finchley and travelling to Uxbridge. Staying for more than one would just have seen the hours pass by. Oh! How that was to change in the coming months lead quite often by? Yes, one George Talbot.

I got used to the club and the game, learnt a bit more about non-league and most of all, I was playing. Then it became a matter of if you can't beat them, join them. A few beers after the game became the norm. Most of the lads, win lose, or draw started their evening in the bar and I joined in.

It was a great upbringing (really). You let off steam, you didn't carry problems around with you and it was what everyone else did. Sometimes it would just turn into a session and we'd be there till 2am...no mobiles, no-one chasing you. 10p in the phone box meant a quick call to say you'd be late as the coach had broken down! I even pulled that off more than once for a home game! (I wasn't married then, honest).

A couple of examples of George at his best: We played and lost at Edgware in a Middlesex Cup Quarter Final. They were in a lower division, but you'd never have known on the night. Come Saturday, and George is in a silent dressing room, everyone still smarting a bit as he reads out the team: *"Sean Dawson, no1 Just about.... Number 3 Fergus Moore just about, 4 Paul McCluskey just about...."* In his own way, George let us know exactly what he thought about the defeat earlier in the week.

When you were on a downer though, he'd always pick you up with a smart comment. He hated defeat but didn't dwell on it. After that Edgware game and the team announcement we lost again, at Abingdon Town, 2 or 3 nil. Quiet on the way back, we eventually got to the Uxbridge clubhouse which as always was busy and especially on this night with the hall let out for a private booking. It got to about 8 or 9 pm and the lot of us, George to the fore, bowled straight into the wedding reception that was going on in the hall. It was our club after all!

Finally, I remember an away game at Billericay. It was another defeat (did we ever win?) and after the game we made for the bar. The lady serving said they were shutting as their players didn't drink after about 5-30 as they all went home and there was a 'do' on in the evening. George being George started banging on the doors chanting *"we shall not, we shall not be moved"*. It worked, the bar stayed open and we were still there at about 8. Talby started his sing-song (San Francisco by Tony Bennett was his favourite opener) with the whole team doing the doo-wops in the background. Then the regulars started coming in for the 'do' which turned out to be a karaoke evening. The lads put me down for a song, so I did Teddy Bear by Elvis. Then there was a raffle for a crate of beer which of course, we won.

The evening went on and we were still there at about 11pm, when I got presented with another crate of beer for being the best karaoke singer on the night! Everyone including Uxbridge President Dave Tucker, who was the coach driver, was still in the party with us. Things finally wrapped up and we got on the coach, beers in hand, ready to go. As we pulled out of the car park we were stopped by John Kendall, then the Billericay Manager. He came out with another crate of beer for us in his words: *"just for being the best crowd of footballers he'd ever seen"*. A non-league crazy gang with three cases of lager on the bus! Great fun and great memories. God bless, George.

In a few years, maybe one of my players will write a book (or if he's any good have it ghost-written for him). I wonder if he'll look back on his time as a player for me and what he'll say...

THREE YEARS, THREE CLUBS

It wasn't what I expected, changing my club year on year. I thought I'd done alright on the field and I was glad when George Talbot called. It meant I dropped back down to Division 1 although I wouldn't be playing against Yeading as they'd been promoted. I suppose that alone justified their decision to release me in favour of others!

We played Corinthian Casuals away on a training pitch in what if memory serves were my first match for the club and we got off to a flyer. I scored an absolute cracker, 25 yards out, centre of the goal. I took a touch and the marauding left back (that's me in case you were unsure) fired it into the top corner. It was one of the best goals I ever scored and a great start at a new club. Sean Dawson and Paul McCluskey, Gary Downs were all there. These guys were to become friends and they still are. It's amazing that in and around a club you come across so many people, some pass by but some stick with you. You don't see them or ring them for weeks or months, but you know they are there if you need them and vice versa. Real friends even when you don't speak for ages, then when you get together it's like you've never been apart. Part of great team spirit, a hidden factor maybe but it's important in a side that wins or loses to get everyone pulling together.

It was good to be playing again and building new friendships. I started the season as captain, but Talby took that away from me about half way through the year when he signed Gary Downs, one of his former players. It was fair enough, he had more experience. I was a bit young and I think the weight of captaincy had brought my form down a bit too, so it was a good move all round though I wasn't too keen at the time.

Overall, it was a decent year. Mid table, semi-final of the Middlesex Charity Cup (where we lost a game we should have won) and some good results too. We went Bishop's Stortford at New Year. They were unbeaten at home and we won, then they went on to win the league. It was Uxbridge all over. We had lots of players in the side who could do a job on the day and make a difference, but we weren't consistent. The club couldn't afford to pay big money for players (me included) so we'd have good spells but really weren't strong enough to maintain the challenge all year.

For me it was a good settler, good banter and I felt part of the place. Some might say that the drinking culture wasn't right and now it wouldn't be, indeed couldn't be with tighter laws on drink driving and such like, but these were (slightly) different times. By the way, for those of you concerned about my liver in the later stages of my career, it's now normally a Lucozade (other sports drinks are available) to get the aches out and the bits working again then I'm off home to the family! And for once, at the end of that season I wasn't off anywhere. I was invited back!

We continued from where we left off, similar results and similar position, but with the bonus of another cup final. My second was the once prestigious London Challenge Cup. In previous years all the top London sides had graced the competition but by the nineties most of these had gone by the wayside, just the odd lower division side using it as a run-out for Reserves and Youth. That didn't take anything away from our victories though. We beat Football Conference Club Welling United in the final, Dagenham & Redbridge and Leyton Orient away at Brisbane Road. In the game against Welling, I marked a lad called Steve Finnan and he got substituted. It didn't ruin his fledgling career though. He went on to sign for Liverpool and won a Champions League Winners Medal in 2005. It no doubt sits alongside the 52 Republic of Ireland international caps he won. In fact, he is the only player to have played in the World Cup, UEFA Champions League, UEFA Cup, Intertoto Cup, all four levels of the English league football and the Football Conference *and* lost a London Senior Cup Final where he was marked out of the game by a young – well 20-year-old – full back from little old Uxbridge. We beat them 3-1. It was good to play at a couple of decent grounds during the cup run and I capped it all with my first Winners medal, it felt great, a real highlight.

The following week we had an end-of-season jolly to Blackpool booked and that was a great trip. The journey up was spent showing off the pictures of the final and the celebrations, in fact we stuck them all over the train carriage. You can't imagine what 20 non-league footballers would have for breakfast when catching the 8 o'clock train either. Well-oiled doesn't cover it. Still the same Uxbridge though, we could beat anyone on our day but weren't consistent enough to do it week in week out.

We played Yeading in the Middlesex Senior Cup that season. It was one of the first times I'd seen Gordon Bartlett since I'd left, and we won that night too. It was the start of something of a jinx as almost every time I've played against him, I've got the result. I must have one of the better records against him of all the players he's ever managed as I can only remember losing against him as part of a fledgling Edgware side, (we wuz robbed) and it always spurs me on. It's just the way I was as a player. I wanted to get one over on him. See? You were wrong to let me go…. Now, as a manager, when I come across a former team-mate or a club I was at (there are a few!) it spurs me on just a little more.

The following year at Uxbridge, we desperately wanted to build on the success. We didn't want to be mid table again and re-instated as Captain I wanted to ensure we took a step up. Unfortunately, it didn't come off and we mirrored the previous two seasons, winning against the better teams, good cup wins and runs, but lacking the consistency. We never really got into the promotion mix and it was a shame as we had some good players who should have been able to do a bit more.

It meant that by the end of the year I had itchy feet. I wanted more on the field, I wanted to win. Socially, Uxbridge were great, but I wanted a big crowd and a winning club, so I moved on. Sods law, I left, George stayed, and Uxbridge won a couple of trophies over the next couple of seasons! (Mind you I got a few too). It was solely ambition. I was sad to leave Uxbridge, George and the lads after three years as I'd enjoyed it, but I wanted to be a winner again.

There were a few shouts of mercenary when the lads found out I was getting a rise to £70 to join Wealdstone. I knew the club had been in decline and were fast approaching rock bottom, but they still had decent crowds, potential and ambition.

WEALDSTONE FC

There was a free paper given out around the Borough of Harrow called All Sport Weekly, which carried match reports and news during the season on the local sides - though mainly about Wealdstone. I was looking back through a couple of old copies (to be honest, to see if I got a mention at Uxbridge, but I didn't) and I noticed that the 'Stones fans were mentioned almost every week. They'd brought in my old Yeading gaffer Gordon Bartlett as boss and he rang me and asked me to go along for the start of the 1995-96 season. A club that had taken a voluntary demotion to Division 3 seemed a big step down, but there was a passion about the place. Gordon was building a brand-new team (as just about every player they had the previous season had left) and I know I got a bit more money to go there, but that wasn't the driver for me. (Note to GB. If you'd offered me the same money as at Uxbridge, that £45, I'd probably still have joined). Looking back, it was the best thing I ever did. I could have been at Uxbridge forever, I'd have been 100% loyal and enjoyed the craic, but football and winning spurred me on, this was a new challenge.

Gordon knew me, and I knew the ground as the 'Stones were ground sharing at Yeading FC - or so I thought. I was almost right... they had just moved to ground share with Edgware Town, but logistically that suited me better as I lived in Finchley at the time. GB said that he felt I'd got the attributes to be a winner and that was what he wanted, and he said he thought I'd relate to the fans and vice versa.

It meant dropping down a couple of divisions, but it really wasn't the money that sold it to me, it was Gordon with his talk of the 'big club' and 'on the way up' and 'getting the success back'. It all appealed to me and I joined them for pre-season to have a nose around and see who else was coming on board. I knew I'd probably sign and after a couple of sessions at Stanmore Polytechnic (where lots of bodies had been involved), Gordon asked me what I thought on a few. Some good, some not so. I recommended a few more likely players for him. Players come and go quite a bit in pre-season, especially at clubs where there isn't silly money on offer.

On the following Saturday we had an inter squad game, a few trialists, a few of the previous season's Wealdstone fringe players (John Shanahan and Terry Birch spring to mind) and as we went out to get warmed up I was stunned. There were about seventy or eighty 'Stones fans along the touchline to watch a bloody training match! I'd never experienced anything like that, it was as many as Uxbridge would get for a home game! It really fired me up, a great adrenalin rush. It was what I thrived on as I'd always loved to play in front of a crowd (normally the other side's fans) but this was different. These were my (well, our) fans.

That buzz is great but there are often nerves too, because the last thing you want is to make a mug of yourself. That's even worse when it's your own fans because, and this was multiplied at Wealdstone, they're not shy of reminding you the next week (and the next week, and probably for a few weeks after that as well) if you cock up. (Christ, even if I go back now *someone* will mention Hertford Town! – see below). Thankfully, that day I was fine, and I was still buzzing with a pint in my hand after the game.

I signed league forms and as the season loomed large we ended our pre-season schedule with a four-team tournament to be played at Harrow B*rough and Edgware over a weekend. (Not quite up to the standard of The Emirates Tournament, eh!) We beat Edgware on the Saturday and were set to face the clubs most local rivals Harrow B*rough in the Sunday final. B*ro were the senior side being two divisions higher up the league and although Wealdstone lost by a couple of goals, to play a friendly in front of a couple of hundred partisan fans was a great boost with the first league game a week away. I'm sure both B*ro fans enjoyed it too.

The season started away to Cove and we won 9-1 with me playing left back. It was a great start for a whole new side, and it really was a new team, only a midfielder called Roddy Braithwaite played from the previous season's side. Well over a hundred 'Stones fans travelled down and that was more than most Ryman Division Three clubs would get week in week out. It was still a time of change, though, as Gordon looked for the right formula and the right mix on the field, so there were still new faces coming in. To be honest, perhaps he tinkered a bit more than he needed as he sought the right balance which eventually cost us.

On a personal note, I wasn't the star player I and a few others thought I would be, having dropped down from the first division. It meant the fans had a few doubts. 'The jury's out' was probably fair after the first few games, but they soon saw I was steady, turning in 7 or 8 out of 10 performances every match.

Wealdstone FC was then (and still is) a different beast. The fans build the pressure and players either sink - many do - or swim. I wanted and needed the fans and the buzz they gave me, but I still had to overcome them mentally to get to the top of my game. Now I don't play for them, yet they still bloody get to me! Many have watched me at other clubs as a player, always saying hello and I've always been pleased to see them. In fact, when the news broke about me becoming a manager, I reckon more than half the congratulations messages by text and on Twitter were from 'Stones fans, so I must have done OK there, eh!

That first season I started as left back and though I didn't mind that, I was hardly a wingback bombing up and down the line. My best games were to come at centre half, but the full back slot gave me the chance to use a range of passes in and out of the midfield or long to the forwards. It wasn't strange to me, it was just a bit more restrictive and I didn't get the chance to win as many headers! I was steady but wasn't setting the world alight (and despite the odd big win, nor was the team) but I was there week in, week out. When the results or the team performance aren't great it can knock you back into your shell a little bit and I'm still no different in that.

The side got to mid-season and like Uxbridge previously, were still inconsistent. We lost to Leighton Town, Windsor & Eton and Horsham in a short spell and that was a signal for a couple of new bodies to come in. One was to become a good mate, the mercurial talent, wide boy and nutter that was (and still is) Lee Walker, aka The Devil. At least, the devil if he didn't like you but a smashing bloke if he did and thankfully, we're still good friends today.

Looking back, he started unbelievably quietly. It took him a couple of games to get used to us, the system and the crowd. Their first impression was always scepticism. No half measures. Wealdstone could have signed Bobby Moore the day after he won the World Cup and he'd have had to prove himself to the fans. Then as now, players must start to prove themselves as soon as the team is read out. No bedding in, no finding your feet. It really is sink or swim from your first touch in the pre-game warm-up.

The club and the fans have been through the proverbial wringer since topping the Non-league tree with a Conference and FA Trophy 'double' in 1985. They were the first club to achieve the feat but were denied promotion to the Football League under the old 're-election' system (a couple of seasons before automatic promotion came in). Then they tripped over the top of the mountain, slid down and spent the best part of twenty years trying to scratch their way back up. (As I write, they're almost there finishing in the top half of Conference South and on the up).

They'd stopped falling at least when I joined, but only because there wasn't much further to go. They'd lost their ground - and then the money that was due in a fraud - and had been homeless nomads since 1991, playing in front of fewer and fewer fans in a financially-strangling half ownership of Watford's Vicarage Road, before escaping just about intact to play in front of even less fans further from 'home' at Yeading FC's Beaconsfield Road ground. Falling crowds and falling income were topped by increasing travel costs in the Beazer Homes League Southern Division, and the decision was made to take a voluntary transfer to the Isthmian League. A league at the same level, but much more South East and London orientated. The problem was, no-one of similar status, i.e. Division One would swap, so Wealdstone had to start at the bottom of the league in Division Three.

This was Wealdstone. Ever looking to the positive the publicity machine took over: New Manager, great squad, new ground (a share at Edgware, at least), then a 9-1 win away from home at Cove in the first match of the season. As if there wasn't enough hype around the club, the bloody Chairman went public in the local paper telling the world that we would win promotion at a canter. Christ, most of us didn't know everyone in the squad's first names! There were more promises in the papers by Christmas of promotion, success and a new era of Wealdstone returning to the top of the non-league ladder. Just the four divisions to win and over a hundred places to climb, then. No half measures!

The twenty of us in the dressing had to cope with this as our reality. Walks made a big difference as he changed the dynamic in the squad. He wasn't afraid to dig people out, but he'd include everyone in the banter as well, it was a bit all for one and one for all, or perhaps more accurately, all for Walks and Walks for all……

After a couple of games to settle in, he also struck up an affinity with the crowd and that helped a few others by taking some of the pressure off. It also helped me as my relationship with the crowd strengthened after a spell where things had been a bit rough, especially after an FA Cup tie. I'm known for a few high points in my career but there have been a few lows along the way and Hertford Town away was one of them. We were drawing but on top. I sprinted down the left wing (really!) and cut inside then tried to knock the ball wide to young winger Gavin Hart but the intended pass was intercepted. They broke away and with no defender to beat on our left-hand side, scored the winner. Another cup run over. The fans dug me out for a few weeks for that one. It was a game we should have won and worse still we had a player's night out planned for the evening. (Weeks? As I said before it was over 20 years ago, and I go to Wealdstone now to watch a match and someone will bring it up!)

In true non-league tradition, it had all gone sour for me on the pitch but after a few liveners the evening went OK! We were up in Northampton so we all stayed over and the next morning met up early to get away. I was stood in the hotel lobby with Steve Bircham and a few of the lads when all we could hear was retching from the gents. Moments later outwalked our very own Mr Bartlett. Players 1 Manager 0.

We were in the mix for the promotion places throughout the season and we had some good results, but late on we stuttered and lost a couple of games at home. We just missed out, finishing fourth by a couple of points and really, we were still a work in progress. Instant success with a new side is rare and we were no exception, but a good base had been built for the following year.

My first or second game nemesis, Steve Croad was Gordon's 'Commander in Chief' at centre half that year, but he missed a few games during the season and as a result, Gordon made me skipper. It was an honour and a great boost personally. I didn't even think I'd get the chance to 'point the finger' either. Not at all. Never. Not once. Nada.

Captaincy by that time was worth an extra 10% I reckon. I'd learnt from Uxbridge and it didn't weigh on me anymore, as I didn't shout and bawl as much as many, my way being to lead by example. Throughout my career as a player, I've stuck my head in where I shouldn't, or others wouldn't, and I'd put the extra yard in every time. I'm proud that managers have seen that in me and I have skippered every club I've played for. That's an honour in itself.

Wealdstone started the following season with most of the same squad though there were still a few ins and outs, most notably Bomber (Darren Bonfield) in goal and a mix of full backs in pre-season and the early games. I'd moved into centre half but there is no truth in the rumour that it was to stop me sprinting down the line. Also joining were Bryan Hammett up front and veteran Roy Marshall at the back. Very experienced and cool headed he had played at a very high level in non-league and was a real no-nonsense centre half who replaced Croady, partnering me.

One of the incoming full-backs was John Massey on the right. A decent tigerish little player but he couldn't drink! (Looking back over this, it's a typical non-league comment of the time, his name followed by his drinking capability. Not for us his speed, strength, dead-ball delivery). I remember another night out (Northampton again, as the Chairman Paul Rumens lived there and was often involved in the organisation!) where he had a couple of pints and he was well past merry by the time he finished the second. He was a newbie and could have been taken advantage of, but on this occasion, the lads looked after him. From then on, for every round we ordered, he got a weak shandy. He didn't notice, and it made no bloody difference anyway, he still got hammered. He must be the first man ever to get completely blitzed on lemonade with a hint of lager.

Another addition was Paul Mckay signed from Harrow B*rough which would give him an extra hurdle to climb in the eyes of 'Stones partisan fans. A lovely bloke and an unbelievable player at that level, he could play anywhere and take it in his stride (except maybe in goal as he isn't the tallest). Right back, sweeper, centre midfield, left midfield, it didn't matter, he'd take on the role and look like he'd played there forever.

My old mate Bomber was in goal. I'd played with him at Watling Boys Club when we were kids and he joined from Kingsbury Town. Like myself wasn't used to playing in front of a large crowd and for their level, Wealdstone had a decent number of followers. As I said, they'd let you know they were there, good or bad. Being Bomber, there was an occasional ricket in among some excellent saves, but like all 'keepers there is very little tolerance in what mistakes you can get away with. Being the last line of defence, a mistake often meant a goal conceded, and he probably didn't need 300 people there to remind him!

Terry Hibbert was another that had joined, a goal-scoring midfielder with a great touch and another than could fill in as a sweeper too. It gave us options. Alongside 'Powders' (Steve Bircham) we really could move the ball around with ease. It made it easier for everyone to raise their game as these players came in around us. Those that did stayed, some with a cheeky arrogance about them (Bircham especially), one or two others got left behind and moved on but as they say, that is football.

Bircham, Walker, McKay, Chrissy Walton and I were the ringleaders off the field and the centre of a good changing room. We had a great team spirit and we'd welcome everyone who came in, but they would get their share of stick as well. Never nasty, but there was plenty of banter!

As much with the way the fixtures panned out as anything else, we didn't take the division by a storm though we were always there or thereabouts. One highlight was a match with Braintree. They, Harlow Town and Northwood were our rivals for promotion and it really looked as if it would be any three from four when The Irons came to visit us. A real six-pointer on a cold crisp February Tuesday night with a particularly partisan crowd of over 400 and a great atmosphere.

The White Lion Ground with its one long side of cover opposite the main stand meant that the sounds and the songs were amplified and projected across the pitch. It was quite an intense atmosphere for the home players and it gave us a boost, but with the fans no more than a metre from the touchline, it put away teams under some pressure if they didn't have strong characters. And the Wealdstone fans could (and would) soon work out the weakness and their target for the night.

Boy, what a game. We (in my best Norwegian*) gave those boys one hell of a beating! Just one of those nights. From minute one we clicked. We scored the first goal early doors through a Roy Marshall header I think. They were top of the league and we were second if memory serves but we absolutely destroyed them. It was the best performance I've ever been involved in. We scored six without reply. Simon Garner of Blackburn Rovers fame had joined us after a spell at Her Majesties for contempt of court and he got a couple that night.

(*Bjørge Lillelien was commentator for the Norwegian Broadcasting Corporation. In September 1981 he came to international prominence when he said: *"Winston Churchill, Maggie Thatcher, Your boys took a hell of a beating"* in commentary following Norway's 2-1 victory against England in a World Cup qualifier).

I don't know why I did it, but you know all this crowd surfing that they say has been invented recently? Nah. I invented it that night I reckon. I went on a couple of runs down the wing (so moving me to centre-half didn't work), we were so much in command the adrenalin took over and the discipline was forgotten. For one of the goals I, Fergie Moore, one-paced centre half, left back, whatever, went on a mazy, yes mazy run, beat my man, cut inside and got a shot away. The force of the shot was so great that the 'keeper could only parry it and Garns was there for a tap in. Probably the easiest goal the amazing Simon Garner ever scored, and I made it. That's an assist I'll remember!

6-0 and at the final whistle, Fergie invents crowd surfing, diving over the barrier full length into the 'Stones fans in The Dog Kennel as they had christened the long-covered side. I was pushed backwards and forwards before eventually getting back onto the pitch. What an amazing night and one I'll never forget.

Garns was different class. Gordon had signed him, and no-one knew. We were playing away at Hertford Town (NOT in the FA Cup) and kitman Graham Smith found out. He came up to me and said we'd signed Blackburn Rovers' all-time leading goal-scorer! I think I was stood with Lee Walker just looking at the pitch at the time, I went: *"Yeah, all right, so we've signed Shearer then…. well done Graham"* and I turned to Walks and laughed. *"Don't believe me then"* Graham said as he walked off.

A couple of minutes later we walked into the changing room and sitting there was Simon Garner. Sitting on the bench, legs crossed having a fag (he'd got into the swing of non-league quickly) with a copy of the Sporting Life. It's the picture I have in my memory because that was just the way he was. We all got changed, Gordon said a few bits and we went out to warm up, then I looked round and no sign of Garner. He didn't do warm-ups!

He hadn't played for a while, but game by game he got better and better. He just oozed class. He was knocking on a bit but over two or three yards and with a little shuffle on the ball, no-one could get near him. He had strength on the ball and the ability and vision to bring other people into the game so easily. Dangerous in and around the box, he scored a few goals and I reckon in the season or so he was with us, he played more passes off his chest than most players could dream of in their whole career. I was in awe of him, a real special signing. He was the one that gave us that little bit extra. He joined in the banter, he and Walks got on well and he partnered well with Bryan Hammett up front, they soon struck up a decent understanding. We were all guns blazing!

It wasn't quite all roses though, as we suffered a couple of nervy hiccups losing at home to Northwood and Harlow, both promotion rivals, both games 0-2. We followed those with two 0-0 draws (one in the league and one in the cup), marking the longest spell without scoring for a couple of years. Despite a recovery from then on, we went into the last league game needing to beat Northwood away and they were unbeaten at home. On top of that, to win the title we had to hope that Braintree lost, I think against East Thurrock, who had nothing to play for and who we'd beaten 4-1 a few weeks earlier.

Perhaps unsurprisingly, we were a bit subdued pre-match. It should have all been wrapped up by then, but we'd let it slip. Being another local side many of us knew a few of the Northwood management and players like Chris Gell, Martin Dobinson and Tony Millard at the back and it was going to be a test for us with them also needing the win to guarantee their promotion.

As the whistle went and with well over 350 'Stones fans in a crowd of 500, we sparked into life. No-one let us down. Dominic Sterling was another that had signed after his release from Wimbledon, a solid defender and a great player.

Touch-tackle was his nickname as he loved nothing more than taking a touch to give the opponent a chance to nick the ball then he'd tackle through them to keep it!

After a cagey first half we went one-nil up early in the second kicking towards the Graveyard End. Northwood's ground has a graveyard behind one goal, odd, but true. Often, you'd see hearses and such like and people visiting graves with flowers and all sorts as you looked up when attacking or at a corner.

Northwood's fans were less in number and less vociferous than many, but God alone (well, God and a few of his residents) knows what they made of the 'Stones fans in full voice that afternoon. A couple of years further on, and Wealdstone moved in to ground-share at Northwood during a less than successful period on the pitch. Some Saturdays with perhaps another home defeat looming large, Rest in Peace wouldn't have cut it!

Back to the game: Almost immediately after we'd scored (and cleared a few exuberant fans off the pitch) Northwood got an equaliser as Millard came up from the back to head home. It meant an edgy last ten or fifteen minutes as we brought on Tony Smith, Walks and Peter Greene, trying to create an opening and it worked. Hammett got through and dinked one over the home keeper, Lee Carroll to restore the lead, having scored our opener. Then Roy Marshall got his head on a corner to make it 3-1. Cue mass hysteria, fans on the pitch and crying with joy. It was the first trophy the club had won 'on their way back' having gone through administration, being homeless and seemingly eternal ground-shares. If it meant a lot to the players, it meant a bloody site more to the long-suffering fans that afternoon.

It was fantastic. Scenes I'll never forget, fans on the field, champagne and Simon Garner as happy as anyone. With all the games he'd played and everything he'd done in his career, this was the first (and only) Championship he ever won. I can imagine his house; match balls from famous hat-tricks, shirts exchanged with some big footballing names, and there, in the corner, his ICIS Isthmian League Division III Champions medal…. I wonder!

The party had started well before the trophy was presented. Despite the odds being well stacked against Wealdstone winning the League at kick-off, Alan

Turvey who was League Chairman at the time had for some reason decided that he would bring the Trophy to Northwood rather than visiting Braintree who should have been odds-on to win the league that day.

I remember coming out of the changing room well after the game, probably around 6 or 6-30 after we'd been presented with the trophy (small) and had a few slugs of Champagne and Lager (large). We had the End of Season Dinner for the Supporters Club to attend. What a night to arrange it. What would have happened had it all gone pear shaped? We might have lost and not won the title or promotion, but who cares now? We had won both!

With no club of their own, the 'do' was booked at Wasps Rugby Club in Sudbury. Walks, myself and an old fan, 'super' Val Shearer, in his eighties were given a lift by Gordon. Val was a real Wealdstone fan and once signed as a player (in his seventies, Val was signed by the club as a protest on signing rules a few years previously). He'd been at the club forever and the fans even sang songs about him. People joke about me making my debut in black and white, but Val actually remembered the club playing in black and white (hoops) in the 1920s.

When we arrived, most of the fans with tickets and a few gate-crashers were already there. It was a packed house, about 150 tickets sold and about 200 in the room! We got a standing ovation as we walked in, shaking hands and cheering as we moved slowly through the crowd, and Val lapped it up too, welcomed with equal measure. The feeling was amazing; relief, ecstasy, exhaustion and elation... great timing.

As skipper, I had to make the Player's Player of the Year award. Apparently, I made a speech, but I don't remember a word of it. I'm told I managed to complete it and I presented the award to Roy Marshall who had been outstanding. It was fitting that he'd scored on the day as well. He didn't get forward too often, but he had been an inspiration alongside me at the back. I looked at him then and hoped I'd be able to play into my late thirties and still do it as he had. Here I am now wondering if I'll still be playing at 50!

The beer and songs flowed throughout the evening, led by the fans or led by the players, it didn't matter. We'd won on the day and were going to celebrate with the biggest hangovers we could get. The players ended up going to the Middlesex & Herts Country Club once the 'do' finished around midnight. I had the trophy, (well, cup) and I ended up putting it in the cloakroom with my jacket for safe keeping.

A few more beers and somehow, we got invited to the Case is Altered, a nearby pub for a lock-in. It was that far after opening hours, I reckon they must have reopened just for us! The usual suspects, Bircham, Walker, me, Leo Morris the assistant manager. I remember leaving (just about) and I remember waking up the next morning. The jacket was there but the cup wasn't. I'd bloody lost it! I remembered having it just before we left so I started to ring round the lads to see if anyone knew what had happened to it.

I didn't know it at the time but after I'd made a couple of calls the jungle drums were beating and the lads were all ringing each other making sure that no-one let the cat out of the bag. Every one of them told me I'd lost it. Bastards.

It got to about two o'clock and I'd been ringing everyone, then ringing them again, fretting about it and what I was going to do. Four or five hours it was before I found out that Birchy had it all along. He'd picked it up off the bar at the pub and taken it home with him. I didn't have a clue. You wouldn't believe the relief that ran through me when I found out. Bastards.

That fearful couple of hours aside, I was buzzing all weekend. It was probably the greatest day of my career winning that day and only winning the FA Sunday Cup (an FA competition in which I can claim to have won a few games!) a few years later has come close.

We had won the league, but our season wasn't over as on the Tuesday following, we had a cup final to play. It was another major competition (not) the (un-sponsored) Associate Members Trophy Final. Not for me the League Cup or a run at the FA Trophy or FA Vase, this was a competition basically for Division II and Division III (that's ICIS Isthmian League Division II & III) clubs, who were so low down the football ladder that they were not allowed to be full members of the Football Association. They couldn't hold a full FA Share, so they were only associate members.

It was against Leighton Town who despite being from the division above, were the underdogs. They arrived with almost no fans though the match was played on their doorstep at Hitchin Town, they wore a washed-out kit and to this day, I don't know how we lost that match 1-0, but we did.

Still, there was another end of season booze trip to Blackpool (again) planned for the weekend! Suffice to say that, that was great fun, far too much drinking and laughter with a great team and every one of them got what Wealdstone was about. Every new player came in had to be on their game straight away and if they had a bad spell, they had to have the character to get out of it. If they didn't they were gone. The crowd were loud, harsh and direct but they were in the main, good judges and fair. The whole package justified my leaving previous clubs to win things. A happy summer. Thinking about it now, whenever an end of season trip to Blackpool has been planned, I've won a league or a cup. Now, where's the brochures?

I spent the summer looking forward to my third season at the club, a long time for me, and as always there were a few new faces in the squad when pre-season started. Wivenhoe away on a bright sunny afternoon was met with (as always) a decent turn out from the fans. Stuart Atkins had joined as a centre half and the enigmatic Stan Bowder was in at full back. We lost but the stand-out memory was walking past the home dressing room after the game with their players shouting *"Welcome to the big boy's league"* as they thought we'd struggle. I know we'd lost but I also knew we were good enough to compete, even with what we'd shown that day.

The following Tuesday we were at home to Leighton Town and it was Paul Lamb's competitive debut. He'd played a few in pre-season but missed the Wivenhoe trip as he was banned. We took a two-goal lead and then Lambie 'threw the nut' headbutting a Leighton player off the ball and in the box. It was a reaction to something not seen or heard by anyone but Lambie, but everyone unfortunately including the referee, saw the retribution. Penalty awarded, Lambie was sent off to firmly mark the night in the memory. They scored but we hung on to win. Lambie started the next three or four games, then took his enforced three game rest courtesy of the suspension!

That win / lose start was reflected through the first eight or nine games and in typical Moore fashion, that included a defeat at the first hurdle away to Leatherhead in the FA Cup though we did nick a win after extra time away to Hornchurch in the FA Vase.

We were still settling in as a side but soon started to turn defeats into draws and draws into wins as the season progressed. We had some luck to, not least on one game versus Canvey island at home when we got absolutely battered but drew 1 – 1. They had a decent side and were fancied to do well, and they tore into us from the kick-off. We were decent but didn't get much of a look in that night, but a bit of luck was with us as we didn't lose. That night really gelled the squad and fired up the spirit in the side.

Around the start of November Dom Sterling was having a bit of a rough spell and the gaffer asked me if I'd play left wing-back. He wasn't expecting me to be up and down the line too much, but to make it solid defensively and get forward when I could. Paul McKay was playing a similar role on the right and we had a competition between us to see who could go the longest in a game without touching the ball. We'd just be there, running up and down the line in support (Macca a bit quicker than me more often than not), just doing what we were meant to do, albeit without the ball. When we did get involved it seemed as though it mattered and to be fair, though it wasn't my normal game, I quite enjoyed it.

We didn't give up and managed to stick around fifth or sixth in the table for quite a while. We even won three games in the FA Vase before we lost at Great Wakering Rovers, when to be honest, we didn't turn up for a game we should have been good enough to win at a canter.

One other new face in the side at that time was the now infamous Mario Celaire. Gordon had a contact at Feltham Young Offenders and this lad was an inmate, playing well for their football team. Nearing the end of his sentence (and we never really found out what it was for, despite several rumours), Gord went to watch him, liked what he saw: a big forward with great pace, and got him down to training then into the side. Quick didn't cover it. He really did, in one game at Chalfont, jump to win a header, flicking the ball on from a goalkeeper's clearance, then he sprinted and beat the defender to the ball, he was that fast.

37

Sadly, injury finished his season early and he moved on before becoming known nationally as the first person convicted under the double jeopardy law in England, being convicted of the murder of his girlfriend seven years after first being cleared of the crime. He was convicted after boasting about it and trying to kill another girlfriend if memory serves. He'd even changed his name to Mario McNish after the first acquittal, continuing his football career along the way.

As the season progressed we suffered the odd defeat but were winning more than we lost and we were keeping pace with the leaders, but for some, that wasn't enough. Early in the new year there was an incident with one of our own fans. At Wealdstone, it didn't matter if you were in your first game or your hundredth, you had to perform and one of the fans (who I do get on with now) was giving me some grief online on the Fans Forum and from the terraces. I scored against Wivenhoe at home and I knew where he was, so I ran over shouting something like: *"what do you think of that then"* but I may have emphasised it a bit. It was passion and an auto-defence mechanism I suppose, but I shouldn't have singled him out. Neither of us would back down until other players arrived and pulled me back to continue the game and nothing more was said. It was just passion from both sides, he's still around as a passionate supporter and I still love the club. Together we both can share a hello and a chat if we meet.

Come March and we were right in the mix for promotion though no-one really said anything, then we hit a bad run losing three on the bounce, but we picked up and started grinding out results rather than setting the world alight. We lost after a poor performance at Barking and then three days later we were away to Braintree Town who were top of the table and unbeaten at home. It was also transfer deadline day and the gaffer brought in a couple of new faces, Andy Peakes from Rushden and a lad called Richard Dobson. They both started though I don't think either knew anyone's name!

It was a master-stroke as we won 1-0, Dennis Greene nicking a late goal. The whole season really hung on that result as we went unbeaten till the end of the season securing a second promotion. Third place, fifteen points behind Champions Canvey Island and Braintree who were only second on goal difference, but we were five points in front of Bedford Town in fourth.

Promotion was confirmed on the last Tuesday of the season winning an away match against our landlords, Edgware Town. They'd been in the mix for most of the season but must have hated playing Wealdstone home or away that year: Stones were victors in numbers on the terraces and four times on the pitch winning both league games and a couple of cup-ties for good measure. Personally, it was bragging rights to me, as I had a lot of friends including Steve Newing on the other side. Straight after the game fans and players alike headed for the Change of Heart, the local pub where, as the song goes we got the party started!

The summer couldn't end quick enough for me as I wanted to get back to playing. It was another step up and with only a few additions to the squad we started the 1998-99 season OK, only suffering two defeats in the first ten games. It was a decent start, but we didn't really kick on and it soon looked like we'd be out of the race for the promotion places. We also conspired to knock ourselves out of the FA Cup after a poor performance at home saw us travel to Newport Isle of Wight for a midweek replay. Not great for a non-league player with a job. It meant time off again for a lunchtime start-out, and we looked tired as we lost in extra time. It was my FA Cup hoodoo again I'm sure, but a few weeks later (with, at the time, little but pride to play for in the League), we got a bit of a glamour tie in the FA Trophy, drawn to play Dagenham & Redbridge away.

On matchday the weather was miserable and despite standing water on the pitch, the match started only to be abandoned after about 15 minutes. We went over to applaud the numerous 'Stones fans that were under the cover in one corner and as I approached I realised that the pitch on that side was flooded, so what better opportunity? I took a full-length belly-dive and floated / aquaplaned / skidded fully twenty yards up to them. I nearly drowned in the bow wave!

For the rescheduled match on the following Tuesday evening, I was marking England C international, Mark Janney and to be honest, I did a job on him, and kept him quiet all game. We took the lead when Stuart Kent scored, and we should have made it two when Birchy (I think) missed a penalty, but even then, we held our own and soaked up the Dagenham pressure throughout. With the ninety minutes ticking down, it looked as though I was going to get a decent result in an FA Competition after all, but I must have upset the football gods somewhere down the line, and in traditional fashion, they kicked me firmly in the bollocks.

With both feet.

Just outside our penalty box I was running with Janney and I made an innocuous challenge for the ball. Now, I'm the world's worst at saying I didn't deserve this and that but this time I really didn't. It was a ball in the air down the flank, he ran across me as I jumped and went down pole-axed and the Ref sent me off almost before he'd landed. I was fuming. It was unjust. He really did just run into me. That was it though, I was off, and they had the free kick, which, just to rub salt into my wounds, they equalised from.

I didn't see it. In fact, I couldn't see much at all through the red mist of anger and frustration. I trudged off and made my way down the tunnel and into the dressing room kicking everything. I nearly took the door off. I think I put my foot through it in anger and nearly had it off the hinges trying to get my foot back out.

I got suspended, a straight red no matter how unjust was three games and that started the end of my first spell at Wealdstone as I struggled to get back into the side. A couple of weeks later and I was a forlorn figure as I took the field in a Middlesex Cup tie. It was a run out to keep me sharp. I wanted to play football and I wanted to play for Wealdstone but now I was on the fringe of the side, not leading it.

I've always thought if you aren't in the side, give yourself a month or six weeks to get back in, maybe as a sub or when someone is injured, but this time my six weeks was up. I hadn't played again and one Thursday night at training I felt I was on the outside. When I'm not involved I get a bit into myself, introverted and quiet, which is not me. A few of the lads gave me some stick and for once I didn't respond. My time had come.

We went to the Change of Hart after training and I remember thinking something was going on as Leo Morris called Bomber over and I thought it was away from me. Then Gordon called me to one side to have a word. He told me he had to let me go because I needed games and I was falling down the pecking order. Basically, his first choice was now Dom Sterling. I had to take it on the chin, but I was devastated. It was the first time it had really happened to me and Wealdstone had become my life. It was a love affair that lasted three or four years but now it was over. I genuinely thought about packing up as I thought that there was nothing left in football after what Wealdstone meant to me, and that had been taken away.

I went around to mums and I was there again on the following Friday when Gordon rang me on my mobile. He'd had a word with Tony Choules, Manager at Northwood and had rung to tell me that there was a chance there for me. To be honest, I let him have it a bit, to my mind he was trying to make himself feel better by moving me on and to a team in the division below at that. He got an earful as I fully vented my frustration and anger. I didn't contact Northwood and a day or two later Chertsey came in for me. They were due to play Wealdstone in a couple of weeks so that was decision made. A chance to show him he was wrong.

I got a great reception from the fans when I turned up and again when I walked on the field. There was even a report saying the game was like a charity match for me. League positions and points meant nothing, it was me being back. As it happens it was a decent game and we, the new Chertsey 'we' earned a 2-2 draw.

From mid-table at the start of February, Chertsey and I remained there. Wealdstone, similarly placed when we played, cut the budget as the money was tight, but the fans rallied round and dug deep to raise a big proportion of the player's wages for the rest of the season. The team repaid them, winning 19 drawing 1 and losing only 1 of their last 21 games to achieve third place and promotion once again but I still don't think Gordon was right. Well, maybe.

During that run-in, they played a game at Chesham against homeless Romford and I went along and watched. I said hello to a few fans but stood on the side lines, the opposite side from the bench and though a few of the players, Jonah (Brian Jones), Rocky Baptiste and Carl Holmes all picked me out, Gordon didn't. Stones were outstanding. They won 4-0 in first gear, but I wasn't going to tell

Gordon that. Not being part of it still hurt.

The promotion they deserved was eventually denied them over a ground grading issue. The club had done all they could and were told verbally and unofficially that it was enough, but the 'official' decision was made against them. Despite not being there that decision hurt me. I was no longer at the club and yet it hurt. I couldn't imagine what it did for the players (and my friends) who were still there. That one bloody suspension was unjust and cost me my place and it still rankles today.

AU REVOIR, NOT GOODBYE

I didn't know it at the time, but when I left Wealdstone it wasn't final. I'd lost my place in the side and they felt it was time for a change. I disagreed but couldn't really do much about it. I just knew that if I got another opportunity it would be to show him he was wrong. Nothing personal, you understand!

Part of the attraction of Chertsey was the potential. They had some decent players from the non-league circuit, the likes of Jason Shaw and Martin Carter and I knew goalkeeper Graham Benstead from Brentford. Oh, and as I said, they were due to play Wealdstone in a couple of weeks....

There was a good spirit there when I joined, and I became good friends with Richard McDonnagh, another now former team mate that I still see and touch base with. A real live wire and great banter but he backed it up by putting himself about on the pitch too. My little rat of a player. Bloody everywhere.

It was only a short spell at Chertsey but long enough to add another trophy as we won the Southern Combination Cup, but the stand-out memory was that trip back to play Wealdstone at The White Lion Ground.

Things changed over the summer and once again it was time to pick up the boots and move on, this time a little closer to home at Hemel Hempstead Town, a division lower (why did I always drop down a division?) but again a club on the up with ambition and a flamboyant Chairman (who is still there) in Dave Boggins. It's fair to say he's not the most educated Chairman in football (though he'd probably add that he has been educated in life), but he loves his club and he's always been happy to splash the cash for the right players or a party. My ambition to be a winner was the driver, but financially I gained as well. Win-win.

I said not long after I joined that despite his style, or maybe because of it, Dave would do good things for that club, truly a nice guy and a fan as much as a Chairman, I'm glad to say he's proved me right over the years and is, with Hemel, settled in the Conference South alongside Wealdstone.

My first training session with them was a return among friends. I suppose after a few years on the circuit and a few clubs, you'd always bump into someone you knew, but I seemed to do it with spades. The same managers, the same team-mates, it was just a different coloured shirt.

Steve Bateman was there at the time as was Tony Kelly, a real tough tackling midfielder who wouldn't shirk a challenge (even at 30/70 against). He played out his career there and eventually took over as Manager. Josh Price was there, (the Managers brother), a former pro at Watford and another Brentford friend in big centre half Lee Thomas. Lee, Marcelle Bruce and I were going to be a solid back three that year!

Maybe it was the management thinking they knew enough or whatever, but in advance of the 1999-2000 season, we had the shortest pre-season I've ever done. It consisted of a handful of training sessions and just three games. Two against local sides from lower levels, Leverstock Green and Tring Athletic, (fairly comfortable as we won by eight and seven) and then we scored four in our final friendly without reply, but it hadn't been challenging and wasn't good preparation for what lay ahead. A week later, we went into the first league game away to Wingate and Finchley and got dicked 3-1. We were slow, unfit, lacked cohesion and in the eyes of the management it must have all been me as I was bombed. To be honest, after a few games, I couldn't see a way back either. I'd already spoken to a couple of mates, Jon Turner and the late Paul Sweales at Yeading about re-joining them. Then, just as I was about to leave I got back into the starting eleven. I didn't miss another game that season. Funny like that, football.

After the dismal opening, the side only lost three games all year (maybe the Management were right during pre-season!) and all to teams beginning with a W: Wingate, Wivenhoe and Witham. A couple of new faces came in including McDonnagh from Chertsey. He tidied up in midfield, made us look composed and he always got the forwards into the game. Butler and Sozzo up front were decent players and the hard-working Vinny Somers out wide scored a few as did Mark Lyebird. It gave us two good wingers pivoting off Kelly who was just hard as nails. Despite my personal start, we became a very good side.

At the end of the season we were fighting for the Championship with Ford

Sports. They were finishing their season playing one game a week, while after postponements because of our poor pitch we were left with three and four games a week to catch up.

We learnt about the pitch issues early in the season when after a bit of August rain our first home game was postponed. Dave Boggins had, had new drainage installed over the summer but it simply didn't work. We were fighting a losing battle just to get games on and by the run in, we were playing on a sand-pit. It was testament to the players that we were still winning. The season came down to the Horsham game at home, our last game of the season and we had to win to win the league and we did.

It signalled the start of probably the best party Hemel Hempstead had ever seen! Everyone turned up in fancy dress and I ended up doing an Irish Jig in the bar, then we all trooped off still in fancy dress to a local nightclub. The party carried on there and when the bar and club closed, we went back to the Hemel clubhouse! It was a great night and a great way to celebrate our promotion. Or so we thought.

As with the let down the previous year at Wealdstone, there was a temporary stand on the far side of the Hemel ground and they'd been told it was good enough for them to achieve the required ground grading for promotion. Given a timeframe and plenty of assurances from those in charge, when it came down to the decision they were refused and told that they wouldn't be going up. I was devastated. I'd even been telling Dave Boggins for a while that he had to get the assurances in writing after what had happened at Wealdstone, but it wasn't to be. Stitched up again. I found out first-hand how the 'Stones lads must have felt the previous year. It was soul destroying to win the league and not go up, but most of us decided to stay and give it another go. It was a real low point, but we had to get on with it.

The following season, we were to find out that winning the league a second time is a hard task. I don't think anyone thought it would be easy, but we got off to a flyer winning the first three or four games and then we struggled. We didn't perform as a unit and individually players didn't reach the heights that they had the previous year. A few players moved on and there were internal squabbles – mainly over money as always at this level. It was a tough year. I

45

was playing and doing OK but then I had a fall-out and Chris Sparkes was brought in which meant once again, I was in and out of the side.

Manager Neil Price was another to sign me twice. Originally at Staines where he eventually got the sack, he had re-signed me at Hemel Hempstead Town. I'd joined a squad with a few players I already knew and a management style I also knew. A bit roughhouse and with Neil 'being one of the lads'. At least he had given up the playing side, so the indiscipline was less of an issue, his at least, but our relationship really came to an end after I was sent off. That caused a spat between Neil and I and I was dropped before my ban had even started.

Frustrations growing, we even got to the Associate Members Trophy Final that season and ran out of time to play the match. There were just too many games to fit in, so the final was held over to the following year by which time most of the side including me had moved on, so we never played in it. I can't even remember who won!

SWEET FA

You'll notice having read this far, that despite mention of a few cup finals, wins and losses, there has been little mention of the FA Competitions, The FA Cup, the FA Trophy or FA Vase, and what there has been hasn't exactly been positive. In the non-league game each offers a much-needed chance to win a few quid to top up the clubs no doubt depleted coffers and it's also a chance for players to get a bit of fame and glory if they win through a few qualifying rounds.

Well, don't sign me then. In the history of the FA Cup I must have the worst record bar none. And the FA Trophy and FA Vase aren't much better either.

From the very start of my career I have never ever had a sniff of a big game or League opposition in the FA Cup, in fact I don't think I've ever made it to the late qualifying rounds. Many a season I have looked on in envy of teams and players that I have played against or with (just got the timing wrong!), as they bask in the spotlight of cup success and glory - without me!

It hurts a bit I suppose, even in a career where I have won a few things as it's always been a major ambition of mine to get to the 1ˢᵗ Round proper and get a little bit of fame. Even to get on either the BBC or Sky - some players get lucky and even achieve this two or three times in their career! Me? Two qualifying round wins in the same season has been rare.

Almost every year, even now, I get a chance to correct that, though it does get harder. Even in recent years (including a season where Edgware didn't even enter the FA competitions, no doubt as with me in the squad they thought they'd save the entry fee), in the FA Cup Qualifying Rounds the football gods conspire against me. Not the team. Just me.

A couple of years ago in my last season at Cockfosters, the Extra Preliminary Round of the FA Cup had opened our competitive season and we were drawn at home to Hullbridge Sports from the Essex Senior League. A game we should have won, and we did although we made it difficult for ourselves. In the first half we were awful but managed to take a 1-0 lead before half time. Then the game changing moment occurred ten minutes into the second half when the old boy (that'll be me, then) knocked in a trademark powerful header at the far stick. It was a nice moment for me as I had my two boys there and I could see that they were delighted for me. I did wonder if it would be the last time they'd see me score though, and it might even have been my first FA Cup goal…. I'll have to go and check!

After an hour, we were 4-0 up but they pegged us back to 4-2 before we scored a fifth. They got a couple more to make it 5-4 and we were lucky to hold on. Conceding four goals took the gloss of me scoring to be honest but we'd got lazy and tried to cruise which as a side we were not good enough to do.

Personally, I didn't have a great game and felt a bit lethargic throughout, that a good reminder that you must play at 100% to help cut out lapses in your game. The result got us a bollocking, but we were in the hat for the next round and hoping for another tie with a team lower down the pyramid.

Football gods intervening we drew Waltham Abbey from the Ryman League away. It was a tough ask and we found ourselves 2-0 down versus our higher placed opposition after about a quarter of an hour. It could have been worse if it hadn't been for Sam Styles in goal. We pulled a goal back with ten to go in the first half and even had chances to equalise, but it wasn't to be.

We got the classic half time team talk of: *"next goal is vital"* and: *"we had 'em rattled when we scored"* but to no avail. We gave away a penalty five minutes into the second half although we did get another goal back, but despite our pressure they broke and scored a fourth. We nearly nicked another goal, but the gods were toying with us, it went 5-2 then 6-2 as the dream crashed around us for another season. Even though Adem Ali scored the goal of the game late on, at 6-3 it didn't make for much consolation.

I'm sorry but I've never been consoled by a late goal in a defeat. It's still a defeat, it still hurts, and this might just have been my last realistic chance for a glory moment in the FA Cup. Even being praised for my performance by the management didn't do anything more than way-lay the self-doubt demon for a few hours. We still bloody lost and I'd rather have played like a wanker in a win!

Last chance? Well, there's one thing almost as bad as losing in the FA Cup and that is not entering. At Cockfosters, I'd been the oldest player in the Competition for two consecutive years, not a win or a record but something I was personally proud of. Moving on to Edgware Town as the newly re-formed club phoenix-like returned to playing, and an administrative error meant that the club didn't even enter for the year. Cue Fergus Moore not happy, then well-travelled ex-pro bloody Barry Hayles played for Chesham in one of their ties and he's older than me too. Next year, Ferg, next year….

So, twilight of my career. FA Cup gone (at least for another season), we needed a good run in the FA Vase which I'm pleased to say, both Cockfosters and subsequently Edgware Town had entered. Not quite the kudos of the senior competition, but it's still one you want to win. In the 2014 competition, Cockfosters had despatched Hoddesdon 5-0 at home at the beginning of October – job done with some ease, and we then drew Ipswich Wanderers away. A lot had been made of this game by everyone around the club but in my preparation, it was just another game in the twilight of my career (except that it was an FA competition of course!).

One big difference from a normal Cockfosters away-day was that we were going on a coach. As it turned out, it was a good journey with plenty of banter but there were a few thoughts and comments about the long journey home if we lost. For me it was another new club and ground to tick off on my football journey, while for the younger lads and my two kids it was exciting. Aaron and Callum bless them were counting down the days till the Saturday when they could be in amongst the lads and the lads fair play to them let my boys join in the banter. They even cleaned it up a bit!

It was a big game for a club like ours and a hot topic was what the team would be. Unsurprisingly, everybody in the squad (including Dennis Marharjan who only does Saturday home games) had made themselves available! It was going to be hard whatever the side picked, but Rochey and Fab went for experience over youthful exuberance. Credit to everyone though, those that were left out took it on the chin and gave those picked all the support they could.

On to the game and Stuey Blackburne missed his trademark early chance. In a game like this an early goal really settles the side but it wasn't to be, then the

49

footie gods took over and the Witches scored with their first chance after about 20 minutes. For fully ten minutes after that we fell apart, we were disjointed in midfield and no-one got a foot on the ball. To be fair we weren't at the races during that spell, though the hosts didn't extend their lead.

For the rest of the half we got settled but didn't really dominate as we should have, and we went in 0-1 down at half-time. Getting our heads right and getting each of us focussed, Rochey sent us out for the second half. As it turned out, a second half of one-way traffic with us creating chance after chance after chance but we just could not find the back of the net. In fact, when the full-time whistle blew it was eerie, almost as though Ipswich were a bit embarrassed to celebrate, such had been our dominance as the game played out.

It didn't take long for the lads who hadn't played to vent their feelings in a cutting but (I think) good natured way, primarily on WhatsApp, a social media site, as well of course as on the coach, face to face. Our experienced midfield (who lost it in the first half) and Stuey who missed a couple you'd normally expect him to score took the full brunt of it but for me personally it hurt deeply. I couldn't face the bar for twenty minutes or so after the game, but I eventually mellowed as the journey home progressed.

At least, my boys enjoyed the day out but even that was tinged with sadness, as I realised there won't be many more – if any more – chances for me to give them a day out on the coach with the team as a player. It was FA Football Gods 2 Fergus Moore 0 for another season. Why always me???

You don't believe in the football gods? Well, how about this then. I'll explain later why so many of us from Cockfosters moved on with the Management Team to Edgware, but this particular season, 2015-16, (takes a while to write a book doesn't it!), Edgware won their first Vase tie with some ease, then drew Ipswich Wanderers at home. Most of us were keen to get our own back. We'd moved to a reformed club with little money, a mix of old players and a few youngsters, and a chance for revenge. Ipswich Wanderers (who have got a few quid) had continued their upward progression and a 3-1 home defeat later, we were out once again.

Despite my abysmal record in senior FA competitions, one has also given me my proudest moment in football, as I was in the Duke of York side that won the FA Sunday Cup in 2002-03.

I was playing for Hemel Hempstead at the time and Lamby asked me if I fancied a crack at the cup with his (Northampton based) Sunday side. It was one of two 'premier' Sunday competitions, the other being the Carlsberg Cup and a lot of my mates and old team-mates had won that playing as West Hendon Ex-Serviceman's Club, affectionately known as 'The Madhouse'. They won their final at Wembley following a semi-final victory at Anfield, and they went on to win an International challenge between the UK and Danish Carlsberg Cup winners, another victory at the home of football. In fact, they damn near repeated the feat with a similar semi-final victory the following season, though that time they lost in the Wembley final. Mates they may have been, but you will understand I wasn't part of their success with my FA record, so bragging rights were certainly firmly held in their hands... they weren't shy in reminding me of their exploits at every opportunity and to be honest, I was gutted that it wasn't me. Just to have played at Wembley would have been the ultimate experience.

I finally did get a call from The Madhouse, only to continue my FA record as we were beaten in the quarter finals, so when Lamby asked me to play for his team, I think I said yes before he'd finished the question, but in truth, I was a little reluctant as I'd be putting myself under pressure to perform, self-doubt was rife: What if I made a mistake that would cost this team (whose players I didn't know) the game? My internal demons were getting in the way of what was to become my greatest moment on a football pitch.

Lamby contacted the team manager, Neil Twelfree and he came to watch me play for Hemel – a Sunday side running the rule over me to see if I was up to it, that's how serious the Sunday Cup's had become. He chose a good night at Wembley FC, as I had a decent game and scored a goal. It made up his mind and I was going to be part of his plans. The only non-Northampton based player. No pressure, and we agreed that I would travel up for the next game where I would be a substitute, I'd get to know the lads and all being well, work my way into the side.

Twelly announced the team for the game and I was starting. I was nervous as I didn't want to let anyone down, not least Lamby and Twelly, as both had shown great faith in me, but I needn't have worried as I settled in well and we cruised to victory. For me there's no better way to earn your team-mates respect than to perform on the pitch and I felt I did in that first match and our progression to the semi-final, to be played at Solihull Borough's ground. As it turned out this neutral venue most certainly wasn't, as it was on the doorstep for our opponents, a local side called Travellers.

I don't know what it was that got to me, but I didn't feel right on the day. I'd been nervous before, but nothing like that, it was almost intolerable. I knew if we won, the final would be at Anfield, the home of my childhood and adulthood heroes, Liverpool. Perhaps that was my problem, but I just wanted the game to fast forward to the end, so I'd know the outcome. It's a cliché, but my legs felt like lead and I didn't want the ball anywhere near me for fear of making an error. A prestigious final at a dream venue was so close and the pressure I put on myself was immense. Losing wasn't an option.

The game was a blur from start to finish. The odd vague memory recalls that with about 10 mins to go the Travellers were 2-0 up. I could feel myself welling up inside, my fears were being realised and we were going to lose, but the last ten minutes was mayhem. We scored three to take the lead the third with just two minutes to go. I was welling up inside again, but now because we were so close to my dream. Pure relief, ecstasy, then shock and fear as Travellers equalised. My mind and every thought I had were thrown into a liquidiser, closely followed by every muscle and bone in my body. I'm sure I realised what soup felt like. Utter turmoil. I won't look this up, but I can't even remember if we scored another two or three in extra time, but after that extra half hour I really didn't care, I was Anfield bound, as pure unadulterated joy and relief overcame me as the final whistle went. I have never experienced such nerves or tension in my life as I did that day. I'd played most of the game as though I was playing in fog. To this day, I don't know how I got through the game, a truly horrible experience that eventually satisfied a lifetime's ambition, to play in an FA final at a major venue. My evening with the lads was spent enjoying a beer or two, interspersing each mouthful with phone calls to The Madhouse lads. My turn for the bragging rights.

The final came along and once again we were to play a 'local' side, Allerton FC. On the Saturday before the game, I must have been the only one of the twenty-two to play for my club, but to me, that game was important as well. Christ knows how I would have felt if I'd picked up a knock! Even Lamby had a convenient injury that needed a bit of a rest, so he was on the bench for Hemel's trip to Barking. How's that for twenty-four hours? Barking FC's Mayesbrook Park to Anfield, chalk and cheese.

Lamby's dad, Dave drove us to Chester to meet the rest of 'The Duke', and it seemed everyone had been given the Saturday off by their respective teams. They were all set for dinner by the time we arrived, and Twelly was already keeping tabs on the alcohol consumption as he didn't want anyone over doing it. I went straight to the bar as I needed a drink to relax otherwise there was no way I'd have got to sleep as the realisation of what tomorrow could bring was looming large.

I don't think we had dinner, I remember Lamby and I had a couple at the bar with Twelly, chatting about my semi-final performance. I told him that I was too wound up and I let the occasion get to me. He said that he understood how much it meant to me and he hoped that I'd raise my game for the final. Demons aside, I promised him I would and thanked him for giving me a once in a lifetime opportunity, then we were off to bed, though Lamby and I did order a couple of cheeky pints on room service before we went to sleep!

No surprise that I woke early and got straight into mental preparation for the game. I had family over from Ireland for the game as well as Hayley and my two brothers travelling up. Even my mum was going to be there, so it must have been something special, though unfortunately, she and dad had fallen out at the time, so he couldn't be there. It's a big regret, but that's family for you.

A gang of the Hemel lads had also travelled up: Bomber, Richard Mcdonagh, Dan West, John Lawford and even gaffer Tony Kelly had decided to have a night out in Liverpool and then come and watch Lamby and I. We were very grateful for their support, as I was that of best friend Dennis O'Rourke, who made the journey up with Hayley's dad Alan. Alan has since passed away and I will be forever thankful that he was there to share my greatest sporting achievement. Love you and miss you Con (that's what Alan was known as) xx.

It was funny but from the minute the semi-final finished, I knew that I'd be OK for the final, nerves wise. It was just getting there that caused the anxiety, and so it proved. I enjoyed every minute of the day. Once I saw the famous Kop end from the car park, I felt like the tallest man in the world. The usual pre-match nerves were there, nothing was going to phase me on that day. I set foot on that hallowed turf having touched the famous Kop sign. It all felt surreal after a lifetime of dreams. We were in the away changing room but that didn't really matter much as it was quality anyway. As the match started, being the home side seemed to put all the pressure on them and we were 3-0 up after about seventy minutes. They pulled one back with about ten to go, but it was never going to be enough. The match finished, and I was a Champion at Liverpool FC. Unbelievable!

Make no mistake this is a competition, especially in the latter rounds, of high pedigree, so to win it was an outstanding achievement. The Duke were basically made up of United Counties League players who were mates, but what a bloody good team they were. Stand-out was Russ Dunkley, two goal hero on the day, and sadly on a much better day later in my career, he tore me a new one. More of that later.

I must thank Lamby and Twelly for making a dream come true, letting me be part of the victory in a national competition. They know how grateful I remain to this day as I tell them every time I see them. It meant that much then and still does now. The celebrations were a thing of legend and I felt like a real Northants boy. Even now, I still love going to Northampton as it reignites all those scintillating moments. For the one FA competition I do have a decent record in, The Duke, I love and thank you all. xxx. Fergus Moore, National Champion 2002-03. And to top it all, I got bragging rights over The Madhouse boys for a while.

KNICKERS CAUGHT ON THE DOOR HANDLE

Not quite, but at the end of that second season at Hemel, I think we all knew that the side had gone as far as it could, and it would break up. I was one of those that moved on.

Since I'd left Wealdstone I'd kept in touch with Gordon Bartlett occasionally (at least, once I was over my release the first time round) and by this time the club was in transition. It had started with their non-promotion. That had really knocked the stuffing out of the players and they struggled the following year. It also cost an already cash-strapped club a lot of money.

A lot of the players had begun to move on and I re-joined a much-changed side for the start of 2001-02. Gordon rang at the end of the previous season (was I the only left footed player he knew?) and offered me a chance to return. He asked about a few of the other lads as well, and after the non-promotion at Hemel, Richard McDonnagh, Bryan Hammett and Vinnie Somers moved with me. Jason Shaw (who I knew from Chertsey) was also brought in, but things don't always pan out as expected. Jason, Bry and I were fine, but Richard and Vinnie found it tough and were soon on their way again.

The season started with a new side, another limited by a low budget, made up of a mix of youngsters and experience like Shawie and I. On a personal note it started with one of the best games I ever had in a 'Stones shirt. We won 4-1 against Bromley who were fancied to do well, and I felt like I was dictating the whole game from the back. Ten minutes in we got a free kick, McDonnagh rolled it across and I spanked it into the top corner, closely followed by a reprise of my crowd surfing exploits in the Dog Kennel with what seemed like the whole place chanting: *"Fergie is back Fergie is back"*. Great memories. Brilliant.

I was absolutely dictating the game. Maybe the fans won't remember it so well, but I can. For the first and possibly only time, I heard the opposition manager Dave Garland say to his defender and midfield player: *"get hold of the left back"* and: *"close him down"*. It was seventy minutes into the game and I was running it from left-back! I was getting down the line, getting crosses in, tracking back and going again. One of the best games I'd ever played.

Five minutes later, and, just as they do, those football gods kicked me in the bollocks again. Garland's instructions got through to his players and I think it was his son who took me out with a kung-fu kick that Bruce Lee would have been proud of. The ball bounced, and he launched at it. I reckon he had time to wave as he went past it and he connected with me around waist high and wiped me out. There I am lying on the pitch and he got up and laughed and gave me some verbal. For once in my life and I really think it is the only time, I completely lost it on the field. I spat at him. Never before and never again and I know it was a million percent wrong but there it is. Off I went as the referee had seen it. Gutted, stupid and wrong – me this time. Lesson learned.

I'd let myself and the club down, especially after I'd done so well in the seventy-odd minutes I'd played. It also meant another three-match ban, and I knew what happened last time I got one of those at Wealdstone. I can't even remember if Gordon or anyone else gave me a roasting after the game. I didn't hear anything, so deeply was I digging myself out.

After a decent start, the lack of money at the club meant as the season progressed, more and more of the kids were being brought through. Tunji Bamgbola, Matt Perry and a few others did OK, and a certain Jermaine Beckford who was eventually signed by Leeds United broke through, but we couldn't support five or six in the starting eleven. Walks, Andy Carter, Robin Tucker, Jason and I were the old heads trying to glue these youngsters together. The league form was up and down, but we did get to the Middlesex Charity Cup Final though we lost on penalties, ironically with one of the experienced players, Tucks seeing his kick saved.

I'd missed a penalty in a shoot-out for Madhouse, a Sunday side I played for a year or so before and it put me off taking them to be honest. That night against Enfield, it was no different and we lost, but in recent years I'm 4 out of 4, four scored, four won. That night, despite my misgivings, I was sixth in line.

Plenty of young players had got their chance and a few of them took it like Marvin Morgan and Jermaine Beckford. David Godfrey, a massive young goalkeeper also was expected to go on to better things but one referee the following season insisted on a game being played in icy conditions. He only abandoned the match when a serious injury to Godfrey meant that even a blind man or a corpse would see the risks. He never really recovered and drifted out of the game soon after. Sadly, the referee continued until a couple of years ago.

It was the end of another season and though it had felt good to be back at Wealdstone, it wasn't really the club I knew. Results hadn't gone our way and a lack of experience let us down a bit. I spoke to GB in the summer. I wanted to build on the core and push on again in a winning side, but he said there was no money available. It was to be another season of the same. He wanted me to commit and stay but Tony Kelly (another former Wealdstone player) who had stayed at Hemel had taken over as Manager and he'd brought in some good players as well as another former 'Stone who I respected in Chrissy Walton as Coach. I said to Gordon I'd like to come back and do pre-season to see what developed but he'd not been able to retain some of the players he had wanted and with little money, it was hard to get new and experienced players to join.

One newcomer was a coach called Fred Cummings, an ex-player who was a good mate as well. He had his way and says it how he sees it which some people can't take, but I've always loved that about him. He's happy to coach and doesn't want to manage, so he must be a manager's dream. He does the work, enjoys the craic then has a beer and goes home. Old school. He's still someone I look to for advice today.

During pre-season I went to a couple of sessions early doors at Wealdstone and then did the same at Hemel. With a heavy heart, I knew Hemel would be the choice. They had the budget – not that it made a difference personally – but it meant they could bring in better players and really give it a go. Wealdstone were still hamstrung and would have to use the youth players and I just wanted to feel more of that winning sensation. Losing that cup final wore on my mind. I wanted to win. I didn't want another October night like the one at Bishop's Stortford where we were beaten 7-1. It wasn't that players didn't try, they just weren't good enough and we weren't good enough as a team. You think that night hurt the fans? Well, get inside my head and see what it did for me.

I signed for Hemel again for the 2002-03 season and we ended up third or fourth, just missing out on promotion as Northwood and Hornchurch went up. We'd given it a good go but fell just short. Perhaps we should have done better, but it wasn't to be. On a personal level, I felt we were close and could push on the next season which we eventually did.

I had the bonus of scoring for Hemel at Wealdstone, at the White Lion Ground. It was a trademark header at the back post and I beat big Dave Ryan to the ball to power the ball home from a John Lawford corner as we went on to win. At the end of the game I reminded him of it as we walked off the pitch. Then in the bar I reminded him again and I reminded him in the Change of Hart as we popped in for a couple of pints of gloat with the 'Stones fans and a few old mates on the playing side. Thankfully, the fans always welcomed me back no matter what the score line was. That relationship I cherish even now. Long may it continue.

Postscript; I played in a Wealdstone Legends match with Dave a season or so ago. I reminded him of that goal then as well. He's a cabbie now and if he ever picks me up, I might just remind him again. It's all part of the banter.

As for Hemel, we thought we'd regroup and go again the next season, but for me it was injury and suspension hit. I missed more than I played in the first few months and with me not playing, the itchy feet started once again. I had a call from a lad called Matty Howard. He was another of the lads I was with at Brentford and his father was on the Board or Committee at Boreham Wood. They'd seen I wasn't getting a game and he asked if I fancied the move. Unofficially of course, as that would be 'tapping me up' and as you well know, no-one does that in non-league football. No-one would contact a player directly before asking permission of his club or before making an official approach. No. Never.

The system in non-league is a little different to the professional game as so many players aren't on contract. With a contract player, the rule is the same at any level, make a bid, discuss with the club and then if it's acceptable, you'll be given permission to negotiate terms with the player and the move goes through, or not. With non-contract players (like me) unless it's during the close season when players are free to talk to anyone, the procedure is to contact the players club and to give them a Seven Day Notice of Approach, which means after seven days you will talk to the player to see if he wants a move. You'd negotiate with the player for up to a maximum of 21 days to agree terms and once agreed, the player is free to move on, with no fee or recompense to the club required. This system as you can imagine is strictly adhered to throughout the non-league game.

Boreham Wood then as now, is two minutes from my house. It was a whole new experience for me, being so close, as I'd always travelled to home and away games alike. Now, half the matches were on my doorstep, and 'Wood were flying high in the league too.

Ian Allinson was trying to refresh the squad with a few in and out which lead to a bit of a drop in my form, but while I was there (like my nemesis) Gordon Bartlett and the 'Stones visited. Fergus Moore and Boreham Wood won on the day, but it was Wealdstone that went up at the end of the season so fair play to them. The Wood hit a bad run late on in the year after looking good for promotion and missed out while Hemel went up as well. I'd moved on to play and win things and with great timing (again) I was the one that got left behind. It was a blow, but I was happy to be playing and walking to games. It also meant I could have an extra couple of pints after a game and stagger home rather than having just one or two and driving.

As the season ended I think I'd only played about fifteen games, yet I was runner up in the Player of the Year! I was a bit of a local celebrity with the fans as I lived on the doorstep, so I suppose that helped, and it's still something that I'm proud of.

Boreham Wood is Chairman Danny Hunters club - and it really is. It's his show, he puts the money in and there is always a feeling that he's watching you. I can't knock what he's done for the club, but it's his way or no way, no matter who you are. I found it oppressive and soon learned to steer clear of any confrontation with him because he wins.

I was able to build friendships with a few people, Noel Imber was there, the former Wealdstone goalkeeper from a couple of years earlier (you're spotting a theme, right?), Sammy Winston became a mate having been an opponent on numerous occasions, and God rest his soul, Ryan Moran, a good player and a very funny lad who sadly lost his fight against cancer a couple of years ago. I played in a benefit match for him, but just a few months later he passed away. A great centre half and one of the nicest guys you could ever meet, that was a very sad day. These things happen, but it knocked me back, the funeral, his family and the emotion of it all hung over me for a while.

Typical of a non-league footballer, I eventually got married and picked a Saturday in the following pre-season to do it. It was one of the, if not the best day of my life when I got married to my gorgeous wife, Hayley but back to the football. Someone once told me that when you get married, that next season you're never at your best. Managers, Coaches, Chairmen and even players become wary of you, and I think it was to be proven true.

Boreham Wood played Arsenal in a friendly, another of the single match highlights of my career. It was a Friday night a couple of weeks before my impending nuptials. It was a great occasion with a decent crowd and we were up against it from the off against an Arsenal Reserve and Youth side, containing a few lads that have gone on to have decent careers albeit at other clubs. They scored midway through the second half and yours truly nicked a late equaliser. Arsene Wenger then presented me with the Man of the Match Award and spoke in the press about how I was a good player, then I think someone told him my age. It's still a great personal memory and a highlight pre-marriage.

About a month into the season, we were away to Stanway Rovers (back to reality) and Ian and I had a bit of a run in. Nothing major or so I thought; he shouted down the pitch at me and I replied. I got into the dressing room at the break and got the rough end of his tongue as he bawled me out for taking back to him. I apologised and thought that was it. It was frustration not disrespect. I apologised to the chairman too, because he always knows exactly what is going on, there or not, as he's told by his manager, his coaches or his players everything that is said and done. Make of that what you will, but I apologised, and both accepted my apology.

At the next training session, the team was named for the following match, and I'd gone from being the first name on the list to not even being in the squad, a bit of a clue that something had gone awry. I asked Ian what was up, and he said it was just football related. The following Tuesday, the same thing happened and not long after I was released. I was told again that it was nothing to do with the spat, but I never kicked a ball for them again. It was the first time in my career that mid-season I was without a club.

Leighton Town made an offer as I was working with their manager but eventually Del Deanus (who sadly lost his battle against motor neurone disease a couple of years later) called. He was assistant manager at Northwood and he invited me down to the then high-flying Ryman Premier League club. A step up this time and to a club that needed a left sided defender, it was like a breath of fresh air, knowing I could be myself, play my game and not worry about who was watching or talking to who.

I joined at a good time. The club were near the top of the division and were playing good football, but they lacked a bit of defensive nous. They used my experience well in a young side. There were a few old heads like Dean Clark who remains probably the laziest player I ever played with (at Wealdstone and Northwood) but what he could do with the ball at his feet. So much skill and a tremendous strike on him too. Plus, he could see a goal from anywhere as he was to prove a few years hence when we were re-united, once again at Wealdstone for a season in the Southern League. Away at Stamford and under a bit of pressure and if memory serves, losing 1-2 he collected the ball in the centre circle and with a touch to control, he then launched a shot over the home 'keepers head for the equaliser. The team and the fans went nuts. He just looked like he did that every day and to be fair, he probably could.

Mark Dennison, Johnny Moore, were both already at Northwood had decent non-league careers, as did Danny Yeoman. it was a team with a good hard work ethic, some young legs and skill, and a couple of old heads to steady the ship. We didn't manage to keep the winning run going to the end of the year, but we finished in a respectable seventh or eighth with a good squad to carry that impetus into the following season.

There were some good guys there. Del did things his own way, and Luke Evans was a character in the Lee Walker mould as well. I was to team up with him again at Hanwell Town later, but it was a good feeling to be at Northwood at that time. There was just a good feeling around the place.

61

Over the summer though, Del had his doubts and early in the following season he left. Manager Micky Harvey then brought in Keith Scott and Terry Back to help him on the coaching side, a couple of old pros who had experience at Windsor & Eton and Leighton Town.

With the changes in the Divisional structure, Northwood found themselves transferred to the Southern League from the Ryman, with all the additional travel and expense that incurred. Expense that might well strangle a small volunteer run club like Northwood, but there was no appeal. The first game at home was a visit from Merthyr Tydfil. Straight away we were tipped to go down because the limited funds would have to be spent on travel getting us to the West County, Wales, Birmingham, Bristol, Bath. No one was close by, it was just a shame you couldn't earn coach miles like air miles. We could all have had a holiday at the end of the season.

We did OK in that first game, leading for a while before conceding a late equaliser and that was the run of the season, we won a few, drew a few and lost a few then about six or seven weeks into the season away to Grantham, I was benched for no reason. It wasn't just in my eyes, as in fact Mickie Harvey became the first manager to be unable to tell me why I'd been dropped. He said he couldn't think of a reason to leave me out, but he was just leaving me out anyway.

We or rather they, lost.

On the Sunday, I got a phone call from someone at the club to tell me Mickie was gone. Gary Farrell stepped in for a game as caretaker, then Colin Payne took over, but he wasn't the Colin I knew.

MANAGERS

When I signed for Chertsey a few years before, I knew of Paynie through other players on the non-league circuit. As a manager then, he was in his early years and Chertsey were at the time a growing club with a bit of money from a benefactor (until he pulled the plug!) He was always prone to an occasional flip and some overzealous punishment for a minor infringement of rules or protocol, but most of the time at Chertsey he seemed fairly relaxed, perhaps as things were going better all round.

I was only there for a short time and maybe I only saw the good side. I knew even then he was very passionate about whatever he did, and perhaps that's why we clashed towards the end of the season. We played Hitchin at home in the last league game of the season and we had a bit of a spat over a throw on of all things. Early in the first half and we were losing 0-1. I took a throw in, but the defender cut it out and Paynie had a dig from the bench *"throw it down the effing line"* or some such rang out. I shouted back, telling him to sit down and thought nothing of it, (really, I know that's twice in a few pages, but it's not like me). Little did I know he saw my outburst as a show of disrespect. It wasn't the case, it was just an outlet for my passion, the heat of the moment getting in the way I suppose. He misconstrued it and at half time he dragged me to one side and told me in no uncertain terms not ever to speak to him like that again. I was off and that was that.

Except we had a night out planned that night and Paynie was coming along, then there was a cup final on the following Monday.

Fair play though. He told me on the night out that he wouldn't stand for it and I apologised, the conversation ended with him saying I was still his captain and he wanted me there on Monday leading out the team. We beat Walton & Hersham in the final and I had a beer with him afterwards.

Now, six years later for the 2005-06 season I was at Northwood, struggling in the Southern League and Mickie Harvey and Keith Scott (I'll come back to him), were sacked. In came Paynie mark II? He'd been out of the game for a while, and I thought he'd lost it a bit, but Colin is Colin. He always has and always will do things his way.

We got a few decent results and a turning point was when he brought in Fred Cummings as Coach. Straight away he started to focus on the defensive side of the game, keeping it tight, clean sheets etc. and it worked. We played the away match at Merthyr and got a great result coming away with a win but come Christmas we were still too close to the bottom of the league for comfort. In a strange show of support, the Board then cut the budget. There just wasn't the money to support the side and the travel. Bottom of the league and a fifty percent cut in wages and I was back down to £45 a week. A few new faces came in and a few of the senior lads left, but to be honest I had nowhere else to go. I liked the club and was happy to stay and fight with a few of the boys who had been there for a long time.

One that left was Luke Garrard, who was on loan from Boreham Wood. They transferred him to AFC Wimbledon, quite within their rights of course, but he had been our skipper. That meant we needed a new captain and for me it showed where Colin wasn't quite the Manager he'd been before, as he held a sort of competition; *"Fergie, Wayne Carter, Dean Clark, line up",* he said. The rest of the squad were then told to stand behind the person they would like to be the next Captain! I mean, I know it's good to have the lads onside but how would the ones that picked the wrong guy feel?

Carts got three or four as did Clarkey and the rest lined up behind me. That was the Thursday night. Come Saturday, pre-game the team is announced, and the new captain read out: *"Wayne Carter!"* I still don't know what that was about. If that's what he wanted, why not say so in the first place!

I didn't mind, I was in the team, and I only play one way, but it was just the start of things to come. I though he was getting a bit strange. He'd bring players in for a game and you'd never see them again (Eddie Dour, where are you?) and in training and even matches, he'd shout things for no reason, but luckily, all the while, Fred was doing a good job and we nicked a few results.

Come the last game of the season, we played away at Cirencester knowing that we couldn't afford to lose. The final relegation spot was going to be decided across the three feeder leagues on points per game average.

Middlesex Under 16's c1988

Back: Jason King, Simon O'Shea, Fergus Moore, Alan McCarthy, Jason Winters, Giles Jacobs, Freddie Leonard, Kofi.

Front: Vic Hardwicke, Andrew Driscoll, Ted Dale (Manager), Paul Dale, Andrew Impey.

[Back Row] **Kevin Godfrey, Simon Ratcliffe, Keith Millen, Terry Evans, Graham Benstead, Jamie Bates, Gary Blissett, Dean Holdsworth, Marcus Gayle** [Middle Row] **Joe Gadston, Robert Peters, Allan Cockram, Jason Cousins, Ashley Bayes, Stuart Cash, Fergus Moore, Khotso Moabi, Roy Clare** [Front Row] **Mark Fleming, Paul Buckle, Garry Brooke, Keith Jones, Phil Holder, Richard Cadette, Neil Smillie, Andy Driscoll, Eddie May**

Football League	Division Three
Manager	Phil Holder
Asst. Manager/Coach	Wilf Rostron / Graham Pearce
Physio	Roy Clare
Captain	Keith Jones
Final Position	6th & Play-Off Semi-Final
FA Cup	3rd Round
Rumbelows Cup	2nd Round
Leyland/DAF Cup	Area Final
Leading Goalscorer (all competitions)	Gary Blissett – 15 goals

The Class of '92. (Just not *THAT* Class of '92)

Reproduced with kind permission from The Big Brentford Book of the Nineties ©

If Panini did Reserve Teams......

Country; Eire, England
DoB; 19.02.1972
Position; Full Back, Centre Half
Married to Hayley
Children; Callum, Aaron and Holly

* * * * * * *

Debut; n/a
Appearances; n/a
Goals; n/a   * * * * * * *

In his own words; Someone said I was so old I still get changed in black and white, and the first time I got booked, the Referee used chalk and a slate to write my name down. I think I'm a bit like the last bottle of a favourite wine – maturing with age, kept on show, never poured.

FERGUS MOORE

FERGUS MOORE

Reserve Team player and Captain of the Brentford FC Youth Team 1989-90

Reproduced with kind permission from The Big Brentford Book of the Nineties. ©

67

Uxbridge FC, London Challenge Cup Winners 1994

Reproduced by kind permission of The Middlesex FA ©

Back: Ernie Kempster (Physio), Lee Hannratty, Mickey Creighton, Steve Toms, Darren Wolfe, Mark Gill, Fergus Moore, Gary Downes, Paul McCluskey.

Front: Alan Gregory, Gerry Crawford, Sean Dawson, Jamie Cleary, Troy Birch, Nicky Ryder.

Wealdstone FC, the first time, 1995 and back as a 'Legend' 2014
Photos reproduced with kind permission of Graham Smith & Steve Foster ©

At Wealdstone FC: ICIS League Division III Champions

69

Champions!

Photo reproduced with kind permission of Graham Smith ©

Back: Chris Walton, Roy Marshall, Darren Bonfield, Simon Garner, Terry Hibbert.

Front: Ian Waugh, Fergus Moore, Tony Smith, Dominic Sterling, Steve Bircham (civvies!),

Foreground: Bryan Hammatt, Paul McKay.

Presenting Roy Marshall with his Player of the Year award at the Wealdstone FC 'Championship' Presentation evening!

Photo reproduced with kind permission of Graham Smith ©

71

Duke of York, FA Sunday Cup Winners

Photo reproduced with kind permission of Peter Norton Photography ©

Back: John Considine, Graham Markie, John Carley, David Faulkener (Chairman), Ross Harris, Jimmy Leah, 'Broomsy', James Twelvetree, Gerry Moss, Russ Dunkley, ?, Paul Lamb, Tom O'Brien, Dan Vesy, Dean Chapman, Scott Marshall, Roy Leah, Brendon Healy, Paul Edgeworth, Steve Ringer. Front: ?, ? (Physio), Steve Jelly, Ben Foster, Paul Wagstaff, Matt Green, Mark Hofford, Matt Finlay, Adam Parker, Paul Birch, Jamie Kearnes. Foreground: Erika O'Grady, Ellie Markie, Fergus Moore, Mick Heath, Ben Heath.

Hendon were in the mix in the Ryman and we need to equal or better their result to finish mathematically above them. At half time, we're drawing 0-0 and Hendon were winning.

Ten minutes into the second half it was 'all-out attack'. Panic stations. Long balls into the box to try and score then ten minutes after it was 'relax don't concede' as the news came through that Hendon were now drawing. A mad afternoon, something I've never experienced since. We didn't have a clue what was going on. It got to the end of the game, we'd drawn 0-0 and it wasn't until about twenty minutes after we finished that we knew we'd stayed up. (As it happened Hendon got a reprieve and stayed up as well).

For me, it was right up there with my best achievements! The Southern League was a tough league, always up against big strong forwards and maybe that suited me a bit, but it was a battle week in week out. Bottom of the league and with the budget being cut, we ended up with a squad of fifteen I think, yet we survived. Wow, did we get hammered on the way home! It was a great achievement against the odds even if the club did get relegated the following season.

Lo and behold, during the close season, back came Gordon Bartlett on the phone with yet another call to Wealdstone. You know the story. Off I went again. Sadly, I left Northwood on a bit of a sour note. An article was put in the paper after I'd spoken to Colin and told him I was going. At the time he had said he was happy for me to leave as he knew Wealdstone were close to my heart and I'd done my bit helping keep Northwood up. In the paper? A quote from Colin the following weekend that *"I have retained all of the squad from last year who helped the club survive, but I've released Fergus Moore"*. He made it read as though I was surplus to requirements and he was glad to see the back of me. Thanks, mate.

Longevity is rare in football management, so it has to be hat's off to Gordon Bartlett. Howard Krais, Wealdstone Chairman for ten years announced he was standing down in 2016. Gordon Bartlett, twenty-three years on, was still there and surely created a record as he managed the side for his fourth Chairman at the same club. Some Chairmen have had four managers in a season! (Gordon agreed to 'move aside' in 2017).

INJURIES, SUSPENSIONS AND POSTPONEMENTS

I've been fairly lucky throughout my career with injuries. There was a run of minor pulls and knocks at Hemel, and later three months out with a twisted knee and ankle later at Bedfont. Those, other than a 'hammy' (yes, really) are the only serious knocks I've had (touches wood).

Suspensions? Well, a bit of a different matter I suppose. I've not counted them or indeed the actual games missed, but as you have read thus far there have been a few, the difference being with a couple of exceptions, once served, I've got my place back. With injuries, it's always been a bit harder.

More recently, it was an old enemy, Sciatica. I've suffered with this on and off over the years, but thankfully, it generally only takes a few days rest to clear and I can get back to playing as, the older I get, there is less I can do to play through the pain. Sure, I can manage it for a short spell, and perhaps set myself to run and jump slightly differently to compensate, but that generally makes it worse later and it can be bloody painful. I've tried to explain it to the younger lads, but it falls on deaf ears. They don't care as it is apparently an 'old boys injury' that won't affect them for many a year. Thanks for the sympathy and support, lads!!

I know it's for the best but when I'm suffering slightly, and I get rested so it doesn't get any worse, I hate it. I never have and never will like not playing but sometimes you have to think a little bit more long term (said the dinosaur).

Injuries to other players play a part in any season too, and often show up the spirit that can keep a side together. We had an example when young Sam Styles, Cockfosters goalkeeper, got injured late on in a match early in the season. Somehow, in the process of being smashed in the face by the ball at point blank range, he managed to injure his shoulder ligaments. (You can feel the sympathy there already, right?).

To be fair he was knocked unconscious by the initial impact and I was first on the scene and could tell that he was all over the place. It's a hard life being a non-league footballer, Sam woke up and went off only to receive dog's abuse from all the lads in the dressing room at the end of the game for 'having a chin like glass' and 'legs like jelly'.

There was an upside though, as out of all this we finally found a position for our team utility (aka play anywhere to get a game) man and wordsmith, Mark Blackburne. He went in goal for the final 15 minutes and had a blinder. In fact, some would say he was better than his brother who is a recognised goalkeeper, who had a couple of torrid games for us in the not too distant past. With Sam injured, Mark was in the frame for a run in the side.

Truth be told, I'm a footballer, I want to play. I can't hack it sitting on the bench and I hate watching when I'm injured or suspended. It puts everything out of kilter and I get moody and restless. Equally as bad are postponements. We had a batch that one season at Hemel when the new drains didn't drain and at Cockfosters with the overall poor state of the pitch we knew in advance if it rained Thursday or Friday, there was a 99% chance the game would be off on the Saturday. With little money around at these clubs, that's unavoidable. The ones that really get to me though are the late call-offs. The most frustrating thing in football. It just seems officials are now so quick to call a game off on a pitch we'd have played on happily a few years ago. I've looked at pitches in some grounds when the games been called off and cannot see a thing wrong with them, only for the referee to blather something about health and safety. Now, having moved on once again to Edgware, at least at home, the problem has gone away. We shouldn't get too many called off on a 3G pitch, but I'll have to let you know what it does for the injuries and old bones.

IT'S IN THE BLOOD

Football gets in your blood, and sometimes, clubs get in your blood. Wealdstone have certainly got in mine. I left Northwood as they returned to the Ryman (Isthmian) League and the phone rang once more from Gordon Bartlett, still at Wealdstone (they're in his blood too). He had been to a few matches to watch us and I'd had a couple of conversations with him about my game and the league, but at the time I had no idea that that would lead to my return. At the end of the season, the 'Stones had suffered the same re-shuffle that cost Northwood a couple of seasons earlier. The Southern League experience was coming to Wealdstone, or, with their fans, more correctly look out Southern League, because for 2006-07, Wealdstone are coming! GB wanted me and my experience back on side for what was expected to be a difficult campaign.

He also asked me about a few people I knew at Uxbridge; Mark Gill, the Coach, who since George Talbot had moved on was metaphorically kicking his heels, and knowing I still had lots of connections (mainly in the bar) at Uxbridge he also asked about a couple of players and whether I thought they'd be up for a move. We had a few conversations about Gavin and Stuart Bamford and Chrissy O'Leary.

He'd asked me back as Player / Coach but to be fair I said I preferred to play and that was around the same time he mentioned Gilly. Everything seemed to fit, and I was back for a third spell in blue and white. I remember texting Paul Rumens the Club President just to let him know I was back on the Wealdstone roller-coaster. He called me for a chat and it was then I realised just what it meant to be back. I thought my time had passed, though my love for the club hadn't.

It was a different direction both geographically and in terms of the squad requirement and a different mentality was needed. I'd been there and done that and gone back and done it again. Playing centre-half (by my own admission) I'd had a good season. So, no surprise then, as we started pre-season, I was back at left back! Stuart, Gavin and Chrissy had joined and so had another centre-half in Kevin Swift. It was a much more physical and much changed 'Stones side that took up the new challenge and with the experience throughout, expectations were quite high as the season began.

We should have started better than we did. We got beaten in a poor game at Mangotsfield to start the season and to top that, goalkeeper Lee Carroll was sent off. That was followed by a home draw with Hemel Hempstead who had also transferred across previously, Wealdstone turning a comfortable 2-0 lead into a struggle to hold on at the end.

Basically, it wasn't going to plan. Good games, bad games, we seemed to alternate until we went to lower league Potters Bar Town in the FA Cup. They weren't a good side, but that day we were worse and lost 1-2. In all my time at Wealdstone that was the first time I'd really seen the 'Stones fans turn. They slaughtered us, the players and the management, as we walked off the pitch. Even in the dressing room we could still hear them and when we'd showered and changed and came back out, there were still plenty around to let us know what they thought. The following week we lost at Halesowen but then strung together a little run of seven or eight unbeaten. It was looking better, it still wasn't right.

As if to prove it, we then lost five on the trot including another early exit from the FA Cup and another club earner fell by the wayside. Despite a win in the London Senior Cup we then drew and lost two more league games, the second high-(low)-lighting the deepest darkest point of my Wealdstone career(s) as we got beaten at Banbury.

The fans were getting on player's backs as they felt one or two weren't up for it. Gavin Bamford got sent off after giving away a penalty I think, and the fans jeered him. Apparently, as he left the field, he 'threw the finger' in their direction and that nearly started a bloody riot. From the pitch we saw Wealdstone fans running from all round the ground towards the tunnel intent on letting him and anyone else in the vicinity know exactly what they thought. That was if he hadn't been flailed, hung, drawn and quartered first.

He made it down the tunnel as stewards and the 'Stones bench escorted him to the relative safety of the dressing room, the management trying to calm things down off the field while we tried to play out the game on it. Did he do it? Was it frustration? I can't tell you because I don't know, but it was effectively the end of his time at the club and that of his brother as, as you'd expect, blood runs thicker.

The season continued in the same way, stuttering at best. We'd go unbeaten for three then loose three on the bounce, firmly establishing us in the bottom half dozen throughout the year. On a personal level, it wasn't working out for me either. Early in October I got 'rested' for a Middlesex cup-tie. Told it was to rest me for the league game on Saturday, I missed eight of the next nine games before I got another run in the side. It put me on guard a bit but as much as I could I made sure when I got back in, I stayed in.

The run-in that season was manic. On 31st March we still had nine games to play before the 28th April. We started with three home draws which meant with six games to go, four away from home, we realistically needed at least nine points to avoid relegation. We'd also lost Lee Carroll some weeks earlier, or rather, he lost himself. He just disappeared. Expected to play against Bath City at home on the Saturday, he didn't turn up. We started the game with a centre half in goal while the youth team goalkeeper was called up and named on the bench to give him time to travel to the game and come on when he arrived. He did at half time, but we were 4 or 5 down by then. Lee didn't reappear for a couple of weeks until he finally got in touch with Gordon, but he never played again. A series of incoming loan keepers were tried out short term, but despite best efforts with the transfer deadline, the club couldn't get an experienced keeper signed.

It meant that we went into those last six crucial games with an inconsistent side and a young keeper in Mitch Swain. The gaffer had also brought in two Watford reserves on loan, Theo Robinson, a young quick striker and John-Joe O'Toole, an Irish youth international midfield player. All hands to the pumps and ready for the battle, we went to Hemel Hempstead Town and got dicked 5-2.

Perhaps one of the goals was down to Mitch but those in front of him hadn't helped and the 'Stones fans were in full voice once again to let us know. Old hands like me, though it hurts, can get over it. Mitch coming from the youth team into this cauldron took it to heart and there were more than a few arms round his shoulders from the management as we tried to see out the season with enough points gained.

Two days later we faced Banbury at home in a performance that was the polar opposite of that at Hemel and we ran out winners 4-0. Mitch held his own and focussed on his game, and Theo Robinson and Dean Papali scored a pair each to secure the points.

Then on the Saturday we were away at Gloucester City. I don't know what the odds were on Wealdstone getting a result that day but in front of over 150 travelling fans (for all their anger and attitude they were and still are intensely loyal) 'Stones won 2-0. Siege mentality was setting in and everyone fought for everything, winning the ball and feeding Papali and Robinson up front. They shared the spoils once again.

The pressure was eased a little but there was still plenty of opportunity for the three clubs below to overtake the side had they won their games and next up was a trip to the desolation of Corby at their old ground, in a sports stadium. It's always windy, always grey and always bloody hard to get a result, but in a tight game we came through 2-1.

The games were still coming thick and fast and, on the Tuesday, we were off to Yate Town. A few weeks earlier, we'd been to Yate to play the match which after three or four floodlight failures was abandoned just after half time. Yate were on a good run and Wealdstone the opposite, losing match on match. In fact, I think we were losing when the game was called off. Now, we went back looking for a further win on the bounce. Again over 60 'Stones fans had made the trip (midweek) and they were in full voice as we ran out winners 4-2 with Papali and Robinson again equal partners in the goal-share. We were safe.

Just as well really, as on the Saturday we travelled for the last game of the season to promoted Kings Lynn Town. There was a party atmosphere all round as they celebrated their promotion and the Wealdstone fans had celebrated survival with quite a few early beers on their train journey up. The 0-1 defeat was a bit undeserved and unlucky, but we'd survived another year and I'd survived a blip in confidence when in and out of the side earlier in the season. Sometimes, people on the outside don't realise how difficult it is mixing football with life.

During that run in, the match at Gloucester was on Grand National day. It was one of my very best friends, John Montgomery's stag day and I spoke to Gordon a couple of weeks earlier and asked not to play as I was booked to be in Liverpool with the rest of the party. He understood but couldn't let me go. I felt the emotions rising and I was gutted not to be there for John, but I also knew Gordon was right and how bad I'd have felt if I'd gone on the stag do and Wealdstone had lost.

A couple of weeks later and we were at Yate. Preparation for that fixture? Paul Rumens and I were at a funeral in Northampton. Former 'Stones skipper Paul Lamb had very sadly lost his partner and we had to be there for him and to pay our respects, as well as to represent the club. We went to the funeral, stayed on for a while and had a bite to eat then drove from Northampton to Yate almost in silence. I promised Lamby as we left that we'd win for him and we'd be back straight after. Immediately after the game, we were on our way back. The emotions really flowed as we went to the fans on the pitch at the end of the game. It was about Wealdstone and what the club meant to me, but it was also for Paul, which very few people knew about. As promised, we got back to his place as the wake was dissipating. We were going back win lose or draw.

That was my last game of the season as I had a Christening to attend on the Saturday. That too would have been missed had the dogfight continued, but we were safe, so I wasn't missed. I still ducked out a couple of times to get the score though! Looking back, I don't know how I'd have explained the absence at the Christening that day if it had been required. It was my best mate and I'm Godfather to his daughter!

It was hard in the Southern League, but that year like others we always knew when it was half term (Gordon Bartlett is a schoolteacher). He'd have a bit more time and could put up a few motivational posters and form guides, points dropped tables, that sort of thing in the dressing room, all because he had a bit more time at home on the computer. I should check the results and term time to see if they worked!

I've upset the missus, the family, friends — all of them. It's always me that's missing from the wedding photographs or not at the service and late for the reception, but football has always come first and even now in the twilight of my career, nine times out of ten it still does.

I went to the End of Season awards that season, and it was Chrissy O'Leary that won Player of the Year as he had, had a good solid season in a struggling side. I'd had that blip in October and November, but Gordon came up to me and told me that he thought I'd been the best player in the side since Christmas. It meant a lot and sent me off for another happy (and relieved) summer. Disaster averted, passion on a high.

Wealdstone were transferred back into the Ryman League for the following season and I was looking forward to defying my age once again. I was thirty-five and more than willing to dig in and give it another go.

Preseason, I'd played most of the games in the build up to the first League fixture away to Folkestone and then a midweek fixture with a resurgent AFC Wimbledon side. With a fortnight to go, I went to a wedding, missing a pre-season game but with everyone's knowledge. It was a match against Hayes and Yeading at home. What we didn't know at the time was that Gordon would pull in a player as cover for me for that one game (at least that was the intention) and the bugger stayed around for a couple of years. Stand up Alan Massey, on loan from Wycombe Wanderers and a left sided centre half to boot!

I went to the wedding and Wealdstone drew with Mass having a decent enough match for people to want him around. I went to the Chesham friendly a few days later and saw him for myself alongside another new centre-half, Marcus Gross. Supplemented by Carl Martin, they were the back three that looked set to start the season and that one wedding had put me back on the side lines.

As the season started I was on the bench for the trip to Folkestone. It was a big pitch and against a fancied side, but Carl Martin wasn't available, so I thought I'd get the nod. I didn't as young Jomo Faal-Thomas (who sadly died a couple of years later from cancer) started. Marcus Gross got injured after about twenty minutes and I did get on and had a stormer! I had a point to prove and

I set up one of Peter Dean's goals in a 4-1 win. He celebrated the goal and I made bloody sure then bench knew who had made the final pass. I ran over turned and backed towards the bench pointing at the number 14 on my back and screaming as the frustration and even a bit of anger came out. I carried on in the dressing room too, letting everyone and anyone know what I thought of being a sub that day. It may have been a bit over the top, but it showed what playing meant to me. I can be quiet and sit on the bench, but when I cross the white line I change. Passion takes over and I go out there to do myself and my club justice.

It got me a start for the next game, in fact the next three games, and we lost all three. I got subbed in the third one and that really signalled the end of the line. I'd been playing OK (at Ashford Town (Middlesex)) but at right side centre-half a young lad called Scott Todd turned me inside out. I tried to get my balance back as I tackled him, and I brought him down for a penalty. They scored and won, and I lost. Mentally, it was getting to me. I felt there were some people waiting for me to fail and to all intents and purposes, I had.

I dual signed for AFC Hayes under Joe Mitchell. (It's another thing unique to non-league non-contract players. You can sign, with a parent club's blessing, for another club in another league. It means that squad players can get games elsewhere and is used quite often). This sub-consciously was probably me preparing for the inevitable.

I played four or five games and was doing OK and then Wealdstone were due to play Horsham away and I got called back to start. We lost 0-4 and the cracks were beginning to show as one or two players were having spats with the fans. They were on top of their game and a decent side and we weren't. I went back to AFC Hayes for a midweek game and I remember that Gordon hadn't been at Horsham for some reason. Then I remembered a conversation in the past about loans and dual signings and how they were rarely to get players games and get them fit, it was generally goodbye. He said it wasn't the way he worked, but as it turned out for me, it was.

Joe Mitchell pulled me a few weeks later and said Wealdstone had stopped paying me! They'd been helping AFC Hayes out with my wages, it was only about a £20 contribution, but it had stopped without a word. The money didn't matter, the lack of contact hurt. I remember a conversation with Fred Cummings at the time; he'd been to watch Wealdstone play and had a chat with the bench. My name came up, and when asked, he said I was doing well at AFC Hayes. The reply was something along the lines of *"these things happen in football"*. What things? No-one had said anything to me, but I never played for them again.

A month or so later I did get a call from Gordon and he told me that they couldn't afford to keep paying the £20. I told him I already knew that as it had stopped a few weeks earlier and I reminded him that I'd said: *"once out of sight, out of mind"*.

Once again, he said it wasn't like that, but, as time proved, it was. I was gutted and angry. I'd helped keep the side up and done everything that was asked of me. It wasn't leaving the club that hurt, but it was the way it had happened. Cut me and I'll bleed blue and white, but I wasn't even worth a phone call or a conversation? Players are asked for loyalty but sometimes you must give some back. It ended with bitterness and that was unnecessary. To this day I think it should have been handled differently and it made me very bitter towards Gordon, my 'football father'. I'd played for him four times, been released a couple of times previously, but this time, I felt cast aside and forgotten.

If I hadn't gone to the wedding perhaps it would have been different, but I doubt that The Mass came in just to cover for one game. Gordon and I had known each other around 18 years, the whole of my non-league career at that time and half of my years on God's earth and it put a major rift in our relationship. We'd gone from speaking once or twice a week whether I was at the club or not, to not speaking at all. I knew there were thirteen or fourteen in his squad that would take priority and he was under pressure with results. That I understood, but...

NOT ALL A BED OF ROSES

Eventually, I signed for AFC Hayes for the next season. They were pleased to have me, and I was pleased to play. Joe Mitchell was a nice guy and one of the most attack minded managers I've ever come across. Certainly, the only one who would be happy to win 6-5 every week, so he was a bit thin on defensive set-up!

We were reasonably successful at the start then before Christmas, we struggled and had a bit of a bad run results-wise, and I became the scapegoat purely because of my age. I didn't spit the dummy though I was in and out of the side almost on a weekly basis. It was not something I enjoyed, but I thought I'd see the season out. Until I got a call.

This one was bad news. My mate Steve Newing was joint manager with Del Deanus at Edgware Town. Del's motor neurone disease was becoming slowly but severely debilitating and invariably would be terminal. He was still involved but on occasion found things difficult and with his treatment and such like, he just couldn't be there all the time, so Steve asked if I'd join them to help.

I wanted to play, and I wanted to be among friends, so I moved and did a bit of coaching as well. Actually, it was enjoyable, and it gave me a new lease of life, a new hunger for match days! There was a great spirit in the club and a good bunch of lads brought together by Steve and Del. They all pulled together, perhaps galvanised in spirit by the sad news of Del's illness. It made the club a good place to be. Del was still involved, and when he wasn't up to it, I stepped in and the lads responded well. Paul Marks and Dennis Marharjan were there, lads I've been with at Edgware Town again, Richard Morton and Bomber were there to, as were Rory Smith, Gavin Hart and Johnny Moore from Northwood, so there were plenty of friendly faces. It was an easy dressing room to get onside as I knew or had played with most of the lads previously.

Off the field, though all was certainly not rosy at Edgware. The club had been notified that they were going to lose The White Lion Ground as it had been owned by Scottish & Newcastle Breweries, but because of problems with paying the rent and the general upkeep over the preceding years, relations between the football club and the landlords weren't great. Along came a developer who succeeded in buying the site and that was it Edgware would be homeless at the end of the season. There was a public outcry, a lot of support in local papers and such like, but little anyone could do, though the 'Dunkirk' spirit of the lads certainly grew. It was also the closest I got to my five minutes (well, nearly five seconds) of fame on the TV as the BBC did a feature on the club and the situation and used some footage of a game: more precisely a Dennis Marharjan goal against Dartford. Look closely at the background and you'll see me (somewhat belatedly) celebrating the goal. Not that I ran sixty yards to join in after remembering that the TV cameras were there. Not me. No.

The piece was three or four minutes on Edgware Town, the lack of funding at this level, the lack of support from the local council and the sad story of one developer who would get very rich by building around one hundred and thirty houses and flats on the site, and me. All to no avail.

We had a decent year on the field and we had a chance of promotion in the last game of the season even though the club was finished with nowhere to play and no money. Unfortunately, we didn't quite make it, just missing out on the play-offs. The club disbanded, keeping the name alive and registering with the Middlesex County Association but not playing, at least preserving the chance of a phoenix club rising at some stage in the future. It did, and as I write this now, I'm Edgware Town Manager.

That mid-summer Steve and Del were offered the opportunity to take over at Leyton FC and I went with them, this time officially as player coach and most of the Edgware squad trekked along behind us. Leyton FC is not in the most auspicious surroundings, the dilapidated ground sitting behind a night club owned by the then chairman, Costas Sophocleous, but there we were. A mixed pre-season was set up, some sessions held on a local park in Leyton, and some at the old White Lion Ground (which at least hadn't been locked up or knocked down at the time) and that gave me my first experience of the infamous Trent Park Triangle.

Pre-season was ok, but once the matches started, I struggled with the player coach role, especially as Steve had brought in another left sided centre half and that limited my games. It really got to me when I wasn't in the side for the first game of the season, then, because the team started well and went on a bit of a run, I missed the entire first month.

It was hard to remain focussed and sharp as I wasn't getting games and that showed a little as I became less motivated about the coaching and then, to top it all, in came another coach as well!

I knew had to play games to keep fit, so with Steve's blessing I dual signed at Berkhamsted Town. That just didn't feel right. I was the outsider at Berko, a club that were suffering with their own mainly financial issues, I didn't really know anyone, and everyone thought I'd only be there short term. As it happened, mental state of whatever it didn't really help in terms of sharpness or getting minutes under my belt as in four games, I was sent off twice. (One harsh, one stupid and borne once again out of frustration).

I went back to Leyton, Berkhamsted continued a downward slide and eventually went bust and I almost got banned from all football, as no-one there had mentioned that I had to pay my own fines. In the past, as is the norm, the clubs pay their players' fines for bookings and sending's off as its part of the game. Some clubs will then fine the players internally aka Yeading in the early days as a sort of informal discipline. Generally, the fine money, which can be added to by turning up late, missing training and a plethora of player's fines, will normally find its way into a Christmas or end of season player's fund. I thought Berkhamsted would be the same but with their money situation i.e. they had none, they hadn't paid the fines and I received a warning from the County FA that if I didn't cough up quickly, I would be banned until the fines had been paid in full. I ended up paying just in time, but it was a bit of an eye-opener. It just added to the general malaise I was feeling at the time.

The malaise began to spread to Steve and Del at Leyton as well, as the chairman Costas (who had previous for this) decided he would get involved in the football side of things, making sure certain people (including his son) got a game, changing formations and such like. It was his money alright, but he couldn't see that he was just undermining his management team. With that in their heads they were finding it tough enough and didn't need me in their ear every time I was left out or benched, but that's the way it was.

It all came to a head in my mum's pub where Steve, myself and a few of the local lads were having a drink. I was having what may be described as a one-way discussion with Steve. I was bawling him out, not letting him get a word in and I was shouting to be heard over the music. Then the music suddenly stopped but I didn't. I think that was a bit of a shock for mum as much as anyone as she hadn't heard her little boy (35!) like that before... she just hadn't seen me in and around the football environment!

Looking back, like so much else, it's in the folder marked experience I suppose. The upshot being that I don't think it's much to ask to be treated honestly and fairly, and I thought I wasn't. Whether that was because or Steve and Del, Costas or my own failings I suppose is all a matter of opinion, but I just wanted to play. Now I've stepped into the management arena I hope I can always be 100% honest with players, good enough or not. It'll certainly be my aim as I know from experience how much it can hurt to be cast aside or ignored with little or no reason given.

Steve and Del had, had enough and left after another run in with Costas and his meddling, (something he cannot do now as he's serving a rather long sentence for VAT fraud, courtesy of Her Majesty, so it wasn't his money after all) and at the same time I got a call from Peter Grant who'd heard I was unhappy and not playing to see if I wanted to join Bedfont Green, then ground sharing at Windsor.

SUPERSTITIONS

I've mentioned that one night as I left home, my young daughter Holly asked why I was going out. As I'd explained, she was used to Daddy being at home when she went to bed and now I was going out to do something she didn't understand. I left her with a questioning look and my heavy heart. I should have guessed it wasn't going to be a good night from that, but off I went.

The same routine as always, driving to the local newsagents for the usual pre-match snack of a Wispa bar and a Red Bull and they didn't have any Wispas. I had to settle for a Wispa Gold. It's just not the same.

Then I got caught in the traffic on the hottest evening of the year so far and I ended up arriving late. It threw things out a bit, but to be honest not my warm up as I don't really need to warm too much up, I wasn't exactly blessed with sprinting muscles as a teenager let alone as a forty-something. Mentally, I'm prepared as I always am, it's just without the Wispa and then the delay, things get a bit out of kilter. And the game was a disaster. We got dicked 5-1 by a team from the Division below. Superstitious? Moi? Is this 'Chapter 13' after all?

I don't have any others really which perhaps is unusual as I've been around so long, but aside from that bit of preparation, the only other thing that comes close is if I'm not skipper and leading the side out, I'll come out last. I don't even know when that started, but it is something I'll do. It's even caused a clash once or twice with other players that must come out last. We'll start side by side, both last, and then maybe I'll stop and re-tie a shoelace at the last minute, just to make sure!

It is amazing how superstitious some players and managers can be. Putting on the same clothes / suits and all in the same order. Some grow their hair, grow beards, some tie their laces in a certain way and then if they lose, they change that for the following match. Even managers get caught up in it with lucky cup suits, the same pre-match routine, all those you'd expect I suppose.

For me, anything that changes the 'norm' can play tricks on your mind and that means you cannot concentrate fully on the game, so actually, these things tend to be habit rather than superstitions for me.

Perhaps if I'd have thought about it earlier in my career, I could have won the same tie-ups or something after an FA Cup or FA Trophy or Vase win... it might have got me that little bit of glory!

DEFEATED, DEFLATED, DOUBT-FULL

Losses come in all shapes and sizes every season, some because you were straight-up beaten by a far better side. If you give your all, then though it's a defeat and no-one likes losing, it is just a little bit easier to bear. A loss to side you should beat or who are patently not as good really hurts and in cup competitions they hurt more than most (and I've made a bloody career out of those). Worse still, when it's your fault, your error (not a career, but I'm sure any Wealdstone fans reading this are immediately thinking Hertford Town again).

You see, most footballers at any level tend to be fragile little darlings really, inside at any rate. Now, I don't mean that Billie Bremner, Ron Harris, Neal Ruddock or Vinnie Jones would burst into tears at a misplaced pass that lead to a last-minute goal, but I'll bet they weren't cock-a-hoop at the loss especially if they were partly at fault. Me? I take it on the chin and get on with life.

No, I don't.

Defeat itself I don't like but you learn to accept it. When It's my fault I can go into my shell a bit and I'm sorry to say, I might carry the baggage around with me for a few days after, unless there's another game on the immediate horizon where I can put it behind me. I don't mean to, but when we lose, the family will get a somewhat less bubbly husband and father home in the evening and I think that perhaps they keep a little bit out of the way at times as well.

One thing is certain. If you lose on a Saturday, you want to put it right midweek. That is assuming the cock-up wasn't so bad that you don't get picked God forbid, and if that happens the old paranoia rears its ugly head once again! The what-if's and the will I ever's increase in intensity every time you are benched and if you don't get on 'to put things right' the darker the gloom of self-doubt becomes. Believe me, if I get dropped then sit on the bench for a couple of games it really starts to get to me. Frustration, even anger. I suppose its part of the passion I have for the game. We all make mistakes. It's just they hurt a lot more if you can't or don't get the chance to put them right.

Just as bad is a defeat that is followed by no game and that, at this level can sometimes for a fortnight. That can be unbearable even though no-one is in control of the situation. Early season cup games in the early rounds, either for you or opponents, often mean that league games are called off, then the weather can have an impact. You just can't imagine how I'd feel if I cocked-up, we lost, then a couple of games were postponed, and we didn't play for a fortnight and then I was on the bench and I didn't get on. Safe to say, I don't think I'd be ready for a night at the Comedy Club!

A couple of years ago, 2012-13 I think, Cockfosters played Hillingdon in mid-September. They were a new side, not part of the old Hillingdon Borough club that folded early in my career, (was it really the nineties?) although they've taken the name. The game didn't pan out as we expected, being 0-2 down at half time in a match we were expected to win. They broke, I anticipated a wide pass to try and get their winger round the back of our line, so I dropped off my man to cover and I got mugged. In came an early ball to the forward I should have been marking and he was running at me. Forwards, I'm no sprinter. Backwards, well the mind is willing, and the body is trying, but as he twisted and turned one way then the next I reckon he started to plait my legs. That gave him a yard and he duly drilled the ball into the bottom corner for a third, which they quickly followed with a fourth. It knocked the wind out of us and although we did eventually get on top, we could only bag three as we slipped (me literally) to defeat.

I apologised to the lads at the end of the game, because that third was a bit of a turning point. Most of them tried to soften the blow with good old dressing room banter. Things like: *"are you still dizzy,"* and:" we *nearly called for a spanner to unwind you"* but it didn't shake my mood. That night it was a quick pint and the journey home. Loyal sons in tow, they tried to find other people and odd errors to blame (they can usually find someone else to blame instead of me, bless them) but I think we all knew it was my fault.

Winning Player of Year for the previous two years didn't matter. A single error like that is hard to take. How could I have done better? Will this keep happening? Is it just a one off? All questions I asked myself as I lay awake the whole of the Saturday night. The minute it happened I knew my weekend was finished. I can't help it. It's the way I've always been. My poor family see a forlorn depressed figure until I get the chance to put it right. Even a couple of beers don't help. Undeserved, they don't taste as nice!

It's easier when you are young and naïve, you are still indestructible, fearless and full of self-confidence, but as an elder statesman you get a bit more fearful and realistic and doubtful. This time it might be the end.

By the following Tuesday morning the focus had changed. I had a cup game to look forward to that evening and the fighting instinct was back to dispel all the dark thoughts. All except the one that wondered if I'd get picked. The ability to battle on through thick and thin is a big part of what keeps me playing the game into my forties and if picked, a decent game would dispel all my doubts. A win as well? Come on the old boy, you can do it.
We didn't.

First, the positives; I started, and I thought I'd be selfish early doors and look after my own game, (second positive) I won a few headers, and this was against Stotfold, the side we'd beaten in the previous season's cup final. Early doors, the confidence flooded back. Third positive; that early boost in confidence got the mouth going and I was back gee-ing up the side trying to keep everyone motivated and sharp, my weekend of doubts just a memory. Fourth positive; we looked quite decent and made lots of chances. Not so positive was the fact we couldn't score. In fact, I think we'd have struggled to hit a cow's arse with a shillelagh.

Individual errors (not mine) cost us the game but Hammond and Bazza will remain nameless to protect the guilty. A 2-0 defeat and revenge for the beaten finalists. The reality soon restored the gloom. Only one cure. Bring on Saturday, at least for the moment without self-doubt. A knock here and there (they're always more serious when a side has lost a couple of games) and 'work commitments' (as in, I don't really fancy it and can earn a few quid anyway) meant that there were a few missing for this one. I had to play right-side centre half.

Maybe I should say at this point I know where 'right' is, as that's the leg I stand on. In a game, I find it difficult to concentrate on what's going on around me when I have to keep looking at a map and compass to see where I am. That side of the pitch, uncharted territories for a left hooker like me, seems bigger as well.

Honest, though, Guv, it wasn't my fault as we went 0-3 down in twenty minutes. Even at 42 I hadn't realised you could do that much defending in one game let alone one half. My personal (if somewhat unwarranted) despair deepened as the defeats continued. It continued still further the following Saturday too as we got done 3-1 against the League leaders. It wasn't the first time in my career but losing four in a row won't be a highlight on the CV that's for sure.

All good things, and eventually all bad things come to an end. Our bad run like many before and I suppose many yet to come, was finally broken and in an FA Vase match to boot. Not, as you know by now, a competition in which I personally have been on the winning side too often, but a 5-0 victory against Hoddesdon, a team with whom I share a mutual dislike (in fact, since most of 'my' Cockfosters side buggered off, most of the then Hoddesdon players are now at Cockfosters) made a couple of pints taste all the sweeter. Then the cream on the cake was their match report. Apparently, it was down to our luck and the footballing gods being against them as the better side. It's always nice to get a decent win but even more so when it's against a club like that. A bit of bias around your own club I can understand, but a complete cyclops attitude that only sees good in one and bad in the other, especially when you've just been dicked, I find a bit harder to swallow.

What a win can do though! The Moore family would be faced with a much happier and satisfied chappy for the next few days at least!

RUB OF THE GREEN

I joined Bedfont midway through the 2008-09 season hoping that a new challenge would dispel the general fug around my time at Leyton. I hoped I would start to enjoy football again, even if it included another visit to the Meadowbank Stadium, Dorking. (We went there and won, and it hadn't changed).

Peter Grant got me down to the club, but Dennis Banborough was the Manager and a character in his self, his image and personality somewhere between Del Boy, Billy Liar and a style idol.

In a nice way, if there was a pound to nick, he'd nick it, even the player's wages. I heard him once or twice use the: *"sorry I left the envelope at home"* line if he thought he could get away with it. A nice guy but get to close and you'd count your fingers. I never knew a manager like it. He'd get ribbed about everything, what he said, what he wore, everything. He was full of bull about where he went and what he did, but at the heart of it all was a decent enough bloke and it was all fairly harmless. He was an OK if a bit interesting manager and he put a smile on people's faces, so he was good to have around the place. He even got the nod to stay for the next season, and so did I.

Joining Bedfont meant a drop down (again) but it meant I'd play. I joined in late November and they were sixth I think but struggling a bit defensively. From then on, I think we lost once to the end of the season, and we won the Championship. I loved it, winning again had become a habit and I had a really good season. It gave me another spark I suppose. I felt wanted there and it was a great feeling to win the league too. A couple of old boys, me and Jon Barrie-Bates were part and parcel of the side. I still feel that (and I'm normally a bit more reserved and modest) I don't think they'd have won the league if they hadn't signed me. There were some good players there; Chrissy Henry who's gone on to play at a decent level, Gavin Hart who had been on the fringes at Wealdstone, both good going forward and a kiwi, Russ Minor. Those three must have scored sixty goals that season. They were great going forward, but the side were a bit leaky at the back. JBB and I gave them a bit of security working with the young lads around us, as much with the voice as with the head and feet. Before he and I there was no-one used to winning things and that does become part of the mentality, so when things get tough, you have that extra push because you want to win again.

It did clear away the fug and I felt like I'd been given a new lease of life. Being there and winning the title put a spring back into my step and the club back into the Southern League. The next pre-season couldn't come soon enough. As I've said no pre-season is a chore for me because I prepare, and I know what it means but for this one? I had a new eagerness. I built myself up over the summer as usual and was ready when we started back, ready for another year. The Southern League Southern Division meant loads of travelling just as there had been with Northwood, but it also meant loads of new grounds like Paulton Rovers, Cinderford and Mangotsfield to experience. I was quite content.

With no expectations we started well and got a couple of early points under the belt. JBB and I were still the experience with a few young lads brought in for strength in the squad. If anything, we underachieved after a good start as we lacked a bit of organisation off the field as well as on, and training at Viking Sports, an old and somewhat dilapidated ground alongside the A40 at Greenford wasn't great as the location gave people an excuse to be late or not to be there at all.

We had some good results though, especially when we travelled to Paulton Rovers just after they played Norwich in the FA Cup (them, not me) and we beat them on their own patch. We were another side that could perform on their day. That day, there was plenty of banter during and after that game, just to let them know that they may have played Norwich, but they'd still lost to the mighty Bedfont Green.

I was having a decent year until another daft challenge. I went in two footed at Mangotsfield, got sent off and after the suspension, my season became a bit stop start as I was in and out of the side, but I thought that there wasn't long to go and there was another season to look forward to when I could start again. At the end of the season the club were re-shuffled once again, this time to the Southern League Central Division, which was at least a bit more local.

Come pre-season and Dennis was tied up with some personal stuff and couldn't be around. Jon-Barrie Bates wanted to concentrate on playing, so pre-season training was down to me. I got Fred Cummings involved to help me put together a schedule and it was made tougher knowing that I wasn't going to be a regular at the start of the season whatever. The kids were now at an age where holidays were taken during school holidays and that meant for the first time, despite me running pre-season, I'd be going away with the family early doors.

We had a few hard sessions and the lads were struggling but it wasn't going to change. I was involved and participated (then almost thirty-eight), so I figured if I could do it so could they. As it happened the sessions went down well, the lads enjoyed them and saw the benefit. We also played a few pre-season games, in one of which I took a knock which put me out for a couple of weeks, but we kept going. We looked sharp and were looking forward to the season, and all set for Dennis to return to take charge.

He did, and I got dropped for the first game, away at Northwood. It was a disastrous start as the lads were 3 or 4 down at half time. Dennis panicked (not unusual) and brought on all three subs, me included. We were better and didn't concede in the second half, with me scoring one in our inglorious defeat, but we all knew there would have to be changes for the next game against title favourites, Slough Town. Having been injured pre-season then been told I wasn't fit enough and was benched at Northwood, suddenly after a couple of days rest I was fit enough to start against Slough. I think to be fair it was more for my organisational skills, big mouth and nous than for my pace, but I was quite happy with that.

We started the game much better and much tighter and I was on top of my game until ten minutes into the second half when in a challenge with Sean Sonner, I turned my knee and ankle and I couldn't carry on. Slough scored, we equalised late on, but I was out. My ankle was in bits and I still wear a support on it to this day. By some distance it's my worst injury in over twenty-eight years. I was out for about three months and the lads were by then doing well. A couple of new centre backs had come in and I was limited to turning up at most matches to watch my replacement, Ryan Lake. He had come in as another experienced and good player and he did well, but that meant it was less and less likely I'd regain my place.

Watching one game from the side lines, Dennis pulled me and told me I'd be the next Bedfont manager as he was going to New Zealand and wouldn't be around, then a week later the club announced Jon-Barrie Bates had got the job. Dennis still full of bull to the last. I just concentrated on getting fit and trying to get my place back in the side.

JBB was still playing and he asked me to be his player / assistant manager which I accepted, and I also brought back Fred to coach the side. We had a couple of games where I enjoyed it and got a bit of a buzz, none more so than in a match at Marlow where we didn't start to well. Fred and I changed things mid-half, we settled and got right back into our stride. We won 3-1 and I got a buzz from the fact we'd changed things around and got the result, but it still wasn't the same as playing. It was an insight perhaps in what may still be yet to come, but it was only the next best thing. In my heart I knew I still had to play.

A couple of months into the season, I was fit and wanted to play but couldn't get into the side until one game when we had a late drop out v Uxbridge at home. It was early February, and I got the nod. Twenty minutes in, doing my job and I was playing well alongside Ryan Lake when the ball was pinged over the top. I ran with the forward and took a nudge which propelled me forward and into the ball hand first. The ref gave the free kick and I got sent off. I was livid. I felt it was unfair and accidental but that was that. I sat in the stand and did a bit, shouting to the lads about shape and what-not, but the frustration was building. This coaching for some reason upset the chairman, or maybe he was upset at the sending-off, I didn't even realise at the time.

I'd lost my place again through the suspension, but I hung in there though I didn't play again. Even when results turned for the worse at the end of the season, JBB wouldn't change the side. As it turned out it was the end of me and the club. We'd all taken pay cuts and listened to the chairman's stories about how things would soon turn for the better, but they didn't.

Bedfont resigned from the league at the end of the year and went back effectively to local football, one step above the park. For me, it was another experience for the memory banks, after Leyton and a meddling chairman that was there for all to see, I'd now experienced the politics involved in management at this level. And especially how so many of the board are experts when things aren't going so well.

I learnt a lot, how to talk to players, how to manage them, knowing those that you can bawl out and those you can't. It also taught me a bit about tactics and changes and how you can influence a game from the side lines. Most of all, it gave me some extra legs. As I'd missed most of the season, I'd kept fit and felt there was now another couple of years left in the tank. I was looking forward to a new season, the only thing I didn't have was a club.

DEMONS; INSIDE, OUTSIDE AND THE OPPOSING SIDE

Every new season brings its own challenges. New players or a new team, new managers, you never really know what's going to happen until you start the first competitive match. As the years pass and you start to get veteran status, the old psyche starts to weigh heavily in your mind too. Still got it? Still got the miles in those old legs? Still able to do it week in, week out?

It's amazing that I still get butterflies in the (now slightly larger) belly after all these years but that's what the start of any new season brings. The opposition are responsible in a small part, but mainly and this does increase with age because of the pressure I put on myself and that paranoia, the self-doubt that creeps in. If I don't play well as a 'vet' it is definitely harder to recover. You start to think that maybe time has caught up with you. Reaching my mid-forties, I've battled with this demon for the last ten years at least and believe me, it's a harder battle than most on the pitch. Even after a victory it doesn't go away, the over critical analysis of every aspect of the game, one small error far outweighing the fifty things I did right in the match. Maybe one day, it's a battle I'll lose, and I'll have to hang up my boots, but not this week or even this season. Or next.

There is some relief from the pressure though. Coming up against old opponents, some still playing, some coaching or managing and at the end of the game there will be a: *"well played, Fergie"* or: *"still got it son"*. Believe me at my age that's more refreshing than any beer and more re-assuring than you'll ever know. The game's much easier when you've got a bit of confidence especially when it's originated from your peers.

Over a few seasons I've lined up for the first game as last season's Player of the Year. Another pot on the shelf and more important, mentally, another feather in the cap. Perhaps it's a manager's trick to squeeze that last little bit of extra effort out, like putting a fork into a squeezed orange to drain the last of the juice, but to me it doesn't matter. I won it and I want to win it again.

Joining Cockfosters in 2012, my first league game ended 3-3 against Leverstock Green. As you'd expect from my completely unbiased assessment, they scored their first from a handball, the goalkeeper cocked-up for their second and their third took a wicked deflection. We were the better team throughout even though a few of the lads were lacking the wind and the pace required, their pre-season excuses blown out of the water as they started blowing out of their arses. Maybe as they sharpen up we'll get a bit more effort and few more breaks, you do make your own luck in this game, after all.

At the end I shook hands with a few of their lads and made a bee-line for their 'keeper, an old teammate, Kieran Jimmy. *"Still know how to read the game then, mate"* he said. Self-doubt duly parked till the next game.

At the start of every season, the games come thick and fast. For a 'vet', tough Saturdays are often too soon followed by midweek matches at least up to the August Bank Holiday, and (I'm told) if you get a run in the early Extra Qualifying and Qualifying rounds of the FA competitions, perhaps with a replay or two, it can be twice a week through September. Now as a twenty-year-old, that's great. Every match an opportunity to impress followed by a beer or six to refresh the limbs then you're ready to go again. Apart from growing paranoia, mentally, I still feel the same, but I now have a forty-six-year-old body with a varied collection of aching joints that would beg to disagree.

We followed that opening draw with a tough home game against fancied Colney Heath on the Tuesday. That gave me 48 hours and in truth I'd have liked to spend the best part of that in a hot bath for my warm-down but a family and a couple of days at work soon put paid to those thoughts.

A game is a game is a game, but some are harder than others, Colney Heath being one. When you're playing them, you know from the off what you are going to get. Physical demons on the pitch and they'll use proper verbals across the park to get in your head. They'll try and bully you all night long. That, I suppose is in their psyche they've been at it for years and it's a well-developed style. For them, it works much of the time, especially against the younger sides at this level, as their final placings in recent years tell no lies.

Clubs and matches like these are part of the reason sides further up the pyramid send players down to this level to learn. It's far more beneficial than an U18, U23 or reserve league where they're only up against kids of the same age. 'Down here' you'll get old pub players at their peak, golden oldies like me on the way down and plenty of experience in all things football that don't necessarily involve the ball itself. It's that same reason pro club use the senior non-leagues to toughen up their development squad players. For many, it's the first time they've taken a kick in anger. The same scenario permeates down through the levels.

In twenty-seven or eight years, I've seen it, I've heard it and I've felt it. Often enough I've even thought of the bible. It's far better to give than receive. Even when you know it's coming, it's no easier and you can't let it put you off your game. Sometimes you need to get your retaliation in first.

Ten minutes into the game and we go a goal down. Their tails are well and truly up and wagging, but we dig in and for twenty-five minutes we're on top, only a couple of decent saves from their keeper stopping us from drawing level. Then against the run of play and just seconds before half time, we get skinned down one flank. In comes a cross, the forward gets on the end of it (not my man, honest) and it's 0-2. Disaster, not least because they've scored but as much because the whistle blows and we're off into the dressing room to find out first hand and at close range (as if we didn't already know) what the management think.

Aside from a few pointed comments about positioning and concentration, it was positive. There were no flying tea cups, no hasty changes, just a lot of keep doing the same, get in their heads and get back on top. The usual mental and fundamental stuff.

Out we go for part two, the twenty or thirty fans (and the odd dog) having meandered back to the barriers at the side lines, a pint or a coffee in hand and we're ready for battle. They, however are still buzzing. We can all hear the comments: *"this lot are pony"*, *"we'll get five or six here"*, *"they've got nothing about them"*. You must swallow it because in the same position, we'd be lauding it over them. Forty-five minutes to play and whether they realized or not, they had done as much if not more for our confidence and resilience as any half-time team talk.

We tightened up the formation a bit and after about a quarter of an hour, without really imposing ourselves but at least containing their efforts, we got one back through Luke Durnin. That gave us a boost and territorially we took over the game forcing Colney back, playing in their half but not really creating too many chances. For their part, every goal-kick, throw–in and free-kick seemed to be taking an age as the position of the ball was changed time after time to waste a few precious seconds. That in the end worked against them though as, as we passed the ninety into time added on Ben Hammond pinged a deep cross to the back post and Morts (Richard Morton) cushioned a header back across the six-yard box for Cookie to head in the equaliser. Have that!

Now they were on the back foot, and we were like bloody peacocks in our pomp. Minutes, maybe only seconds remained as we nicked the ball from their kick off. Pushing forward we won a free kick on the edge of the box, central to the goal. As their wall lined up the Ref turned to Ben Hammond and said: *"it'll be the last kick of the game"*. No pressure then!

He produced a worldy. Curling over the wall and dropping sweetly under the bar out of the despairing reach of their keeper. Manic celebrations began, and we were giving it out it big time as they looked shell shocked. The bottom line is, if you dish it out you have got to learn to take it but some of these boys don't seem to have read that page yet. I've learnt over the years that you can't give it large at half-time or even in the last few minutes of a game as it will often come back and bite you in the bum. Maybe its luck or maybe because it breaks the concentration, but believe me, when you nick one like this, you are the demon and can sure as hell give it out at the final whistle. And each and every player on their side was 'gently' reminded of this as we trooped off the field, passing the away dressing room. On a personal level, one smug old man went home very happy, and even temporarily (adrenalin driven) ache-free.

They would certainly be up for it at their place later in the season, but so what? Those few moments were ours to enjoy. And we did.

PASTURES NEW, NOT OUT TO PASTURE

It's not until you write things down and are looking for a new heading for each chapter that you realise how hard it is to find new words for almost every season at a new club. In fact, as I've been fortunate so far that the telephone has always rung, for me, it's harder than finding a new club.

After Bedfont, the call came from Keith Scott who had been Assistant Manager for a short spell in my time at Northwood. Now in charge at the newly re-born Windsor FC, he asked me to sign because he wanted me to be part of an experienced squad, one that would start the club's progression back up the non-league ladder from the Combined Counties League. And the money was decent too.

Myself and a coach, Jim Melvin were there to support Scotty, me as a senior player to help where I could, though once again it was more an informal thing. It seemed like a good club and there were some decent players in the squad, Dave Tilbury, Jake and Ryan Parsons as well as most of the side that had got Windsor promoted once already. With a few new faces added to the squad, we were fancied to be there or thereabouts for the one automatic promotion place. They also had some decent youth players on the fringes, but sadly, they weren't going to get their chance. We soon found out that Keith and Jim wanted experience.

We went into the first league game and I don't think we were ready. We hadn't played enough during pre-season to really get sharp and it showed when we lined up against South Park. They should have won the game, but we got a draw and worse still one of their goals was down to me, as I was beaten to a back-stick header. Maybe with the ball hanging in the air that long, you'd expect a bit of a hand from the 'keeper but it didn't come, and we got done. Scotty gave me both barrels afterwards and I had to swallow it. The goal was my fault.

We played a couple more matches and things weren't going too well as we were letting in goals that we shouldn't have. Not down to me in particular but still goals that we should have done better with. Scotty and Jim were like good cop, bad cop except both played bad cop. Scotty would come in and have his say, then bugger me, Jim would have a go at the same bloke. That was strange and something I'd never seen before. They were direct and rarely let things drop.

Home to Molesey, we were 3-1 up and won 4-3 but they weren't happy about that. Next game I was out. I wasn't told, I was just dropped, but after a few games and with a bit of luck, I got back in the side. I wasn't supposed to start, I was wearing 14 away to Raynes Park Vale (highlife eh!) and one lad turned up late, so I got put back in the XI. I scored, and boy did I let them know! The lads loved it because no-one had stood up to Scotty or Jim before. I'd take a bollocking where due, but I wasn't taking it if it wasn't down to me and this was my way of letting them know what I thought. I ran past them shouting and once again pointing to the 14 on my back.

Sods law, I got back into the side and then I got injured, I pulled a hamstring. Now if you've seen me play at any time in twenty-eight years you'll know I'm not quick enough to pull a hammy, so I just don't know how that happened! It kept me out for a couple of weeks then by the time I was fit, the team were winning. I did get back in the side just after Christmas because Ryan Parsons' missus was having a baby, then I was out when he came back. It got to February and I was still out of the side and getting a bit miffed.

Scotty loved a team meeting as well. He'd call them about nothing. Just repeating himself over and over, they got a bit tedious as we'd get all the usual stuff, then he'd try to start some banter by digging people out. When it was my turn, I let him have some back and Ryan Ashe who's been around a few years pulled me after and said he'd never heard anyone speak to Scotty like that before, but I didn't see why I should just take it. Ashie was wetting himself laughing.

Scotty was another of those managers that had to bully because he didn't command respect or a response. I remember one game when we were 5 or 6 nil up and he brought on a young lad. The boy did OK but didn't track or something at one point and Scotty absolutely tore into him. The kid didn't know what had hit him. No reason, he just slaughtered him. The kid never played again and while I was there he never even came back.

Craig Bartlett was at Windsor at the same time. We played over at Flackwell Heath, well, I say we, but it should have been he, as I was there but suspended. Craig was playing right back but he just didn't look right. At half time 'the bullys' Melvin and Scotty bawled him out big time, but they sent him back out. Luckily the physio and I went with him. I don't know if we both sensed it, but it was apparent something was seriously wrong, Craig wasn't unconscious, but he was unresponsive and had no idea what was happening round him.

We knew dad, Gordon was at a game and his phone would be off and someone asked if anyone knew another number. Off the top of my head I called out his home number, where wife Jackie or daughter Amanda would probably be. It just showed how often I rang the bloke, even when I wasn't at Wealdstone I still called often enough to know his home and mobile numbers off the top of my head. Jackie was in, not too far away and came out to get Craig and get him sorted.

For me, Scotty didn't use my experience or experienced players in the right way. When you were winning it was OK but if you conceded a goal it wasn't experience it was old. He couldn't understand that sometimes, the other side were better and would score. I swear he even thought that sometimes we'd concede a goal just to spite him. From the sublime to the ridiculous.

There were a few odd selections too. At Molesey he played me and Dave Tilbury as wing backs and Ryan Parson, a natural wing back in Central Midfield. At half time we were 3-0 down and chasing shadows so Dave and I got pulled and fair play the lads got back to 3-3 and might even have won it. I just sat there at half time thinking that it was enough. As Scotty laid into us again, I knew I'd had enough, it wasn't the bollocking for not playing well or not doing my job, it was just the fact that there was no pleasure in it anymore. We had a game on the Tuesday and for the first (and only) time in my life I cried off. I spoke the chairman, he rang and asked why I wasn't there, and I told him. I just couldn't be around Scotty anymore. He tried to get me to stay to the end of the season and then after management dropped my money, the chairman said he'd make it back up. But I just had to go.

A week or so later I joined Hanwell Town, then managed by Tommy Williams who was like a breath of fresh air. A nice bloke and a good manager who used experience where it was most effective. I got a new lease of life and was playing well and more importantly enjoying it. my experience being used to bring the kids on and support them. We were plum bottom when I joined but we escaped relegation and I'd scored a few goals to help. We should have gone down in what would have been the first relegation in my career, but we got reprieved when someone else collapsed to preserve my record.

Since then, Hanwell who have always had the feel of a family club, have rebuilt and gone on to bigger and better things so good luck to them. At Windsor, Scotty and his sidekick were moved on at the end of the year and haven't been involved in the game since. Long may it last. I still message some of the lads from over there: *"Have they got jobs yet?"* The answer is always *"no"* It's become a bit of a laugh now even though it's harsh to laugh at someone else's expense. It was just how they made me, and a few others feel. At Northwood as assistant he'd been fine, and he'd seen something in me that he wanted to sign at Windsor for which I'm grateful. I just can't understand why, once on board, there seemed to be no respect or relationship. Did he think I was someone else? Ah well, another summer, another season, time to retire or another club?

Over the summer, Michael Roache had been made up to first team manager at Cockfosters and he took a mate of mine, Fabio Valenti with him as his assistant. Knowing my situation, the phone rang again, and they invited me down to join the club. I'd been through Cockfosters, been round it and been past it but I never saw the ground till I turned up for training. Perhaps that was a good thing.

FOOTBALL IS AN EASY GAME; SOME OFFICIALS MAKE IT DIFFICULT

I know they must learn and I know we're all fallible and make mistakes, but you wonder sometimes if the game would be better off without referees and their assistants involved? I've seen it all; goals given that weren't, goals not given that were, players booked for getting injured, the wrong man sent off, all sorts. I've heard many senior players say that it's becoming obvious that some referees are getting promoted through the system because they can answer the right questions rather than having a grasp of the game, the passion, decent vision and an attention span slightly longer than that of a gnat.

A couple of years into my time at Cockfosters, we were set to play away to the mighty St Margaretsbury, a side we played knowing, like Colney Heath, what to expect. Their management would be on the Referee's back from the first minute, in fact in the warm up if they thought they could get away with it. The players follow suit, challenging every decision and surrounding the referee to waste time (not that we see that every week in the Premier League despite the apparent 'rules' to prevent it). I know it's something that most clubs do on occasion but for this lot, it was just a normal part of the game. It must have been mentioned by the officials in their reports week in, week out so the league must have been aware. We had a bit of history too, games between the two sides rarely being completed without incident of one sort or another. You'd like to think that when there is 'a bit of previous' between the two sides, the League or at least those who place officials at matches would take that into account and perhaps appoint a good strong official?

In the previous season, it was played two, lost two. We wanted revenge and we knew what was coming from the side-lines. They didn't let us down. From minute one they appealed for everything and were baying to get our lads booked after every challenge, but we were solid and held it together (despite some odd decisions here and there) to go in level at half-time. What we didn't realise and hadn't expected was what else the referee had in mind.

Ten minutes or so into the second half our midfielder Marksy made a challenge in our box. He raised a foot, no doubt, but the referee gave an indirect free kick. (See, it's not always a bad decision in favour of our opponents). Their bench went loopy. It was hysterical watching and listening while still trying to concentrate on the game. Ten minutes more and one of their lads 'went through' Adem Ali who got up and fronted the offender, if not actually retaliating. It was a two-footed challenge and the ref called the offender over for a word or two. We expected the two of them to be sent off but no, this master of the laws of the game charged with control on this sunny afternoon didn't even issue a booking.

As though trying to reprise his earlier escape, five or six minutes later the same defender took out another of our forwards and that was it. Handbags were drawn in the classic farce of footballers pushing and posturing. Once the ensuing melee had calmed down (in truth it ran out of steam rather than having been stopped by referee or assistants), the man in black sent off their centre half who had apparently punched one of our lads, Lasalle Simon who just happened to earn his living as a cage fighter. Not the smartest move, but maybe he didn't realise what he could potentially have unleashed. Lasalle was dismissed for his reaction and off he went at some pace to 'continue the discussion' with his opponent in the dressing room. Thankfully however he was stopped on the long march from pitch to clubhouse that St Maggies offers. The original offender that had started the incident? This time he was at least booked.

We were then awarded a penalty with ten to go which Stuey Blackburne duly despatched and then minutes later while their bench was still loudly and pointedly sharing their opinions of the penalty decision, another oldie, assistant manager Fabio Valenti came on for a cameo appearance and nicked another goal to seal the points. The eruption from their bench on the penalty award had to be seen to be believed, the goal increased the intensity and that resulted in their manager being sent off as well.

So incensed was he, he duly took to twitter to vent his feelings about the officials and us, and he labelled the referee the worst he had ever come across. On seeing this I responded, not directly to him, biting my lip a little as I didn't think the officials had been great either, but with the 'previous' it was too good an opportunity to turn down. I sent a general reply, somewhat tongue in cheek to the effect that players win and lose you games not referees, which despite some poor performances from officials, I do believe.

The tweet was picked up on in a few places, not least the excellent Cold End football blog, and as someone who has played over eleven hundred games in non-league (yes, really!) they sort of tabled me as the voice of reason. Needless to say, it started a 'twitter fest' which also involved St Mags players ensuring that the return was unlikely to be a feast of football for the purist. I know it's easy to moan, but just as players can have an off-day, so can officials. Theirs however tend to have more impact and certainly stay in the memory longer.

At Uxbridge, we had an up and coming referee for one game, Paul Taylor. It seemed to me and a few others unbelievable after that day, that he eventually went on to become a football league referee. We were playing away to Leyton. It was a bank holiday and as we travelled over, we passed by a circus on a green in Walthamstow. It was surely an omen? In the game, a decision was given against me and I (unusually) had something to say about it. I think it was along the lines of *"Eh! Coco, you shouldn't be here mate you should be down the road"* and I pointed in the general direction of the circus. That was it, I was called over and out came the book. A week later after a home game I was a bit late into the bar and when I walked in everyone was laughing. George Talbot had got the booking Form back from the FA, had it enlarged and had pinned it on the wall in among the pictures of the good and famous teams and players from Uxbridge's past. There it was in all its glory: Booking section 6 or whatever, Dissent. *"In the xxth minute of the match I awarded a foul against Mr Moore and as I approached him he said "Oi, Coco, where's your red nose and your big red shoes? You shouldn't be here, you should be down the road at Zippo's Circus"*. Honestly, I don't think I said all that that, but what a jobsworth, writing it all down, even if I did. Maybe that rattled me as it was there for everyone to see, but to me it just proved that for him, the forms were more important than the performance.

Too often, and its more prevalent as I progress down the leagues, it's all about the officials on the day. I've lost count of the times I've heard fans shout: *"Come on ref were here to watch the game, not you"*. Less and less do I come across those that you can talk to and have a bit of banter with. I'm sure those referees get an easier game and control it better, but it doesn't seem to be the way they are taught or instructed to play the game.

I don't care what officialdom, the FA, managers or players say in public or in the press, believe me, footballers are elephants. They don't forget, and niggles and battles carry on game to game, even moving clubs with the players concerned, a good referee can manage that out of a game with a few words, but those that carry so much self-importance will generally inflame a situation. Most are players that weren't good enough (did you know anyone at school who always wanted to be a referee?), and that black kit and a whistle on a Saturday may be their only chance of a bit of power. They get a lot of stick from fans and often quite a bit from players: The less they communicate, in general, the more stick they get. It's all about opinion, but they must be bats to choose that role in our favourite game.

And sometimes, I reckon their radar doesn't work.

HOLD THE CURTAIN CALL

Michael Roach, then at Cockfosters (2012-13) and subsequently Edgware Town was just so 'not manager material' in the traditional way. His persona is that of Jack the Lad and lively, we even used to go on the occasional bender together socially. As a player, he was well known on the local circuit playing at Kingsbury Town and Edgware but to no great standard, making his name if that's the right phrase with West Hendon in the Carlsberg Sunday Cup. Oh, and did I mention that he does like a beer. And the craic. And he was the manager, my manager. And he likes a beer.

It was strange at first but there were plenty of old faces from Edgware and local sides in the 'Fosters (see, I didn't go for the obvious there!) squad so it was a bit of a home from home really. Morts, Marj, Rispolli, Marks, the Blackburne's, the list goes on and pre-season was the Trent Park triangle once again. The sessions and friendlies were all leading up to our opening game, another FA Cup Extra Preliminary tie, this time against Sporting Bengal. We won but once again it wasn't to be the start of my glorious run to FA Cup fame and fortune as we lost in the following round.

We had a decent season as a division one side and had beaten a couple of premier division sides in cups and whatever, but disappointingly we lost in the semi-final of the league cup on penalties to Codicote. (I scored mine as I had in two other penalty shoot-outs that year, even though I'm not known as a penalty taker). Late on, we also lost the division one cup semi-final against Kings Langley and we lost in the Middlesex Charity Cup quarter final to complete an unwanted hat-trick.

Those games combined with a few postponements on the boggy home pitch left us some way behind the others in our league fixtures, and for the last month or so of the season, it meant we had to play three and four games a week to catch up. Eventually after a near sixty game season, we approached the final Saturday and we were set fair for promotion as runners-up, if we got at least a draw away to Winslow United. Otherwise, there was every chance that Hoddesdon Town, away to the bottom side in the division would nick the second spot.

The conditions weren't great as it was a blowy blustery day and wind can be a great leveller. It was a day when the big game players had to come out and lead from the front. I think that's me and I played my part in a decent 0-0 draw while Hoddesdon won 9-0 but still missed out, finishing a close third. We got a little bit over excited afterward and even at my age, the adrenalin kicked in and (this isn't an excuse) I sort of lost myself. I sent a tweet out to Hoddesdon saying hard luck, get your chins up, that bit was fine, but I added best of luck at Stoney Stratford away next year. Stoney Stratford is the worst ground in the league. I got untold responses off the Hoddesdon lads. They vilified me, but it was just meant as banter, even an old boy can get carried away now and then. As it happens three or four weeks later my phone was red hot with tweets and texts of: *"see you next year, old man, don't retire, we're looking forward to it"*. They'd gone up in third, through the back door. I'm not really sure how, but I did hear a rumour that one or two of their committee are involved at the FA!

League promotion secured, our last game was the Southern Floodlight Cup Final against premier division Oxhey Jets. We took the lead but eventually lost 2-1. It was disappointing, but still not a bad result as they were well placed in the division above us. On a personal level, I'd played over fifty games that season as a forty-one-year-old. I missed a couple of games through injury and got rested a couple of times in midweek at the end of the season to preserve the old legs, but overall, I was happy, and management were pleased enough to vote me the Managers Player of the Year. I was made up, really ecstatic. I think they signed me as a bit of a mentor to fill in when required and I'd held my place all year and become a lynchpin in the side. Good for the old'un. It also meant I could spend the summer almost certain that despite the step-up in level, this old fella was still going to be around for the next season.

So, it was. Another year, another new division and yet more new grounds in the premier that I'd not been to before. Now, they were not only for me, but for my new regular travelling partner, my son Callum to enjoy. Before all that though, the end of June meant the beloved triangle again, and this year, for the first time I was to miss the end of pre-season to go on holiday with my family. School terms as many a teacher and father knows, do not fit in with a football schedule. Disbelievers you may be, but I really did do my runs on the beach to make sure I kept the fitness up.

Literally just before the first game of the season, Rochey pulled me to tell me I was playing (but with a bit more meaning than George Talbot previously) *"but only just"*. Although he never said as much, I think me being a fill-in was back in his mind and younger legs were likely to be in front of me in the queue. The match ended up in a 2-2 draw and I had a blinder. As a side we were unlucky not to win, but Rochey's pre-game comment still bugged me, it hinted that there were cracks appearing and it put me on the back foot, giving rise once again to those demons of self-doubt. I really didn't think I had too much to prove after the previous year.

Generally, the season started well, and we did OK in the cups and even in the FA Cup! As the oldest player in the competition we had probably my best run, playing five matches over four rounds, ending in a replay defeat at phoenix club AFC Rushden and Diamonds in the second qualifying round. They were a new side born from the ashes of the Max Griggs inspired Rushden side that had collapsed a couple of years earlier. They were on the up and expected to beat us, yet we were five minutes from beating them at home on the Saturday. It reminded me of an old Gordon Bartlett mantra: *"You get one chance, and you have to take it"*.

How right that proved to be as we got dicked at their place in the replay, 8-0. We had a couple out injured on top of the usual midweek no-shows, but we didn't do ourselves justice. It wasn't a great night for me personally as the guy I was marking was Russ Dunkley. He and I had won that FA Sunday Cup together at Anfield playing for The Duke of York and that makes him a legend in my book (this one!), as that Sunday Cup win at Liverpool (my club since childhood) is right up there with the best days in my career. Dunkley scored five on this evening and was named FA Cup Player of the Round. I think he's owes me a couple of beers for that. I hope I get close enough to him to drink them.

Strangely, I was in the area recently and I saw that The Duke of York has gone and is now an off-licence. I popped in and bought a can for old time's sake, and doffed my cap to the memory as I drank it...

The FA Vase was also a highlight (for me) as we got to the second round and were unlucky to lose 1-0 at Great Wakering Rovers. Once again, at four games, it was my best run in the competition! The downside was that those early cup games had once again caused a backlog of fixtures that we had to make up through the year, but there was a spell of about six or seven weeks when we didn't have a home game at all. Then, at the end of the season we ended up losing at Uxbridge in the Middlesex Cup semi-final, having to immediately pick ourselves up as the following night we had a league game. Not for us a day off and a couple of days of light training before the next game.

Cups were good to us all year really, we won at Hoddesdon which was a big win in the premier cup semi-final to get another final against Stotfold who we also ended up playing in the league cup final. Once again it meant that for four of the last six weeks of the season, we would play Monday, Tuesday, Thursday, Saturday. Don't give me all this twaddle with the Premiership sweethearts who struggle to play three times in ten days, we weren't the only club, and this wasn't the only season it happened in non-league.

I didn't even get time to get tired as in three of the four weeks I played all four fixtures. It was another sixty-game season when the manager pulled me just before the first game to tell me I was only just in the eleven! Forty-two, sixty games and I work five days a week to earn a living.

We had to put out some mixed sides with people's work commitments and the odd injury and such like, but we did OK. There were a few occasions where the side was selected for damage limitation, but everyone involved in that run-in pulled their weight and we came through with some good results. I've had some busy seasons with weather issues and such like, but I can't remember another where in mid-March twenty-one league games remained to be played! At least for the most part I kept the other internal demon of my sciatica at bay. Perhaps being completely knackered worked like some magic anaesthetic!

Two cup finals might have been a good swansong to this career. The first on Bank Holiday Monday at Harefield against Stotfold was a tough game defending the long high ball to their two big forwards. We scored a penalty then they equalised with a scrappy goal, but we did enough and won it in extra time when Billal Butt scored the winner. They were gutted but promised us another tough game a few days later in final number two. In between, they also lost in the Hinchingbrooke Senior Cup Final, so they were coming to us the following midweek with the unwanted chance of losing three finals in about ten days. We were going to do our utmost to help.

Rochey changed it around a little bit for the Southern Floodlight Cup Final to give a few other lads a chance of some glory and it was a tight game. About half an hour in we scored then again, they scored an equaliser just before the end. Just like the previous final, we once again scored the winner in extra time. Now it was two cup wins that looked like my swansong, but at the presentation night, I also got the Players Player of the Year and the Sportsman's Award as well as the Chairman's Award for what I'd done to help the young lads out through the season. I was well made up, and I decided that that meant there were five trophies I wanted to win again the following season. One more then. Would it be my last?

WHY?

Football is a drug. I am an addict. There. I've said it.

Football is also an escape. Almost every player, manager and official of a club at this level will handle things by juggling elements of their life around. I've seen managers that have been under a bit of pressure at home suddenly go missing, or with a young family that takes precedence, but for me it's been the opposite.

If there's a problem but I've committed to my club or a game, I go. I can lose myself in football, like it's almost another life and then when the game or is done, I'll go back and resolve the problem at home or work or wherever. It's just me I suppose. I don't know if it's something I should or even could change, and I don't know which, if either option is the best way, it's just my way, and I can't understand those people that bring their outside problems into my Saturday afternoon. For a couple of hours on a Saturday football is 100% of my thoughts and I couldn't have it any other way.

I don't like not playing in the summer, when I'm injured or out of favour, and I like it even less when people don't give their all. I can only play one way and it doesn't matter if the opposition are top, bottom or a Sunday league side I give it everything, and when lads come in alongside me I'm not shy of giving them a reminder to step it up if required. To me, there is nothing better than a tough, backs to the wall victory against a better side when everyone has put everything on the line and come through, and we had a game away to Tring Athletic that was just the way I love it. A real back to the wall victory, epitomising why I still play and why it will kill me when I do eventually have to stop.

With Gio injured and George McCluskey recalled from his loan by parent club, Wingate & Finchley, we were left short at centre half so Morts dropped in alongside me. It was a real oldies double act in the heart of the defence, despite him thinking he's still got enough to run the midfield. His battling style and aerial ability make him well suited for the back line, and in a game like this, as Tring were a good, quick young side, we'd need plenty of nous and hard work to get any sort of result.

We were given an early boost with a goal after about fifteen minutes and the two oldies and our young wingmen, Jack and Brad, stemmed most of the flow as the home side tried to equalise. They bettered us on a couple of occasions, but Sam in goal was up to the task, stopping whatever he faced. We were perhaps a bit fortunate to go in 1-0 to the good at the interval and Rochey and Fab said they were happy with us containing Tring, though we needed to do a bit more going forward on the break rather than just trying to hold on. So be it.

Fifteen minutes in to the second period, we scored again and that really opened the flood-gates! It brought Tring onto us in waves, but we contained them and with great work rate all round broke down their moves while still creating occasional break-away chances for our own forwards. The longer the game went on, the stronger our 'thou shalt not pass' mentality became and though they did get through to get one back in the ninety third minute (which started a couple of minutes like the Alamo in terms of them trying to equalise), we recorded by far the most satisfying win of the season. If they'd scored ten minutes earlier, it might have got a bit interesting!

With my (one) pace, I'd thought for years I was best suited to a side that defends deep and catches out opponents on the break. It quite often forces the opposition into a long ball game to try and get over the backline, but I'm always happy to do my bit in the air in those circumstances to quell the danger.

Personally, once again the doubts were parked up for a while when I chatted to the Tring management duo after the game. I've known them 'on the circuit' for a few years and played against them in the past too. They, with a few supporters in earshot asked how old I was. When I said *"42"* there was a bit of a collective gasp. It said plenty about my performance on the night. Retire? Your 'avin a laugh!

I've been doing this longer in my life than I haven't. Up to the age of eighteen I was playing school and county football, with a bit of time at Brentford in the youth system and reserves, but now, for over twenty-eight years, I've been a regular on the non-league circuit. That earns me some kudos off the pitch and perhaps in non-league discussions. As I've said before, there is a perceived voice of reason element, but the reality is that on the pitch for ninety odd minutes it means the best part of bugger all. It has meant that just like that game against Tring, I often come across old foes or old team-mates, yet in many cases as I've gone on playing, they've hung up their boots and they are more often now the opposing manager or coach rather than an on-field opponent. More recently, I've also started to see a new generation of players starting out with whom I have a sort of spiritual link, even building a new generation of old foes...

First things first then, those new kids on the block. Playing for a Spartan South Midlands League club isn't generally glamorous. No (or at least, very rare) coach travel, as we are expected to make our own way to games, generally accompanied by others who don't or won't drive, playing more often than not on little more than a park pitch with all the detritus and ephemera they hold! I remember one pre-season game away to Banbury United of the Southern Premier League no less, so a few levels higher than I find myself now. We (Wealdstone) were out on the pitch warming up and one of the lads noticed that at least one of the local dogs had been using the pitch for a bit more than chasing the ball. Not wanting to, shall we say, spread the good luck with a sliding tackle mid-game, this was pointed out to the referee who approached the benches to ask for a groundsman to clear away the offending pile.

"Shit on the pitch" he said, garnering a reaction from both benches. From the home dugout, someone scurried away to find shovel and bucket as you'd both hope and expect. From the away dugout, a lone voice in reply, in the person of one Mark Gill, the Wealdstone FC Coach: *"sorry ref, they're all we've got"*. Football humour; that's another story, but either way, an example that you may be a footballer just like Messi (apt), Rooney, Beckham or whoever, but for every one of them, there are literally thousands of us that won't get close to the bright lights and newspaper headlines.

Playing in the Spartan League you won't even come across 'stadia', but Cockfosters had entered the London Senior Cup and had been drawn away to Welling United of the Football Conference. Who would have thought it? At my age playing at a Conference ground. In truth it was against their reserves, but it was a mostly enjoyable experience anyhow.

The journey from my house in Borehamwood to leafy suburban Kent on a Tuesday afternoon was an absolute nightmare. Two and a half hours in traffic with my only company being the lively (not) Luke Durnin. Generally, non-league players find travel a major gripe but to be honest it has never bothered me. I just look at it as being part and parcel of the game. Also, many of the longer journeys end with me playing at a new ground which makes it somewhat of a novelty and this was no different. Except for the semi and occasionally fully comatose Luke, that is.

Onto the game and my usual look into the programme where I find only one name that I can recognise, a young lad called Charlie Penny formerly of Millwall. Just prior to his release at the end of the previous season, he had signed on loan at Wealdstone, my former club, thus the 'link'. Now I'm fondly remembered at Wealdstone for my wholehearted style and never say die attitude (and this is a club that knows what never say die is all about) but after three spells there, I still turn out in occasional 'vets' games or fundraisers for them. Charlie however wrote his name into their folklore in a much shorter spell of fifteen games in one of which, away to Margate, he scored the goal that got them promoted to the Conference South as Ryman League Champions. On this night, I mentioned in a tweet after the game (tongue in cheek of course), there were two Wealdstone legends from different decades on opposing sides that night. I don't know Charlie, but he did come into contact with me at least once during the ninety minutes, in the form of a commonly used and well-timed body check to stop his passage towards our goal. The game ended in a 3-1 victory for us and progress in the London Senior Cup re-igniting the memories of former glory and victory in the competition at Uxbridge FC those many, many moons ago. Perhaps signalling a reprise of the first thing I won as a non-league player? It still holds a special place in the memory.

A new generation of old foes? Well, on a couple of occasions I've glanced in the programme and recognised a name or two as you'd expect, but some of these names I've recognised as they are the sons of former foes and teammates. Testament I suppose to the fact that I seem to have been around for a while, but I'm sure one or two have received a quiet whisper from their Dads pre-game looking for a bit of retribution or to put one over on the 'old man'.

On the field they are just players, but when I look back over recent years, there have been a few times when I've played with or against the son of a former teammate like Paul McCluskey who I played with at Uxbridge. We're still mates, and he's a great character. While we were at Uxbridge, I was working at a Sports Centre and I used to take a 9 or 10-year-old Carl to my five-a-side tournaments. A few years later, I played alongside him at Bedfont and occasionally at Belstone. He's a much more cultured player than his dad who was a real rough and tumble midfielder, but Carl's thirty odd now. There's his younger brother George too. I always thought he could do a bit in the game as a decent full-back, but dad Paul reckons he's a bit like me, having had a bit of a falling out this year at Harrow. All passion, that'll get him into trouble sometimes, but now twenty-two, he's probably on last chance for stepping up.

Another father and son combo are the Meakins, Graham and his son Garry. I played with Graham at Wealdstone and Garry I now come across as a manager on the local circuit. Dad was a big centre half whereas Garry is a little full-back, a real rat of a player. They and the Dickers, Phil and Perry (respectively a play-anywhere utility man 'for' Wealdstone and a battling midfielder 'against' Northwood) are at the top of a list that I'm sure will only increase in the next few years.

EDGWARE TOWN, A PHOENIX CLUB AND PLENTY OF OLD FLAMES

We'd had a decent season at Cockfosters and we wanted to start the following campaign at the same level but a miserable November in 2014 results wise ended up with a change of scenery. Players have always moved on mid or post season and I'm no different as my record and list of clubs will testify, but this time, things were a little different.

As I approached a home match against Biggleswade United, I had no idea it was to be my last game at Cockfosters. It turned out that Rochey and Fabio had, after a long drawn out interview process, been offered the opportunity to take over at a resurgent Edgware Town. A club where Fabio and I and a few other Cockfosters players had previously plied our trade, but also a club that had stopped playing and been dormant for about five years because of financial woes, only being brought back to life for the 2014-15 campaign.

Resurgent they may have been in comparison to the dormant years, but it truth it was a division lower and near the bottom of that to boot! What was the draw? Simply that the longer-term picture and prospects seemed far brighter with a stadium (the old Kingsbury Town / London Tigers Silver Jubilee Park) being re-developed and a 3G pitch installed, the prospects on and off the field looked somewhat more a stable platform to build from. There was also a better financial prospect with the club's owners, whereas Cockfosters like so many clubs in the lower leagues were supported by a plethora of volunteers and the pockets of very few.

Rochey and Fabio had in fact informed the chairman at Cockfosters of their decision to leave just as I arrived at the ground, at which point they told me. I was then summoned to the boardroom and offered the job! I have to say that I have a lot of time for the chairman, Ron Syrrett and club secretary, Graham Bint at Cockfosters. They are very, very nice people and I have a lot of respect for the work they've put into the club and they know that they can't offer any financial incentives to people because they want to run their club on a level footing. They always made my two sons very welcome and went out of their way to do what they could for them while I was playing. Real football people. In my mind, these are the people who should be recognized for what they do as without their input as volunteers their club would not exist. Whether it be the first team, the reserves or the youth, they will be there looking after the officials, clearing out the dressing rooms or serving behind the bar. Whatever needs doing they and their small team of helpers make sure everything runs smoothly. I felt highly complemented and privileged to be offered the job but knew in my heart of hearts that I couldn't accept. I just didn't feel that I would be able to attract players to the club and be able to build on the success that Rochey and Fab had, had. Deep in my heart I also knew that I wanted to keep playing for as long as I was able, and I thought management was a step for the future not the present. I asked for the weekend to decide even though I think I already knew what my answer was to be.

With Rochey and Fab in charge for one last game we all wanted to finish with a win and put an end to a bad run. A trademark back stick header by yours truly was parried by the keeper into Juniors path for an easy tap in to give us an early lead which we held till about the hour mark. They equalised and set up a last half hour that was end to end stuff, but we couldn't quite get the win that we wanted. The pitch had taken another battering, perhaps costing us yet more points as skilful players found it difficult to adapt to the bobbles and bounces and that itself would be a major concern if I took over. How do you attract players to a club where the pitch is in dire need of a groundsman's attention, but the funding just isn't there to provide it?

I left the ground knowing that I wouldn't be back. It was very sad leaving like that. Not only because I wouldn't be manager, but that I'd played my last game at this lovely little club. A club which had given me three major highlights in the twilight of my career. It was time to move on and for another and most likely the final stage in my playing career to start. Maybe in the future, when the legs are shot, and the boots are hung up for good, I'll go back, because I'd love to bring that club and the people there some success, but they are thoughts for another day.

Cockfosters knew that when their management duo went, most of the players would follow and though it wasn't going to be a problem, one or two things like registrations being cancelled got a bit messy. It became a bit 'he said, she said', but thankfully it soon cleared up and we moved on. As it panned out, there was a promising young squad that remained at Cockfosters, though it did lack a bit of experience, but only four of the old hands were regulars in the starting XI when we moved on. Emotions got a bit high and a few thoughts and comments about 'stripping the club bare' were over exaggerated and left a sour taste in the mouth for a while, but that's football I suppose.

The first match for the returning Edgware gang was a new competition for me, the Middlesex Premier Cup, primarily a competition for senior reserve and intermediate level clubs, and for the first time in my career, I had now dropped far enough down the football ladder that the club I was with qualified to play its first team in the competition! We were away to CB Hounslow but with all the latent hassles with Cockfosters we had a real mix and match XI; four ex-Cockfosters from the current campaign, plus one who hadn't played since the previous year, a former Harrow B*rough skipper, a lad from Rayners Lane, a new recruit entirely in JJ Molloy and three lads that had been at Edgware when we arrived. We should have had name badges, but at least a few of us knew each other!

As it turned out, we were too strong for the opposition and won 3 – 1 with the 'old man' scoring a debut goal at 42, a header of course, to help the club progress to the semi-final. It would have been rude of me not to use all the social media available to tell the world about my goal! (Blimey, the first goal I ever scored, we nigh on tied a message to a pigeon's leg...) It felt good to put on that Edgware kit again after the sad decline of the club the first time around. Now we had to get ourselves up the league.

Rochey had been responsible for me signing at Bedfont half a dozen years earlier, and he signed me for Cockfosters a couple of seasons previous, (then nearly dropped me, but it doesn't grate) and now I had become part of his new adventure at Edgware Town. I suppose there must be something there he likes in this old man and he can motivate. I doubt if many match officials enjoy their afternoons when he's around though! Looking back, I'd never had him down as a Master of Psychology, but that day when he told me I'd only just made the starting XI; was that Rochey just using a bit of nous to keep me on my toes? Surely not.

After the elation of a goal-scoring cup debut, the first league game as "the new Edgware" was at home v Codicote at Silver Jubilee Park. Apt I suppose, approaching my 25th year in non-league. The ground holds a lot of memories for me as I had many friends that played for Kingsbury and I did a lot of socialising at the clubhouse which involved the consumption of the occasional pint of lager. The ground has been upgraded with a 3G pitch installed which I hoped wouldn't be a problem. I figured that at my age I was always stiff, so a few more creaking bones and joints wasn't gonna hurt me!!

On the lead up to that game I felt a bit nervous, not so much for me but for Rochey and Fab as it was a homecoming for them and a bit of a gamble as they were dropping down a level. I felt they just had a few doubts as to whether they could attract players to this level, but I told them that the pitch would help, and the fact that they had the rest of the season to set their stall out in preparation for a real title charge the following year. In the back of my mind was the question whether I might be part of it. Far from my thoughts that day was the fact that just a couple of years later all those doubts and questions would be mine, as this time, when Rochey and then Fab moved on, I would be there to take up the reins.

Back to the game! Codicote seemed to pay us the utmost respect as they had heard we were Cockfosters and sat with near enough all their outfield players getting behind the ball at every opportunity. A missed penalty by Stuey in the first half didn't help our cause but he made amends by scoring the only goal about fifteen minutes into the second half. It meant a nice clean sheet in our first home game and nearly another goal by yours truly as I hit the post from a well worked set piece. That really would have been the icing on the cake. It was good to also see a few familiar faces in the bar but there was still a hell of a long way to go before we could say that it felt like the old Edgware, if it ever would.

A couple of training sessions over the following week helped us start to gel the side and we got to know each other's names. All of that helped as we travelled away to Winslow for our next match, coming away with a 6-1 win. The only blemish was us giving away a penalty to wipe out what would have been another clean sheet. I pride myself on not conceding so my team mates old and new would have to start getting used to it or my Mr Grumpy side would certainly be coming out.

That win was followed by a couple of weeks off over Christmas. Only because of the weather, but from a family side, appreciated none the less. From the footballing side, we had won a couple on the bounce, but we didn't want to lose the momentum through an enforced break.

The morning of the next game I was getting various texts etc. from fellow non-league players and mates who wanted tickets for the game. Not because it was a big game, but it was to be one of only a couple of games to be played in the area due to persistent rain of a week or so, that of course making no difference to our 3G pitch. It was good going into the game knowing that there could be a good crowd and that there would be plenty of familiar faces. Saying that it did fill me with a little bit more nerves than usual as I didn't want to let myself down with a poor game for me or the team. As sure as eggs is eggs, if I did, someone would say *"maybe it's time, Fergie"*.

We had been training a lot, but we were lacking in match sharpness after the break and after the usual winter slog on wet pitches, we had to adapt (at my bloody age) to playing on a decent solid passing surface. Eventually, it was our downfall as we didn't adjust as well as our opponents. We took the lead twice and got pegged back twice then they took the lead with twenty to go. That was it. No more tippy-tap football on the surface, we went route one. We won a free kick in the dying minutes out by the corner flag, in came the cross and in came Fergus Moore Esquire, flying like a salmon belying the years that had passed, to equalise with a bullet header. Get in! 2 goals in 4 games, I was on fire!

The game finished 3-3 and I followed a very large grin from the field at the end of the game, cheered on by a good crowd, a good few mates and my brother Neil and nephew Ryan who were down visiting from Preston. Ryan's a good young player who had been at Blackburn Rovers since he was eight. Sixteen at the time, he was about to be told if he'd get a pro contract, but sadly picked up an injury and that knocked him down the pecking order and eventually out of the club. He's since joined AFC Flyde and had a good season in their development squad while the first team have won promotion to the Conference National and subsequently got into the play-offs with a chance of entering the football League. He's working towards cementing a place there in the short term, but who knows what the future may hold.

That day, the beers with a few mates in the bar tasted sweet and when I got home, once again the banter continued on social media. Remember when we had to write things down and read the papers?

WEALDSTONE FOUR, FERGUS MOORE...

I never thought I'd go back after the first time or the second and the third, well, enough said.

There is something about the place and so many of the past players, despite careers elsewhere seem to migrate back either on or off the pitch, as players or fans. Once a 'Stone always a 'Stone they say. Now I'm waiting for the fourth spell....

When I left Wealdstone for the third time the bitterness was slow to subside. Much as I was a player, I was and still am a fan of the club and they say time heals. I focussed on my game, my friends, my new club and doing my best. Sure, there was often a faint hope that if I did well, maybe they'd call me back, but, I don't suppose being beyond the twilight of my career I ever got a second thought. One day I think I'll go back in some capacity and perhaps be able to pass on some of the experience I have. Including man-management. Maybe I can impart some of what the club means to a new generation. One day.

The relationship with Gordon went nowhere for a couple of years, then around the time his book "Off the Bench" was being written I was told I'd got a couple of mentions. I saw some of the text and I could see that maybe he was hurting too. Perhaps it was just two people with different expectations and not a dash of stubbornness, then time took hold and the cracks became a crevice. Perhaps the rights and wrongs didn't matter by then and I text him once I had read a preview of some of what he had written. Probably a little dig or something, but he replied. We swapped a couple of texts over a short period then we met up and spoke about it. I think we'd both said enough. I'd seen what he'd written, he'd heard what I'd said but it was in the past.

We met around the time of my 40th Birthday. Watford were playing Bristol City and both our games were called off. I rang him as he had built a great relationship with Watford through loanees and such like and asked if he could help get a couple of tickets for me and my boys. As it turned out, he and son Craig came along as well, and we had a great day. My boys were really taken with him and Craig and we had a couple of beers at half time. The boys loved it as their first experience of live professional football. There was little mention of the past other than the odd comment about games and situations and we embraced at the end. I wished him well for the rest of the season as the 'Stones were involved in a run to the FA Trophy semi-finals (without me, of course) and we've spoken often since, not least a very long conversation last summer as the management opportunity came up at Edgware, and subsequently when he moved on from Wealdstone.

I also played in a Wealdstone Legends game a couple of years ago with several my old mates from the club, Gordon managed the side and it was like old times. It had been difficult, but I have the utmost respect for him and I think he has the same for me. It's all water under the bridge now. Happy days. And what a day that Legends match was. It had been planned over five or six months and I'd helped Roge Slater pull the side together to play a Watford Legends XI. Between us we'd got Andy Carter, Darren Bonfield, Paul Mckay, Paul Benning, Steve Bircham, Paul Lamb, Tommy Williams, Robin Tucker, Brian Jones, Bryan Hammett, Chrissy Walton, Martin Carter, Lee Walker, Jason Shaw, Mickie Swaysland, Steve Bircham, Dave Ryan and me, Fergus Moore. A decent squad on the day, if I do say so myself.

It was just after Wealdstone had won promotion, so the place was buzzing but with Gordon at the helm, we had a great time. The match was good, and we got a result but leading up to it I was nervous! Everyone had played with a few if not most of the other lads and we'd many of us played against each other too. I drove into the car park and the first player I saw was an even bigger Dave Ryan, a real gentle giant. Then Martin Carter, Andy Carter, Tucks; there was a new (old) face at every turn! The banter kicked in big time, not least when Walks arrived and Jonah too. Could be a superstar one day and get sent off the next, a fantastic talent when his head was switched on and a great pleasure to play with, but what a wind up!

Then in came Williams and Hammett, checking out the mirrors on the way through, the pair of them. Everyone with a smile on their face. A great day. Just to be in that changing room was great. It took everyone back, it was like we'd never left. Macca, Bomber, Carts, Tucker, everyone. Who's going to be captain? I looked round and I reckoned there were six former club captains in that dressing room, so I took the skippers armband off the shelf and went out.

Sod it I thought, it'll be me.

Watford put out a decent side; Gary Phillips in goal, Luther Blissett, my old Manager, Neil Price, Ian Richardson, Steve Terry, Richard Johnson, Alan Smart. There were plenty of appearances under various belts that day. After about five minutes, Smarty was behind me and I thought I'd be clever and knock the ball back to Bomber. Great start. It nestled nicely in the back of the net and I'd scored an oggie! Laughter? Their players, our players, the crowd, just about everyone in the ground except me thought it was bloody hi-lar-i-ous.

It just made me more determined to score at the right end, even from left back. A couple of the boys pulled hammies early doors but there was no surprise it was Lamby and Bircham, then Chrissy Walton twisted his knee. Some of these old joints hadn't done much more than walk up the stairs for a few years, so it was just as well we had a few subs on the day!

We switched players on and off to give everyone a game, and aside from injuries, I think everyone was a bit peeved when they got tugged, even in a legends game. It was a good atmosphere, good to be back together and we all wanted it to last. Bartlett even took me off with about ten to go to get Lamby back on. Miraculous recovery? Hmm, not sure but we did have a free kick in a dangerous position and he fancied his chances!

WELL, THAT WASN'T SUPPOSED TO HAPPEN

Early in the New Year (2015) I got another injury. We were playing against Buckingham Athletic and I made a challenge and felt a bit of a 'pop' in my calf. I thought I could shake it off, but it just went very tight and I had to come off. I've gambled with little knocks and injuries in the past and nearly always got away with it, playing through a bit of pain with no long-term damage, but this wasn't one of those occasions.

I watched the last half hour or so from the bench as we scrapped a 3-2 win, but my mind was elsewhere. I didn't even know where I could get some treatment as one of the many things you have to contend with at this level is a lack of finances and that normally means it's a struggle to get a physio to work on the cheap. Edgware had tried all season but still had no-one. Luckily, I got on the 'old boys' network' jungle drums and rang around – Gary McCann, a mate and manager of Hendon FC was on the list and he came up trumps, offering me the chance to get some treatment from their physio who also kindly obliged. He said my calf had a little tear and massaged it and said it would be a two-week thing, so it meant I'd sit out for a while.

As it happened, the weather gave me an extra week with a postponement and I started the game against Risborough Rangers at the end of January. Getting picked and then knocking a bit of rust off put my internal demons away again, as, as always when I'm not involved I had started to wonder if I'd get another chance. To be honest, that day it didn't take much to impress as we were poor, but we ground out a result with a last-minute equaliser! Not really the springboard we needed before a cup semi-final on the Tuesday! That lead to a quiet(ish) birthday, my forty-third, on the Monday, before the 'big' game.

We started brightly but were then pegged back a little without ever being in danger and so the match continued until JJ Molloy who had scored our equaliser on Saturday coolly slotted the ball past their 'keeper one-on-one for the only goal of the night and resurgent Edgware Town had reached their first Cup-Final. For me, it was something to look forward to at the end of season and it would keep the chaps on their toes. It was also a clean sheet which had been a non-entity recently!

When I got home I looked up the County web-site to see who we might be playing in the Final. It turned out that it was likely to be Enfield under 21s! Yes, a team that would contain players that are all half my age and some that weren't even born when I made my non-league debut as an eighteen-year-old. Old-head nous would definitely have to come into play that night. They won their semi-final as expected, meaning that you could take any two of the opposition and add their ages together and I'd still be older. I'd been playing longer than these kids had been breathing.

We were on the crest of a wave, doing well in the league (although we couldn't get promoted) and it would have been the icing on a very new cake to finish off with a cup win, but our preparation wasn't great to be fair. On the previous Saturday we'd played Welwyn, the league champions. Marksy was sent off after about ten minutes and we played the rest with ten men. Although we took the lead in the second half and held on right till the last minute, they equalised. It was a decent draw but bloody hard work which had an effect on us oldies a couple of days before a big game!

We went into the final (played at Northwood FC) thinking that we'd win it. On the day we didn't really get going though, we had a couple of early chances and didn't take them. Enfield u21s were a decent side but lacked experience, so we had to make our experience count against their 'legs'. I knew their manager as I'd played there when coming back from injury and I'd played with a couple of their older youngsters then as well.

They took the lead midway through the first half, Morts got one back for us then they took the lead again and we equalised again. It finished 2-2 after extra time with some very tired legs on our side (especially mine) and it went to penalties. We'd created much more but just didn't do enough to break them down in the box, they defended well and had pace and youth on their side on the break.

I hadn't missed a penalty in half a dozen attempts, always going third and that night, I think mine was the last of three we scored. The last couple were saved, and we lost to a fourth from the U21s. My boys enjoyed watching alongside my old mate Darren (Bonfield), especially the 'Stuart Pearce-esque' celebration as my penalty hit home.

Since we'd moved to Edgware with Rochey we'd only lost a couple of games and we'd reached a cup final. It was disappointing to lose, but there were good signs for the future. For me, it was another close season for me to work through and decide if there was another year in the legs. And it was a great penalty. It's on the DVD.

It didn't take long over the summer to convince myself that I would start the 2015/16 season as a player and hopefully I'd see it through well into my forty-fourth year.

Pre-season can be a strange time. Some players and managers read a lot into it, some don't. We started like a house on fire with a couple of great results in the first few friendlies and we looked a good side at full strength, leading a higher division Potters Bar team 2-0 at half time. Then as you do in pre-season, a multitude of changes saw trialists come in and we got beaten eventually 2-3 but we'd played well.

For me however the demons were back. I'd gone on with the trialists, not the First XI. I know you can't play everyone and we had 4 centre halves there, but why was I one to miss out? I didn't enjoy the game at all, I let it get to me a little and the demons worried me more than the forwards. My head was all over the place. I knew it was only pre-season but for me, the writing was on the wall and even though I knew pre-game, that didn't make it any easier. I only play one way and I want/need/expect those around me to be the same and with a side of mainly trialists, you don't get that.

A couple more friendlies and a couple more decent results (thankfully with me involved) and mentally, things improved, but then, towards then end of pre-season, we'd faded and lost a couple. It meant that places were up for grabs for the opening fixture... We were still 'Off the Cuff United'. One week, players would be available, the next they wouldn't but I won my first challenge, I was in the side for the first game.

We'd played most of our pre-season on the 3G and were getting used to the surface which was sure to give us a bit of an edge. It certainly didn't do us any harm in the first league match as we beat Winslow United 12-3. It was an amazing start as I think we were 6-0 up after about 15 minutes, everything we did worked, and they couldn't get close. Half an hour in however and that was game over for me. I felt my calf tightening again and I turned to Carl McCluskey alongside me and told him, then the bench that had to come off. I said to Carl to keep the ball away as it would be a couple of minutes while the sub got ready and warm before I could go off and lo and behold, he won the ball, rolled it across to me and as I stepped to get it, my calf went completely. What hurt more was that their centre forward nipped in, nicked the ball and scored to make it 6-1. Perhaps it was the surface, perhaps it was my age, perhaps it was both, but the goal and my calf bloody hurt!

I knew I'd be out for a couple of weeks (again) which was frustrating, but I did get to watch the side and I was still involved. The next two games saw a victory over Southall away and another against Coney Heath who'd approached me in the summer with an offer to become their manager. I turned it down because it was just too soon for me, I felt I still had it in me as a player and though I'd even spoken to a couple of people about coming with me to assist and coach, eventually, it didn't feel right. Not my time, but maybe next time.

I was back on the bench for the match at Buckingham a couple of weeks later as we lost 0-1. They got an early goal and though we were all over them, we couldn't score. I got on at half time as Gio was struggling and to be honest I wasn't sure I was 100%, but that's me, I wasn't going to turn down the chance to get my place back. Luckily, I got through it. Afterwards my calf was like concrete, it was so stiff as I hadn't done anything for a couple of weeks, so I went in for some physio after the game to get it loosened up. I could have done without him saying you can't do anything about old age! My calf muscles do just tighten up after a game now and that's probably what lead to two similar injuries in a short space of time.

I stayed in the side and victories in the league and even in the FA Vase were justifying some early confidence. Wilmslow must have hated us as after we did them 12-3 in the league, we drew them in the Vase and won 6-0. Perhaps they were showing signs of improvement. (Actually, we played them again at the start of October and we were a goal behind for half the match before we finally nicked a 2-1 win...).

In among the melee of early season games, one personal highlight was a match in the county cup away to Wealdstone. I knew I'd always get back to play against them, even in this competition with their slightly below strength side. We held our own and played some good football sitting deep against them, playing on the break and we were 2-0 up at half time. Sadly, it wasn't to be, and we lost 2-3 eventually. My boys were there to share their dad's evening and that as always, was special. There's a 'Legends' board at Wealdstone next to their scoreboard and it has my name on it. I'm proud of that and that night I was proud to show it off too. Most importantly, I had a good game!

The following Saturday was tough. I'd played well at Wealdstone, but we had four centre halves at Edgware and Rochey came up and told me I wasn't in the XI for our next game. I know its rotation and it keeps everyone involved but I was on a good run of form and I wanted it to continue. At 44 I wasn't going to learn much when not involved. I didn't take it as well as I should but that wasn't anger, it was passion, emotion, spirit. All those things that have kept me going after twenty-six years.

Sods law, I was warming up and Carl McCluskey who'd started got injured and Rochey brought on Nick Turner, not me, as I was accidentally on purpose warming up at the end of the ground. Double bollocks, but at least we won. I just don't handle not playing very well. I always want to play, and I still believe I can be there every game. Ironically, the following Saturday I couldn't play anyway as it was my brother-in-law's wedding and I had to be at that, but the boys stepped up and played well. They got a good win and a clean sheet against Chesham Reserves, but now, I'd missed a couple of weeks and the inner demons were reminding me of that more and more frequently! A week later (and I know I couldn't expect to get straight back into the side), the Vase threw up a fixture with Whitton United. I missed out, watching with head and heart in turmoil as I wanted us to win and for our centre halves to have a mare. We won 5-2 and those inner voices soon pointed out that after three games, this was a run in the Vase – one of my FA nemesis' – and I wasn't in the side!

I did get back in the side in midweek as someone was unavailable and I did enough to keep my place that night and in the run-up to the next round of the Vas, against Kirkley and Pakefield. I started, and we played the game like the way we played at Wealdstone, a bit deeper and a bit tighter. 0-0 at half-time we felt was good, but they scored after an hour. It didn't seem to knock us back at all though – if anything we took the shackles of and played with a bit more of our freedom and won it 2-1. A great result away from home and the coach journey back was a bit lively as the lads celebrated by digging each other out about everything and anything. The banter was flowing as were a few beers and to top it all off, my drop-off was at Morrisons, Boreham Wood, a few hundred yards from my house. Still leading the singing as I got off the coach, had I really gone through four rounds of an FA competition? We didn't make it five though as the football gods threw us another tie with Ipswich Wanderers (was there no-one else from Suffolk we could play?) and they did a job on us winning 3-0.

I called us 'Off the Cuff United' as players will turn out for some games, not others? Well, the training session before our biggest game of the season saw all of five players turn up. You'd love to drop those that weren't there, but we simply would never have a team. I can't hack that, that attitude to training. All year, all weather I'll run to keep fit and with less than a handful of exceptions over twenty-five-plus years, when fit, I train, because I love the game and I want to be part of it. Sadly, I don't think many of these boys will still be playing into their forty-fifth year.

I remember spoke with Roachy and Fabio about it, but what could they do? The players weren't paid and didn't even get expenses for match travel let alone training. You couldn't fine them for not being there if you didn't pay them when they were! We truly got found out. We had our pants pulled down in the first minute and simply, we got spanked.

We needed to get that game out of our system, but the weather played a hand and we didn't then play for three weeks. In fact, we only played sporadically for about six or seven weeks. Match sharpness suffered, and we were about to face Crawley Green, the main contenders for the title. They'd won 13 straight at the start of the season. Roachy wasn't about and Fabio asked if I'd help him out on the day, so I didn't play. Another quick foray into management and a win. I had a great game on the touchline gee-ing the side up keeping the work rate up and we won 3-1, a great win for us after so little match practise. It showed what we were capable of, and it showed how much we had let ourselves down a couple of games earlier. Then we followed it with a game against third place Baldock. When you are in the mix at the top or the bottom of the table every game is a big game. Against your peers, against lesser sides that get extra motivation and want a scalp, you must be on your game all the time, but off the cuff, sometimes it's just not there.

When we got over the spell of bad weather, matches came thick and fast. We lost a midweek cup match struggling to get a side out, then Roachy was back for the Saturday and played the same side as the previous week which meant I missed out again. Demons surfacing, I wasn't happy about it, but I knew I'd play on the Tuesday: a midweek away game meant three or four wouldn't be available as always.

The Saturday saw another late winner which we were making a bit of a habit. Tuesday as anticipated, I was back in the side at Bradwell St Peter and we ended up losing to a freak goal. Sam Styles in goal had taken a knock and was struggling when they hit an aimless ball into the box. He went down early but hesitantly as he protected an injured knee and the ball bounced over him. We got on with the game but couldn't get back into it, earning only our second league loss of the season, and poor old Sam was slaughtered for it for a few weeks after... football humour is always a good way to let off steam!

It was the catalyst to a run of six away matches without defeat, one of which at Risborough saw me playing right side centre-half (map time again!) against a side that were unbeaten in seventeen games. JJ Molloy came through and we won 1-0. It put us right on the top of our game, and we all-but continued the run to the end of the season and the title. From defeat at Longford in early February, our record in all games was won 15, drawn 3, lost 1. The 1? The bloody division one cup final against Crawley Green, who paid us back for the League wins.

Typical of my luck the family were at the final, wife, sons, daughter (at her first game), even the mother-in-law, but we didn't perform on the night. We took the lead, should have extended it on the half hour and didn't and they went straight down the other end and equalised. They took the lead with a worldy mid-way through the second half, a free kick from thirty-odd yards straight into the net and that turned out to be the winner. Disappointing not to do the double, but at least we won the league, and by ten points at that. Seven competitive defeats all season, and with hindsight, every-one could be put down to that 'off the cuff' attitude. There was some great banter on the players WhatsApp group, but the defeats still grated. Not because we lost, but because of WHY we lost. But, hey! I was a forty-four-year-old title winner. I'd missed a few games, some rested, a couple injured. My only disappointment was being rested for players who hadn't trained and hadn't been there.

EVERY ROSE HAS A THORN

A couple of days after we confirmed our promotion, we played at Hatfield, the non-atmospheric Gosling Stadium. We beat them 1-0 on a Tuesday night and our 'prize' was to go there again the following Tuesday to play against Codicote who shared the ground. At least we won that one 5-0 to celebrate the Championship in style. We slaughtered them to be fair winning 18 corners in the first half alone!

Fifteen to go we were three up and we got a free kick slightly to the right of goal, so up stepped this old fella to take it, accompanied by groans and: *"what's he taking it for?"* from the side-lines. I hit a worldy! It was up and over the wall and down and into the bottom corner for our fourth and luckily for me Lewis Parry, (son of Glenn who's been playing for us) caught it on video as well. Was I happy with that! (Actually, I still am!) As the ball has gone in I've turned and run across to our supporters and you can see on the video, I've turned to Marksy and said: *"I've got to finish on that!!"*. (I didn't).

I still loved playing. I know I'd had my doubts and during and after the games when I wasn't involved, it was harder to keep the demons at bay, but I knew that while I was still doing myself and the team justice at whatever level, I'd carry on. At the end of every season the thoughts were the same. Shall I, shan't I? Will I be able to keep this up? It's worse over the summer because I can't go out there and test myself and prove I'm good enough to carry on. Fitness is a tick, running is a tick, but there's no competition to judge myself in or against.

May and June are the months of self-doubt, then that first pre-season friendly comes around: will I get the nod? Have I done enough to get picked and take my first chance to put the demons to bed? Or...

I knew there would be a 'last season' as a player, and I knew I wanted to be a manager. I just don't think I could not be involved somewhere. As I've aged, so those demons have become a bit smarter too, alongside worrying if I was good enough to play, they started asking if I'd still 'get the buzz' as a manager. I'd flirted with it a couple of times, but it was always temporary, and I had playing to fall back on. Now, like it or not, my body was telling the demons who were telling me that the time was approaching… and this time playing would not be there to fall back on. The buck would stop with me and I'd be responsible, but could I really make a difference for ninety minutes? Maybe a change of tactics or formation or a substitution can change a game, so that would be great when you go on to win, but what if it doesn't work? I really didn't know if it would 'do it' for me. Christ. Not beating myself up enough about my age and if I was good enough to keep on playing, I was also worrying about a job I hadn't even got!

What you may not have realised, is that all this was going through my head about ten minutes after the last game of our championship season. I was almost in a trance, deep in my own thoughts, but I managed to park it all. There was a promotion party to enjoy first. I'd have to tell the lads about that goal and maybe I'd have the video to hand as well.

Incredibly, just a few weeks later Rochey was gone. His new young family and business life needed more time and that had reduced his involvement in the football. I think we'd seen it coming as there were a few matches when he couldn't be around, then it was confirmed, and Fabio Valenti had got the job. Rochey had done a great job with both Cockfosters and Edgware on a zero budget. Through his contacts, a few of Fabio's and some of mine, they had managed to get successful teams at both clubs. He had a big personality which helped as we had a team of big personalities. He could relate to (and master) them, which was something Fabio would have to learn very quickly.

The Edgware committee never really tried to talk him into staying. I'm sure looking back that they thought it would be a smooth transition giving the job to Fabio. For them, he was a lot easier to relate to than Rochey. Perhaps it was a bit of an insult, as Rochey had achieved what he had set out to do, regaining Spartan League status. We would miss him immensely and if the club weren't aware of that, I certainly was.

Fabio's first task was to ask me, as he had during the season, to help. It was mid-May, I already had to fight the demons as a player and now I had the chance to step up into management, but that would surely reduce my playing time. Tough call. In the phone call I said: *"yes of course I would help but would also like to still play"* and also that: *"I wouldn't be his bitch so to speak!!"* What

I meant was that I wasn't prepared to do everything such as take training, warm-ups etc. while he stood around doing nothing. It wasn't said horribly just matter of factly, which has always been my way.

Fab accepted what I said and that was it until pre-season was looming. I soon found out that the truth was, Fab wanted me to stop playing full stop. It wasn't going to happen like that. All the self-doubt and heartache I'd gone through over countless summers, the only person who was ever going to tell me to stop playing would be me. It was not going to be a 'first-time' manager, who wanted to share the workload, so it was easier for him. But he never said.

It was late June and I hadn't been contacted by Fab about pre-season planning, my role, or, come to that, at all. I had heard through the grapevine that he had employed a coach, Jason Dale, who happened to be a very good friend of mine. That didn't bother me one bit as It would suit my wish to keep playing.

When pre-season did start little was said. We trained and there were several 'management' discussions. At least, I think that's what they were because they happened without me. Strange that, seeing as I was told I was assistant manager...

A couple of weeks in, I could see a pattern emerging in that players weren't coming back. You get it at every pre-season, players would pick and choose when to come back, but this felt different. When they did come back they would suss that it was different, and they would then stay away for good. What was it down to? I think it was because Fabio wanted it the whole set-up to be more professional and he wanted to run a tighter ship. I had to agree a little as we were too 'off the cuff' as I've illustrated. Fabio wanted the players to commit to training more and not pick and choose when to come to training or what games to play in. All the right things, but not something that can easily be imposed on players, especially older players that have been on the circuit for a while and have always been like that. Families and work commitments must be considered and an all or nothing approach will only end one way. With nothing.

It was a big squad of mates and whatever team we put out, we were decent for the level we were at. By giving people ultimatums players chose not to come back and by the end of pre-season, the championship winning team of only a couple of months ago was barely recognisable. The don't train, don't play mantra had to be introduced slowly, as did players that would work with it. Sadly, as the season started, Fabio tried to enforce it and some of the players that had stayed also began to move on. Unfortunately, there weren't adequate (in skill or quantity) replacements coming in, and results suffered too.

As it happens I was going to be away for the first couple of games of the season, so it was no surprise that I was less involved before I went away, then when I came back, I was on the bench. My season was to be stop start throughout as Fabio would play me, then not play me, as he clearly thought (without telling me) that I shouldn't be playing at my age. He and Jason got on with managing the side without my involvement. And nothing had been said to me about that either.

That was how things stayed for most of the season: Fabio would manage, Jason (initially) would assist and coach, though Fab actually went through two or three coaches in short order. By the last third or so of the season, with coach no3 on board, Fab realised that I had more of an influence ON the pitch than he previously had thought. Alongside that, he started to use me as an 'advisor' along with skipper, Marksy. We became a bit more of the sounding board which wasn't a problem, but he still hadn't got the balls to tell me that he preferred me not to play. It was a strange situation: Fab and I had been friends for a long time, he knew my 'bark is worse than my bite' personality and he knew what I was like on and off the field. He even knew, as did some of our mutual friends, that I would have sidestepped playing on occasion to help him out, I just didn't want the whole playing career to finish. Especially as I knew I could still do a job on the field. Sadly, it put a bit of a cloud over the whole season for me. It was the least enjoyable season in my non-league career and that had little to do with the football.

By the final week we had managed to preserve our premier league status which was a massive, massive underachievement considering the squad we had started out with and Fabio resigned on the evening of our presentations. I wasn't there but, by all accounts that was a highlight of a drab evening, pretty much like our whole season. I had a prior arrangement at the dogs in Henlow which I enjoyed immensely and when I was told by players next day of Fabio's resignation, I was neither surprised or despondent. Unfortunately, as good a coach as he is, and even as a good assistant, Fabio wasn't made to be a manager and fair play he has admitted as much. No one could say that he didn't give it one hundred per cent, but things didn't quite go as he or the club would have wanted.

As I always have, because I love to play, I've kept myself 'on call' for another local side, Belstone, and when the season is over for many, they often have a few games still to play so I help out. This season was no different and it was a week later, on the Tuesday evening, I was on my way home having played for them that I got a call from Dan Manzi, of Edgware Town, offering me the role of first team manager.

Honestly? My first thought was no way. I felt that the club had become stale and maybe it was time for me to move on (God knows where) and even perhaps to quit playing. The whole depressing season had shattered me mentally and my mind was at sixes and sevens, but I did say I'd think about it. Over the next few days, I did think about it and my mental strength brought me to a better place. It had become a challenge. To prove the doubters wrong and show that I could still play and manage at this level. What I perhaps didn't realise at the time was that most of those doubters were in fact my inner demons again! After all, no-one outside of Dan and I even knew about the call!

I felt I still had something to give to the team no matter what anybody else thought. I also realised that it wouldn't be sustainable without someone helping me which was when I thought of Julian. He was someone who had experienced managing at this level and could assist me off the field as well as on, resolving any issues around the club as and when they occur.

Perhaps it was now time to take the next step in my career. I knew that it would happen one day, and this would be a start at a club I knew only too well. It seemed that the biggest issue would be within. Not within the club or the team, but within me. I would have to overcome many more self-doubt issues: Can I still play? Am I good enough? Will the players think I just pick myself? Will I be worth my place? Can I manage? Can I do both?

I rang Dan and said "Yes".

II - The Manager

That was it then. The season done and dusted for me. My last as just a player. Management was the future, but I had got over the initial shock.

I had about six weeks to get things organised before pre-season started.

HOW DID THAT HAPPEN?

On 9th May 2017, after a lot of soul-searching, and determined to overcome a lot of self-doubt, I became Player Manager of Edgware Town FC. I had suffered quite badly during the latter part of my playing career with self-confidence, though I had always battled through it and I was able to use it as inspiration and motivation going forward. I would be taking that challenge (and plenty of new ones) into the next stage of my career.

I could have picked up the phone, called round the players and asked whether they would like me to accept or not, but I didn't because I would have been doing it for them rather than myself. I took my time and asked some close friends and people in the game (but outside of the club) whose opinions I respect, and I think they all advised me that it was probably the natural progression. Most thought that this time, I'd regret it if I didn't take it on. Personally, it meant that I'd be able to 'manage' the end of my playing career over time, rather than just stopping or being stopped. Not playing held an element of fear for me, going from forty-odd games a season to zero? I don't know how seriously that would have affected my welfare. How could I cope without the drug of my football? Management would put that situation in my own hands going forward.

A week to decide, then a week making those calls to the players was how it worked out. I called to let them know I wanted them all to be part of the new season. There were some advantages in having no budget as no-one could ask for more money, but with no travel expenses provided, my initial concern was to check that I had enough drivers in the squad to get the players to away games! Out of the first ten of the squad I called, eight said they would stay, one more said he would decide when his long-term injury got better and the last was thinking of going to play for his mates' side. I took that as an 8 ½ and not a bad start.

Just for a change of pace, the next half dozen or so calls were trying to arrange pre-season friendlies. There was no one else to ring round for me here, as at this level it's the manager's contacts that get a game set up. It's not quite begging when you are this low down the ladder, but if needs must...

Then a call to Julian Robinson. I'd got to know him in the lower leagues over a few years and what sprung immediately to mind was that he had managed at clubs with no budget, but with relative success. A wily old character who I felt would know what issues / pitfalls / dramas would lay ahead on this journey, and he'd be there to help me deal with them. Also, when I would be needed to play (ahem, _needed_), my thoughts were that there would be someone with experience left in control on the touch line. I also thought he'd share my desire and that which I want from my squad going forward: To try their best every game, to run through a brick wall for me and their team mates, a never say die spirit and a passion to be a winner, no matter what the game. A big cup game or versus the bottom placed team in the league should make no difference in my mind. I also knew that I wanted my squad to respect me as the manager in the way they respected me as a player. Was I dreaming? I wanted my players to be a carbon copy of me if I'm honest! I did know they'd work bloody hard for us, especially at the back, as I have always had a passion for clean sheets as a defender. That was where I wanted to build from, a solid back line with pace out wide and more up top to nick the goals. Not much to ask, was it? I couldn't understand why no-one else had ever thought of it.

By the end of that first week, I'd been in touch with most of the squad, either on the phone or by individual WhatsApp message. There was plenty of banter back and forth which I felt was a good thing and most of the squad said they'd be up for it which was what I both wanted and needed to hear. I knew that I could stay on the Player's WhatsApp group and it would help me get things organised early-doors (see, manager-speak already). Once we were underway I'd planned to leave as I knew from experience that a lot gets said on there by players that perhaps is a way of letting off steam. It's not for _The Management_ as players need that 'escape'. We'll see.

At home, the news broke with a little less champagne and fireworks. Hayley and I were in company with friends / couples a few weeks earlier and the subject of what I was doing next year came up. She was bantering with a comment like: _"you're too old to play now, you will have to become a manager"_. I'd replied: _"you won't want that to happen because that takes up a lot more time, with extra duties like watching matches etc"_. She then said: _"you're probably better still playing then"_. As you'll understand, when the call actually came I was a bit wary of telling her, but we did discuss it. She had to realise that if I was to have any success, the progress I would make as a manager would mean more and more time away from home in the evenings.

Then I softened that thought down with *"at little old Edgware, it won't come to that"*. I'm a natural!

Edgware's season had finished but mixed in with those early days of my management career were a couple more matches, as I turned out for Belstone in the Herts County League. To be honest it was good fun (as always) just to go out and worry about winning my headers and tackles and it was probably exactly what I needed, putting the management issues to one side for a while and starting the summer with a smile on my face. I did find the time to do a bit of on-field scouting however, as I spoke to Mark Blackburne when Belstone played Evergreen. They had a winger I liked the look of, but I didn't want my first action as a manager to be being accused of tapping him up, so I did a bit of research (via Bazza) to get a number. Apparently, he'd been in and out of the side as he was actually a Northwood FC player, but hey, if I didn't ask, I wouldn't get. I was hopeful, but as it panned out I didn't get close.

Games out of the way, I also spoke to a player we had, had at Edgware a couple of seasons previous, but hadn't been around since due to work commitments. Lee 'Inchy' Inch was not only a good player, but a great character that would light up any changing room. That's another trait I like in a player, so I thought I'd keep working on him too. (another one that didn't pan out!) Then it was off for my first run as a player-manager, after all, I could be (ahem*) needed* to play at any time, so I had to be fit.

The Sunday was a little more glamourous, as my son Callum had a match in the morning, so I went off to watch that, and then in the afternoon we both went to watch Steve Newing's team in a Cup final. His boy, Freddie played, but unfortunately, they lost that one 2-4. Also in attendance was Anthony Manzi, Chairman of Edgware Town. It was the first time I'd met him since my appointment, as his brother Dan, the Director of Football, had offered me the job. Not a problem as such, but I did soon realise that the two brothers had (and still have) different opinions on what the club can afford or what they can contribute on their limited funds. I love Anthony's principles as he is willing to try and fund the smallest of figures, even to try and get the boys some petrol money, yet Dan's response is a blunt *"no"* to whatever I suggest! A song started to play in my mind: *"There may be trouble ahead"*, *only* time would tell how that developed!

I also spoke with co-manager Julian, and we both felt that with the players who said they were staying and with the ones he and I hoped and expected to bring in, at the very least we decided we wouldn't need to run a trials night for all-comers. We might have picked up a possible player or two, but the 20 or 30 no-hopers? Not in my first pre-season. I'd seen so many wasters in my career, I deserved a pre-season without them. I did tell the Club Secretary that if he got what he felt was a legit CV through the post then at least pass it on and I'd do a bit of digging before we invited them in... Second pre-season underway as I write and I'm still waiting!

One thing that perhaps won't be a surprise is, that as football entered the close season, I had more time to think about what lay ahead. Generally, the thoughts were positive and exciting, though I hadn't really had time to dwell on what might happen if it didn't start well. I concentrated on the challenge and giving it my best shot. Julian would take training sessions and so would I, both with our own stamp on things, but I knew I would feel more comfortable learning how to adapt sessions when numbers or circumstances changed, i.e. setting up a session for 18 and then having only 11 turn up. I knew it would happen, Julian agreed, and we decided to try and recruit a coach to come on board. The thought was that I could watch both him and Julian and enhance my skills. We thought that different ideas and variation would also keep the squad interested, on their toes and focussed. That could only be a benefit.

On the playing side, I also had a call from an old team mate, James Duncan, then running a scholarship scheme for Wealdstone FC young players. Any players that he felt needed to continue their education in senior football, he said he would pass onto me. They probably wouldn't be the elite (as James is Manager at Potters Bar Town, a league or two above us), but I did tell him no 'wrongguns'. After all, I had a reputation to build!

All of this took place in about ten days, but it boosted my confidence. The squad was looking OK (without kicking a ball) and I had a few promises for pre-season coupled with my back-up, a few people out there I could turn to for advice. Gordon Bartlett headed the list as what he doesn't know about non-league management after doing it for nearly a hundred years isn't worth knowing. Another was my driver on that first foray into non-league, Steve Newing who had also been in the management business a while. Two mates and two opinions I knew I could council if (and I was sure, when) the need arose. Third was Fred Cummings, a coach on the non-league scene who had worked for various managers and another mate. I knew he too would be more than useful whatever the situation. All three would have seen it all before, but at the end of the day, I knew it would be down to me, or at least Julian and me.

My thoughts were racing through so many scenarios, it felt like I had to take a step back from myself, and I hadn't even arranged the first training session yet! I knew that if the squad was light in areas or if injuries took hold, I'd have to think about loan players, another area where I would have to be careful. I've seen players come to various clubs from a higher level on loan and not produce because their attitude was crap. They thought they could just turn up and it would come easy, but the Spartan Premier will bite them on the bum. With the wrong attitude and too high an opinion of themselves, players will be made to look very ordinary. After all, if some of them were as good as they thought they were, they wouldn't be out on loan, would they? It would be contacts again, and I had a few plus my knowledge of local players. That, and a character and attitude assessment would be undertaken before any loans got brought in.

I considered how We'd get away from the 'Off the Cuff United' attitude, the low turnout and cry-offs of players at training, especially as we still had no budget. I knew what I wanted to achieve, but I'd seen the result of going in too heavy-handed when Fabio took over. It was going to be tricky to deal with and only time would tell if I would be successful, but I felt if we could get a winning mentality within the team in an environment which was a fun place, the problem would go away, happy players being more than willing to train when asked. Was that just wishful thinking from a rookie manager?

Head a little clearer, that afternoon, I settled down to watch the League 2 playoffs. Wow!! I was watching still mentally as a player because within myself, until pre-season was under way, I wasn't really going to feel like a manager. The games were unbelievable, so much drama at the end. I remember the interviews after the matches, especially Luton v Blackpool. The two teams with the best defensive records in the league, yet the score after the two legs was 6-5 to Blackpool. It could have been more, as that's what happens when pressure kicks in. It was great hearing stories about players who have never played at Wembley and how both teams reached the final with last minute goals.

For teams at the lower levels of the game, Wembley is such a buzz, and to get there in such dramatic circumstances can only heighten the pleasure. For me watching it, I wondered what if.... Even now, I feel a bit of a tingle thinking about it. You may think it's sad, but I was wishing I could have been a Carlisle or Blackpool player for the night to be able to feel that ecstasy and adrenalin, knowing I'd be the one playing at Wembley. For a little while I was a very jealous non-league player. It made me think what I'd say as the manager of defeated Luton but looking back I think he got it right. He said: *"I'm immensely proud of my players. They will wallow in self-pity for a couple of days but then regroup for next year"*. Spot on. That's the way football rolls and devastation is normally soaked up in a couple of beers before the realisation kicks in that there is a job to be done the following week / month or year. As I write this now, Luton, one year on, have just gained the second automatic promotion place. I'd love to know what he's said to his players over the season to keep that focus. Good luck to him, and them!

I'M IN CHARGE

Being part of the dressing room atmosphere is a feeling second to none as a player. The positives of winning a game of football and then going back into the changing room to share that elation with your team mates creates a terrific buzz. Even more so if your team mates, through you playing with them, turn into good friends. Imagine winning a League or Cup surrounded by people you have literally grown to love on the pitch and in the changing room. You can't get on with everybody (you may have noticed that), but anyone that shares your desire and passion on the pitch becomes bonded by that spirit, heightening the chances of being successful.

A tight knit changing room remains one of the key elements to a successful team. That 'never say die' spirit and 'run through a brick wall for each other' mentality, both nurtured through dressing room banter and wind-ups. Every club at every level has them; the dodgy clobber team mate, the youngster with no girlfriend team mate, the tight-ass never buy a drink team mate, the managers pet team mate, the bet loving team mate, the sulking because he is the sub team mate. The list goes on and on, but at this level, every player has a different personality, a different day-job and comes from a different walk of life. The one place that brings each of these together is the dressing room and I've been part of a few good dressing rooms and some not so good. The negative side of so many different types of people is that they can clash and occasionally just don't get on. In my experience, that angst causes results to falter and on the few occasions I flirted with relegation in my playing career, it was camaraderie that eventually got us out of the pooh. Getting that chemistry right is target number one for me as a manager. Me as a manager. I had to let that sink in. My season, my last as just a player had finished, now I had six weeks to organise a side and a pre-season!

Over the precious few weeks that made up that close season, I sat back and thought about the previous couple of seasons at Cockfosters and Edgware. I looked at the sides and the players I had played with and in my mind, I picked an ideal team. Not a 'greatest players', but, those that I thought had the spirit and character as well as the ability I thought we'd need, and in most cases, those that I hoped or thought I may be able to get on board. The next ten months and the next few pages will be testament to my success or failure.

I wanted to play 4-4-2 or 4-4-1-1 and starting from the back, I wanted a goalkeeper like Darren 'Bomber' Bonfield. I've played with so many over the years and as a defender, I wanted a big dominating keeper who would command the area, a dominating presence that could collect a cross, and occasionally the forward! Bomber would drop a ricket occasionally (don't we all) but he'd take the pressure off his defenders by being the boss in the box. Strange as it seems, that's a dying trait in the art of goalkeeping!

The wide men in my four at the back would get in for different reasons. On the right, Mark 'Bazza' Blackburne, a real character, Mark gives it with spades in the dressing room with his 'laugh at his own stupidity' humour. On the pitch he's a 'steady Eddie' solid defender who gets forward when required. If only his distribution was better. You can find him in fog when he says *"sorry"* as another pass goes astray. On the other side, Phil Kane. It's a specialist position, left back, as most sides attack more often through the right channel, so a solid defender fitted the bill. Add to that (if you can) a player who is powerful going forward and you have a threat other sides will struggle with. Sadly, Phil got a bad knock a season or so ago and hasn't played since, but I can hope...

In the middle, obviously (ahem) if I'm *needed*, I'd want someone alongside who I could control! By choice, Jack Cook from Cockfosters would just get the nod over Craig 'Gio' McKay, but it won't happen. Gio does get a few knocks and Cookie, tall and quick, could always play a bit which would be an advantage. He also doesn't go out on a Friday night... A mixture of the two might cover for me when I'm not *needed* as well. The decider? Gio will play for nowt whereas Cookie made the step up to play at a higher level with Worthing, a few divisions and a few quid higher up the ladder.

Middle of the park; pace out wide. Two that spring to mind would be Lorenzo Ferrari (really) and Adem Ali. I played in the same side as these two at both Cockfosters and Edgware and they'll interchange at any stage, both preferring to beat their man cutting inside. Adem is by far is the laziest player that has ever graced a football pitch and he has the worst non-footballer body ever, probably down to his awful junk food diet. He stepped up from the ressies at Cockfosters and in two seasons, he almost single-handedly won half our games with his goals. The goals outweigh the laziness...just, whereas Lorenzo is a flying machine. Big, strong and powerful, he scores a few as well. You wouldn't want him running at you full steam as he's known to rarely stop. Mentally, I cross him off as soon as I add him as he's another I won't be able to get on board. He too stepped up to play for St Neots and Dunstable Town and had finally hung up his boots.

In the middle my twin rocks would be Paul Marks and Bilal Butt. You couldn't have two more contrasting figures in the middle, but what a combination. Marksy with his all-action aggressive (sometimes lunatic) play and Bilzy's languid, laconic, almost not bothered style, yet he's another who scores goals from midfield with ease. Marksy is the player that every opponent we play hates, but they would love him in their team, full in your face for ninety minutes, he absolutely loves a tackle. Definitely my type of player with his passion and grit. I love him to bits and look forward to him captaining my team whereas Bilzy can be quiet most of the time, at least until he gets riled by the referee, when he can turn into a nightmare. He's an unassuming guy off the pitch, but he does love a quiet pint of gloat on social media about his goal scoring exploits!

Finally, my forwards. Pace again. Oh, for an Emond Protain from Cockfosters and a younger Stuart Blackburne (Cockfosters and Edgware). What a handful these two would be for any centre-half pairing. Both could leap like salmon and both were mustard attacking the ball. Emond was pivotal in the early success at Cockfosters scoring bundles of goals and his hold up play was top notch. It's hard to believe that season was one of only a handful he had as a front man, his early career played as a left back where he graced the TV cameras playing for Yeading versus Newcastle in the FA Cup 3rd round back in the day.

Alongside, Stuey was a little rat in his prime, a regular goal scorer and someone who never stopped chasing lost causes and won a few of them to boot. He had a spell at a higher level with Borehamwood before he came to us, but he didn't really take his chance there. For us it was a bonus, but a shame that these two didn't play together very often. That, I'd have paid to watch.

Would I get close to a side like that? I doubted it, but I could dream. Some of the players were already on board, some were still playing elsewhere and like Gio, I'd ask them to come down, but there would be a few places to fill. I hoped that a few of the Edgware lads from the previous year would step up and we'd get a team that would be hard to beat and could put up a good challenge over the year.

Silver Jubilee Park, our home ground and the all-weather surface is shared with our landlords, Hendon FC. You'd think that having the 3G surface would be in our favour but the previous season, it had worked against us. All these teams with #ballers came and enjoyed playing on a decent pitch and in the main, played us off the park. Their own playing surface not being as good as ours, they relished playing on it. That was something I wanted to reverse, as we must take advantage where we can. Being better on our pitch than our opponents is a no-brainer, so I reckoned the long ball game would be a non-starter!

Best laid plans, eh? Everything looking positive early days and just the summer to get through when I had a call out of the blue from my intended captain, Marksy. He'd been approached by the moneybags of the Spartan League, Welwyn Garden City. The call wasn't a problem as it was the close season, but it was something I didn't foresee or need.

We are close, we are always honest with each other and that was why he rang to tell me. He had been loyal to Edgware as he loved the club, but deep down he loved to be loved too so the constant calls from the Welwyn gaffer would have been flattering for him. They had money, we didn't, but money is laced with expectation and the pressure to produce all the time. At his age, Marksy said he was unsure if that was worth it.

Initially, I felt confident he'd stay, but niggling in my mind was the thought that if he was thinking of staying why would he call? I had a doubt or two and knew it would be a massive blow if he did move on.

SO, WHAT DID YOU DO IN THE SUMMER?

With no football to watch or play, I became fully focused on the challenges ahead. Not just how I would fare or how the team would do, but I'd never organised a pre-season before either! It was a little daunting but that turned to nervous excitement as I started to get some ideas. My fitness regime stepped up a gear as well, as I wasn't going to be last in the pre-season runs. Work also gave me a change of scenery as I got stuck in Covent Garden for a few weeks. Running in London isn't my favourite thing to do with all the traffic and such like, but those lunchtime runs along the Embankment broke the monotony of the day and were relatively traffic free. I pushed a bit harder than usual as well, as I knew that I wouldn't be able to take part in all the pre-season as I'd be organising and coaching much of it, and I wanted to make bloody sure I was as fit as I could be for those occasions when I knew I'd want (and need) to show the rest of the squad how it's done. I was actually looking forward to the look on some of the 'newbies' faces as I kept up and indeed overtook them on a run or two. Priceless!

I purposely didn't get in touch with my (MY!) players for a while as I was sure they'd need to kick back a bit after the season and the news. I was hoping that a few would be out running and implementing their own training regimes to keep their fitness levels up, but I also knew for certain that some wouldn't do a damn thing. I also knew they'd be the same people that would be moaning during pre-season and most likely, lagging behind everyone else. Oh, the joys that lay ahead.

Going back a few years, I used to read football autobiographies. I really enjoyed reading the 'warts and all' stories from Roy Keane, Paul McGrath and Steven Gerrard as they were my heroes as players. Manager wise I read the great Brian Clough's biography and that of the wonderful Jack Charlton among others. They gave a great insight into what made them tick and the off the field antics of the characters that they had worked with. There sat I with the bar well and truly raised. A veteran, a non-league dinosaur with my thoughts turning to the transition, as a fledgling manager. I wondered, could it get more interesting than that?

In between runs, I examined my Non-League Database, as I knew that a few of the players I wanted I wouldn't get. I needed a back-up or two and the database would provide it. It's something that's been built up over the years as a player and it's easy to carry about as it's all in my head, it's my knowledge of the local non-league scene. Luckily, I can remember many of the players I've played against recently and some not so recently as well, especially those that stood out in a game. I remember their club, the game and what position they played, even what coloured boots they wore. No, seriously, not the boots! Because of my love of the game I've always seemed able to take in a lot of information on team's players and store it. It's been useful in the past when we've met again, and it would be a worthy tool as I started to build my side. I reckon if I could write it all down, it'd be worth a fortune.

Then my thoughts drifted back to Marksy. I was feeling a bit down because my skipper and probably best mate had been tapped up. He was leaving his beloved Edgware. And he was got at. We both know who helped instigate the deal even though in the end it was him that made the decision.

I was meant to go out with him to watch the FA Cup final with a few of the old Edgware treble winning team, (a theme here, I wasn't part of that side, it was before I joined) but many are friends of mine and ex-teammates from my first spell at Edgware. A last-minute change in my personal circumstances meant that I couldn't make it, then, on the Bank Holiday Monday evening, I received a WhatsApp message from him. He was on holiday and he said the decision was tearing him apart, but he was probably going to leave. It wasn't about the money, he wanted to win things. At 33 he felt it might have been his last chance. It was a long night as we exchanged many texts with real emotion in the conversation on his behalf and mine. We'd been together at the same club for the previous five years. That is a long time in football, especially so at two clubs where not a penny has been paid to any player. Five years of phone calls before the game, directly after the game, a couple days after and in the build up to the next game. He was (and still is) a mate but in my heart, I knew being wanted by Welwyn was a big pull. There was also a niggle in my mind that a few others may follow. I knew it may be one or two, but I also knew he wouldn't encourage them. My bigger problem would be replacing him both as a player and as the figurehead in the squad, a leader and the other players loved him. I hoped they'd all respect his decision and wish him the all best. And stay.

The loss didn't kick in for a while. It was the closeness and his presence around the place that I was going to miss, possibly when I'd need it most. He's not a big drinker, in fact two Coronas and he'd be away with the fairies, so we've rarely met up socially if at all. Family life dictates a lot on both sides. The friendship had been built at footy by our understanding of each other. He gets me, and I get him. He'd tell it to me straight if one of my rants was out of order and he always knew when I'd got the hump and when to approach with caution. He also knew when enough was enough and would tell me to snap out of it. It was a relationship more like brothers I'd say. He would probably say father and son knowing him. It felt like he'd moved a million miles away, but I knew the sadness would heal and the banter would resume once pre-season started. He'd become another reason I would want to win at least two games, but I felt with that one change, my job had become a hundred times harder. Selfish bastard. I hoped the greener grass over there would give him hay-fever.

He told the lads in the WhatsApp group and fair play, then told me a couple needed a chat pdq, so I got in touch. One was Adem Ali: His mates had set up a local team in Southgate where he lives, playing in Spartan League Division 2. I figured he'd be off whatever I said and that was a shame because ability wise he was one of the best in our division. He just lacked the desire and motivation because he wanted an easy life. A bigger loss would have been Dan Pett who was the other that Marksie told me to call. They were good mates and that could have clouded Dan's thinking, but I managed to keep him on board.

He'd joined from Potters Bar Town at a time we were struggling but put in some excellent performances to help turn things around. There's a footballing pedigree in his family as his brother Tom is a professional formerly at Stevenage FC and now at Lincoln City. He went pro after impressing in a Championship winning side at Wealdstone. Dan had done enough the previous season at right back to secure the Managers Player of the Year award and when we first spoke he mentioned that he wanted to give midfield a go. Now, I broke the ice by sending a couple of smiley face emojis with the #midfieldmaestro tag. I said we'd try it in preseason and see what happened. I hoped it would be enough.

Shortly after, I got a reply saying he wanted to stay but he couldn't do Saturday's in July as he has got ...cricket! I don't know, commitment levels aren't what they used to be, but I thought that if he could get his midweek training sessions and games in, it wouldn't be ideal, but it wouldn't be a problem. It wasn't something I expected in my first pre-season and I'd handled it on my own. Not because Julian wasn't there or available, but because these were my relationships, I'd been at the club the previous season and knew the players, so I felt it was my responsibility. I think Julian agreed when I brought him up to speed and he did settle my nerves when we spoke. He said it was all part and parcel of the game, losing players, but it was still hard to accept. Those inner demons kept the questions coming too – was it really me? What if the ones we had in mind didn't turn up? What if they weren't good enough? It had not been an easy couple of days and I hadn't even had to worry about any football. Thankfully, the fear of failure was diluted as thoughts of potential success overcame me. At that moment, just getting a team out would have been a major bonus!

Once things had settled down, I relied more and more on Julian. I was in touch with him almost every day regarding players and general stuff. He'd been replying to trialists enquiries and suchlike while I had been sending messages to players that didn't seem to be sorted for the coming season, in the hope that they might give us a chance. All that effort despite knowing that many probably wouldn't even respond because of the zero budget. It meant more calls to Julian for re-assurance. He had an abundance of enthusiasm and he kept telling me not to worry so I tried not to. I knew that the first game would change things, and it couldn't come quick enough for me. Then, I would get a better picture of what we had and what we needed. It would be tough as there would be a lot of decisions to make over a matter of a couple of weeks, but Julian convinced me we'd be fine.

Always happy to return, Fergus captained the Yellows in a Field of Dreams match, where Wealdstone Fans played alongside former 'Stones players.

Photo reproduced with kind permission of Steve Foster ©

The oldest swingers in town, as Fergus Moore (then 42) and Scott McGleish (then 41) line up as opponents, Wealdstone FC v Edgware Town FC 2013

Photo reproduced with kind permission of Alan Palmer ©

100%. Nothing more, nothing less.
Photo reproduced with kind permission of Paul Holdrick ©

It still means a lot to win.
Edgware Town FC Spartan South Midland League Div 1 Champions, 2015-16
Photo reproduced with kind permission of Paul Holdrick ©

Still heading and kicking every ball

Edgware Town photographs (Inc Rear Cover) reproduced with kind permission of Paul Holdrick.©

As another pre-season starts, still leading from the front...

Reproduced with kind permission of Paul Holdrick.©

At this level, the manager's job is more than on the bench...
Reproduced with kind permission of Paul Holdrick.©

….and occasionally, the bench and the facilities need a bit of work!

THE GAFFER
Photo reproduced with kind permission of Paul Holdrick.©

The Family
© Fergus Moore

166

AND THEN THERE WERE THREE

Mid-summer, around the time of my Dad's 70th Birthday, we appointed a Coach, Enda Hennessey who had been recommended by a footballing mate of Julian. I was out of the way as we had loads of relations and friends over from Gods own country for a surprise party that I seemed to be doing all the organising of, but I did manage to arrange a meeting with Enda and Julian to sort how we'd work together. He'd been manager of Hellenic League Rayners Lane FC for the previous four or five seasons and he came across as very keen to get on board. He liked the set-up we had, the ties (albeit loose) to our landlords, Hendon FC and most of all he liked the facilities. He also said that he was very hands-on and was keen on taking training, so with the three of us willing to contribute, we felt that would reduce the load and the problems. He asked all the right questions and we said to him that obviously his opinion would matter, (ahem) especially if I was _needed_ to play, in which case, he and Julian would be in charge. (They may not be in charge long if they wanted to take me off however...).

Being a manager for the last few years had given him the opportunity to have a big input into what went on. Now, as a coach with co-managers, it would be a learning curve, but we didn't foresee any issues. Coming from a local club it also meant that the three of us had local contacts, a view on players and such like and that had to be an advantage.

Speaking of player recruitment, it was hard to work out where we stood. Early days perhaps, but sometimes I felt we had too many then other days, not enough. It was probably my self-doubt, but I knew I'd be happier once we were training and I could see exactly what was in front of me. We were all still inviting players down as well, some would say _"yes"_ then a couple of weeks later we'd speak to them again and find they'd changed their minds or were going elsewhere. I hoped it was the same for everyone, but I knew that it would be different once we could get a ball at their feet.

The last few weeks of the close season flew by as I spent a lot of the time washing training bibs and kit! Really, but at least it helped us to get ready for day one. Julian, Enda and I had a meeting at the club on the Thursday before we were due to start training to check our 'stores'. We had a store – but that was almost all we had. There were a couple of torn match balls, a couple of sets of very smelly bibs and a few cones but sod all else, so we made a list up of what we thought we needed and we passed it on to Dan Manzi, who we were assured would sort everything out in advance of the first session. With no budget, we had to look as professional as we could in other ways. When Tuesday came, I had a decision to make, would I train, or would I sit out (if the numbers were just too high)? That was a decision for later, so in the morning I went for a run anyway...just in case. I followed my normal routine, Red Bull, Wispa, everything – just a bit earlier as I wanted to arrive in good time, but I was nervous as hell. Too many? Not enough? How will the session go? Will Julian, Enda and I have the same ideas? Truth be told, for the first time in years, I really didn't want pre-season to start, I just wanted to go straight to our first match in August and have it all behind me. Then I could focus on being better than last season, finishing in the top half of the table. Not much to ask in year one was it?

For my first session in management I didn't think it went too shabbily. I got there earlier than the players and so did Julian and Enda. We got the few bits and pieces we had from the store but then had to endure an anxious twenty-minute wait until Dan turned up with what we'd ordered, including the new footballs - which unfortunately he hadn't pumped up, but at least they were there. I took on the role of introducing existing players to Julian and Enda and of taking down the names, telephone numbers and positions of the potential new recruits and trialists. Julian also updated me on a few drop outs for various reasons and one stood out. A player who had been contacted because he wanted to play men's football, stepping up from Barnet FC youth. In the previous season he'd been loaned to a Spartan Division 1 side and wanted a chance to progress. Apparently, he'd text Julian and said: *"I can't make Tuesday or Thursday this week as I have made alternative plans, but I will be in touch to let you know when I will be available"*. You can probably guess what I told Julian to send him in reply. Some attitude eh? Wants to make the step up but on his terms? He was the first, but I suspected he wouldn't be the last.

The worst part of the session was the running as I got itchy feet. I just wanted to be involved but with thirty there I knew time would be better spent with my management team sorting who was in, who was out etc. Then, at the end of the session we did some 5 v 5 and I said to Julian: *"Come on, let me join in"*. His response? *"Most of them are kids and I can't let you hurt them"*. Charming.

Overall though, I enjoyed it once we were underway. Julian and Enda took the lead as they were more experienced in coaching, but I got involved, putting my spin on the session with various bits of geeing up and banter. I am a big believer in the serious side but having a bit of fun and chat would help the players as some were nervous. It all helped ease the tension. The turn-out was good and overall, so was the quality. We're not talking world beaters here, but most seemed to have a bit of a game about them and a good touch. It was far too early to raise any expectations, but I had a quiet smile to myself and thought I may last longer than Christmas, at least. No surprises at the end of the session either as I had to go out of my way to give Luke Durnin a lift home. It was a sharp reminder that aside from being good enough to play, I had to sign a few who could not only drive, but owned cars so we could even get the team to games!

First night nerves well and truly put to bed, for the Thursday night session forty players turned up and there were a few from Tuesday missing! I don't really know how or why as we hadn't organised an open session, it just seemed that a few told a few more and some bought a mate...that sort of thing. Anyway, it was a complete 'mare to coach, so I left most of the session to Julian and Enda! I took down yet more names and details and got some of the 'existing' squad to sign Registration forms before they changed their minds. That gave me seven signed on at the end of the session and straight into my squad for the first two pre-season games planned for the Saturday and Monday. (Ahem), eight if I _needed_ a run out. For the rest, and I wanted about twenty to cover both matches, I picked a few trialists out and then told the remainder that I'd let them know by text on the Friday if they would be involved in one of the two games. I also said if they didn't get a text, we'd like them all back for training the following Thursday. With so many bodies we felt it was the best way. Come Thursday, we planned to mix up the ones that had played some part in the games with the ones who hadn't. One thing was certain, we couldn't keep running sessions with forty-odd players.

So, onto the Saturday and my first game versus a Barnet XI. My day started differently as I went for an early morning run. We'd ended up selecting a squad of 22 intending that every player would get 45 minutes and I couldn't fit myself in however hard I tried, well, not unless we had a couple of no-shows! It was my first game as a manager so no surprise, I felt a bit apprehensive beforehand, blimey, it was even stressful sending out all the texts to the players. Ticking off the list and remembering who I had and hadn't contacted. It started to sink in that a Saturdays wouldn't just be about me individually anymore. It was now about my team and everything that went with it. I had spent a lot of time mulling over the team selections then I sent them to Julian and Enda to get their thoughts. I only took the lead as it had been me doing all the administration and I knew who was available. I knew that I wouldn't say *"no"* to anything that they had to say, because as much as possible it had to be a group decision. I sent the texts and waited. Bated breath, then a ping and then another as their replies came back. I could breathe again as the consensus was that they agreed with me, so we went with it.

I named teams for both halves and said that we just wanted everyone to give it their all physically as they were only playing forty-five minutes. The team talk didn't feel much different as I have done a few in my latter years (the last fifteen) and I've always been asked to express an opinion on what goes on, on the pitch. As you may have noticed, I am the sort that would generally chip in even if I wasn't asked. Looking ahead, I was certain that there would be a few more butterflies when I was team-talking my first competitive match. I knew then, I'd need to be more inspirational and put across tactically how we expected things to be done.

This time, I started, but Julian and Enda had their say too. As the 'first team' took the field, Julian went up into the stand and Enda and I went onto the bench ready to bark out instructions. The Barnet side was young as was ours, but we had two full sides while they only had three subs. On a hot day that was going to make a difference and it did, with us running out 3-1 winners. The hour and a half had gone in a flash, my first game in charge finished and my feelings were more of relief than anything else. Relief that we hadn't made fools of ourselves and relieved that Julian, Enda and I had managed to organise the side into a decent looking outfit.

All twenty-two said they were available for the Monday match as well and that was our first problem: There were three more of the squad returning to play, so three of these boys (and me again) would miss out. Even at this stage it was hard to tell the lads they were missing out, but we had to do it. I sorted the two sides again on the Sunday, then got the OK from Julian and Enda before starting what seemed to be another endless stream of texts to the players. Sorted by Sunday lunchtime, it did mean that I could sit down with a pint in the afternoon to reflect on Saturday's game!

That Monday was my thirteenth Wedding Anniversary, but with Hayley pre-warned and a meal out arranged for the Tuesday, I was going to football. It's happened so many times and I really cannot thank Hayley enough for her tolerance. I always said as a player that I'd make it up to her when I finished. Now, I'm saying the same thing as a manager, not knowing if that will last twenty days, months or years. My mind on the game, at about 4:30 I received a text from one of our centre halves. He had picked up an injury on Saturday and felt couldn't play that evening. Normally I'd have been a little irate as a couple of hours' notice is not good enough, but (ahem) we had a more than adequate replacement ready and available. The non-league dinosaur was about to strut his stuff. Get in!

We got a 2-2 draw against a strong Southall side, who had a few experienced players from a higher level dropping down to play for them. It was a decent result, especially as they scored an injury time goal to scrape the draw, and a better performance all round which was pleasing, as for some of our young lads it was the first time they had played 'senior' football. Mikkel up top impressed as did Rio in midfield (he'd made a couple of cameo appearances the previous season) and, young Ethan scored a great goal to show us what he could do. Apart from my return, Dan Pett played well in the new central midfield role, and Bazza starred at the back. It was great seeing him in the first half when he wasn't playing, sitting and chatting with the youngsters despite not knowing them, helping put them at ease. A brilliant character Bazza, and long may he part of this young team. It'll need that bit of experience and wit and he has both in abundance. Alongside the returning players, several the new recruits were coming along nicely. and we had already signed five on the strength of the two pre-season games. It meant I could put football to one side for a couple of days and enjoy my delayed Anniversary meal!

ASTERISKS *

I've seen it at so many clubs over the years. You look in the Match Programme, at the Player Statistics and alongside some of the player's names is *, an asterisk. Look down the page and somewhere it'll say *"* Player no longer with the club"*. If you are that player and you go back as an opponent in the same season (as I did for Chertsey, returning to Wealdstone) you look for your name. There it was: *"*Fergus Moore"*. It hurts. It hurts if it's after one appearance or a thousand appearances, and at a club like Wealdstone, the fans aren't shy about telling players there's an asterisk coming (at least in their eyes). Thankfully, that never happened to me, but I've been in the side with one or two that have suffered the terrace wrath.

Julian, Enda and I had christened the Thursday training session after the opening friendlies as X-Factor night. We could just as easily have called it asterisk night, as we had decided, with the season fast approaching, we had to cull the squad from forty-odd down to a manageable mid-twenties. Not a final cull, as there were still a few we wanted to have another look at, but the first and probably the biggest. In truth, we were dreading it, as we knew even at this level with no money we would be shattering dreams. Dreams that some of these youngsters had of starting small and climbing the ladder into the professional game. Now we were going to tell them it was back to the terrace or the park with their mates. The lads that had already signed and been involved in the friendlies were taken to a grass area behind the main pitch for a training session with Enda while those that hadn't been involved were to have a night of playing 'round robin' training games. Playing amongst themselves, but under the beady eyes of Julian and me. It was the chance for us to take a last look at these boys and see if we had missed anyone or anything previously.

It may seem a tad harsh looking back, that some of these players might not have been given a full game to show their worth but trust me, Julian and I had seen enough after about twenty minutes that night to vindicate our decisions. We already had the best twenty-five and none of these lads were going to make it. We let them play for about seventy-five minutes, then we called a halt and sat the boys down. Julian had experience having been through this process before, but he let me take the lead in explaining who we were keeping. It was a short conversation as a lucky six were told to stay behind for a chat whilst the others were told they would no longer be required. We couldn't go through each individual case, so we explained that some were a bit green for this level and others weren't any better than those we already had. We tried to soften the blow, but I'm not sure it worked, but at least we tried to be respectful and honest. Even to the six lads we picked out; we explained to them that even though they had been selected from this session, it didn't mean that they were going to be asked to sign for us. We told them that in next week or so, we would involve them in a match to see how they performed. Again, we were honest and said that we didn't want to harm their chances of finding another club if things don't work out with us. As it happened, three were selected to play in the next game due to the inevitable unavailability of others.

We had trimmed the squad to twenty-eight, eight to ten more than we expected to start the season with. A couple had already risen to the top of our thoughts with their performances; Cain in goal had had a couple of decent halves in the matches, Rio had been excellent in midfield (as had Dan Pett in his one game) and up front, young Mikkel had been a real find as a bustling striker, which was just as well because we hadn't really got another to keep an eye on! One that could drive would have been nice.

There were still plenty of places up for grabs, not least at centre half. I had seen all four of the trialists play and none had really shone, indeed a pre-season progressed I played with all four – just keeping my fitness up and having a look 'close at hand' you understand – and there were positives and negatives for each. Alongside that, we were struggling where I expected. We lacked a cutting edge up front and as the final few games of pre-season came along that was more evident as we seemed to work very, very hard for our goals, yet were giving simple chances to the opposition. It was all valuable knowledge and experience for me, but the problems were mine to solve, and that was harder.

We changed personnel game to game, mainly because of all the things you expect at this level; work commitments, holidays, niggles etc. and some just plain can't be arsed attitudes plus Dan Pett was continuing to play cricket at weekends. Top all that with four defeats towards the end of pre-season and I was thinking that I may be an asterisk soon as well.

Our first competitive game against Leverstock Green in the Extra Preliminary Round of the FA Cup was fast approaching and out of earshot of all except

Julian and Enda, I jokingly mentioned that we could be out of the FA Cup and bottom of the league before we could get our best team out.

Overall preseason had been OK, it had been quite stressful but quite enjoyable, but perhaps understandably, it became an internal battle between my increasing nerves and my desire to succeed. I wished then, that I could fast forward myself, not to the first game but maybe one or two 2 seasons on, so that I could look back to see how I had progressed through the early stage of what I hoped would still be my managerial career.

SCARED? NOT ME

Julian had watched our opponents in a Herts County Cup match and he came back to report that though they had lost 1-4, they were the better team. They didn't take their chances in the first half and they were punished in the second when Tring, their hosts made the game safe. On previous experience and knowledge, they were going to be one of the mid-table teams in our division and that was the minimum target for us also.

We were a team in transition, a lot of new faces who I felt were good enough to help avoid relegation, but many weren't of the quality I wanted to ensure we'd be in the mix at the top end of the table. With that in mind and following Julian's report, I was instructed (honestly) that I should start on the Saturday. It hadn't been my decision, but it did justify my keeping the fitness up over the summer, as the feeling was that we needed to be strong and dominant at the back and the four trialist centre-halves hadn't shown that often enough in pre-season. The team needed a good start as a base to build on and we had questions over the mental toughness of some of the lads. We'd seen the weakness after a couple of the pre-season defeats, it was probably our biggest issue and the one we as a management team had to address first. We had to know who we could rely on, those players that could pick up the mantle, adding to the good attributes that already existed in the group. Approaching that first game we had a young squad with three or four old hands for experience, so we had the legs to match most sides. We also had some good ball players who did look to try and play football more often than not. The problem was with their rawness, we were also inclined to overplay a bit and that had cost us. We knew it was going to be a steep learning curve for some, and there was no doubt one or two would fall by the wayside when we played pick-and-mix to address the problems.

I desperately wanted a good start, not only in the cup, but in the league. Despite my wants, the reality was that I'd be happy if we got through the first three or four games relatively unscathed. By then a couple more of the more experienced players would be available and we should have been able to put out our expected first-choice eleven.

By about 10pm on the Thursday before the Leverstock Green game, I had only nine in my starting eleven and Julian, Enda and myself were in deep discussion about the other options. By 2:14:59 pm on the Saturday, (forty-five minutes before kick-off to hand in the team sheet) I'd named my first team:

Cain Davies

Mark Blackburne   Luke Burton   Fergus Moore   Alfie Hill

Ethan Mooney   Dennis Marharjan   Andrew Manatou   Samuel Addae

Mikkel James

Stuart Blackburne

Subs: **Luke Durnin, Hanni Berchiche, Darren Bonfield.**

It wasn't the side I expected as at least five potential starters were missing, but it was the best we could do with suspension, injuries, holidays (seriously? Didn't know when the season starts, no?) and bloody cricket taking their toll. It wasn't even the side I'd managed to put out in pre-season, or come to that, the side we had in mind fifteen minutes earlier. At 2pm I'd taken the step of speaking to the players I was leaving out. I wanted to do it rather than hand it over to Julian as it was my call and my responsibility, playing or not. Luke Durnin was a bit unlucky to be on the bench as he wasn't 100% fit having been ill towards the end of pre-season, and he was the first I told. To be fair he took it very well. Then Alfie Hill. I told him that I was one of his biggest fans and that I thought he was harshly treated by the previous manager as he has all the traits and ability needed to be a good left back. Good left peg, good physique and he's quick too. I know If I'd had those attributes at the same age I would have played at a higher level, they were probably the three reasons Brentford let me go. The downside with Alfie was a tendency to play at 100mph all the time, sometimes he needed to slow down and be composed on the ball. I'd told him in pre-season, but little had changed. Maybe this would help? Only time would tell.

He took it on the chin too, which was just as well, as ten minutes later he was back in the starting XI as Manny someone-or-other, the intended starting left winger missed the cut off time of 2.10pm. In fact, he also missed 2:30, 3:00 and by Sunday morning I was still waiting for his call... Non-league players, eh? Oh, wait – there's the phone...not.

The match kicked off and it wasn't really a surprise that we started slowly, kicking downhill into a strong wind (football gods having a say, as this was the FA Cup after all). We conceded early as Leverstock played some good football on the deck and our midfield struggled to get into the game. Thankfully, Cain Davies in goal was on his game and kept us in it, only one down at half time. It gave us a chance to change things a little. Julian and Enda had their say and I did the same. We'd been under so much pressure at times in the first half I hadn't been able to get instructions across to other players, but now, in the dressing room I could. It was simple stuff; find your man with the pass, find space to receive a pass and in the wind, keep the ball down.

In the second half we started better, but we were still struggling until Julian took off Alfie after about 20 minutes, bringing on Luke Durnin. It signalled a change to three in the middle of the park and it changed the game. We pushed forward but still couldn't equalise. With the clock ticking down through the 90th then 91st and 92nd minutes I was convinced my FA Cup hoodoo would see me lose my first game in charge. Another metaphorical kick in the nuts...

With the game ebbing and flowing into the dying seconds, we were awarded a free kick. It was awarded in the 93rd minute, but after much debate and two bookings, Ethan Mooney stepped up to take the kick in about the 98th minute. He struck it from just outside the penalty area and in off the bar leaving the keeper no chance. Have that! Sheer relief all round as we hadn't been at our best, nor had we really deserved the chance to level. We let out a lot of frustration and it was aimed squarely at the Levy players. They had, for the previous twenty minutes taken the piss out of us on the field, lazily time wasting and giving us 'the verbals' across the park. It's all part of the game and when you are three or four up, perhaps expected, but to do it at 1-0? What were they thinking? That equaliser really was a leveller in all respects and in two minutes we gave back everything they'd given in twenty. In spades. They just had time to kick off before referee blew for full time to signal a replay on the Tuesday night. UNBEATEN!

FAMILY

It's a bit unfair on the family I'm sure. Callum and Aaron both play and I like to watch. Holly my daughter and Hayley, I can't say enough about them. Can I carry on, can I support the boys, how do I spend the time with my wife and daughter. I might make the wrong choice and live to regret it. I've made wrong ones in the past and battled on, or moved on, but this one? Management could be a biggie and the guilt that will never go away is the time I miss with the family.

We are not talking here about a premier league player with a premier league salary travelling the world for friendlies, champions league games or internationals. My playing career has been just Saturdays, Tuesday and Thursday nights and a few hours here and there. Now though, I'm a manager. There will be a little more time when I'm not around, so the times when I am must remain precious. And I have a day job. I'm a husband and father coming in from work and then having to rush out again straight away for my hobby basically. And especially in the later years, I've followed this routine for no additional income. Even when I was getting paid it was just used as beer money for after the game or for a sneaky pint on a Sunday.

I have known a couple of players in the past who saved what they earned at football and put it in a pot to pay for holidays but honestly, I've never had the will power (or come to that, enough money) to do that. For me, it's been game over, get paid then either a misery or happy pint. It has been my reward for dedicating my whole week to playing. I'd relax and have a beer. In the past, time away from home wasn't thought of, as my mind was in robot mode; football, football, football. Some people may say that's me being selfish, but I got bitten by the bug and I've been taking my medicine ever since. It's hard to describe what comes over me for the months between July and early May.

Sometimes all compassion and sense drifts out of the window but now, the defence mechanism of missing my family has kicked in. Hayley has put up with me not being there at weddings, parties, all sorts of things and even delaying holidays. I'm nowhere near as bad as I was but close as we are, I don't think she really understands my need for football and there have been times when she's had enough and has rightly vented her frustration and anger towards me. Inside, that tears me to pieces. To see her that hurt is upsetting and very painful. My reassurances are generally shrugged aside, as it will happen again just as it has before. I can't ever promise that it won't happen again no matter how much I mean it. Groundhog Day. I try and make our time special, but sometimes I just cannot control the game.

Even now, I cannot express in words the amount of love I have for Hayley and our wonderful family. To put up with me especially on the days when I've lost, puts her up onto the highest pedestal ever. Whilst I'm writing this, I can feel the guilt building up as I recall the times I haven't been the perfect husband and dad. Not one occasion in particular, but every time I step out of the door she must wonder which Fergie is coming home. I haven't committed the biggest crime in the world by giving my time to football, it's the fact that it is continuous and repetitive. It has a relentless hold on me that sometimes must drive her to distraction. God only knows how I'd feel if this wonderful woman I love spent so much time away from me with her passion? One day when the ball is firmly tucked away and put to bed I will try and make it up to her and show her how much she means to me. Till then...

My daughter Holly is now 6 and she doesn't know any different, sadly. I feel that she asks me if I'm going to football almost every time she sees me, and honestly, that hurts. I try to hide it by suggesting how much she loves having 'mummy days' but it masks my real insecurities. Will she grow up not loving me properly? Does she think I love football more than her? A bit too far-fetched you may think for a few hours here and there, but they are the thoughts and despairs I have. I fight these demons by giving her and all my family as much love as I can. Only they can say if it is enough.

What is the alternative? Give up football I hear you say! Yes, perhaps, but try telling that to a stubborn old fool who knows no different. Aaron is eighteen now. I get some comfort that the time I've had away from him hasn't affected our relationship as we have a loving bond with each other, and Callum who is twelve has been coming to football with me since he was 4 or 5, always taken under a player's mum or dad's supervision while I played. Maybe it is different for boys! Unfortunately, perhaps, Hayley says he could turn out like me and be besotted with the game, but is that such a bad thing? To all my wonderful family I love you so much and I'm sorry if you feel I've let you down! You are my world. One day, I promise. xxx.

UNSWEETENED FA!

I may have mentioned this, but I didn't have a great record in FA competitions as a player, and on the Sunday morning after that first game I awoke unbeaten in the FA Cup as a manager. It was a very small thing in the scope of earthshattering world news, but after a late, late equaliser, it meant a lot to me. It also meant that in forty-eight hours we had a replay. I was mentally and physically drained, not so much with the effort of playing the game, but everything that surrounded it. I was bloody glad it was behind me! I was also lucky that the draw meant I could spend a planned Sunday in Clacton with Hayley and the kids and not have the worries of the world on my shoulders. Nothing would have been worse than to share such precious time with the family and ruin it by my selfish dissection of a defeat. We had a fantastic day and it made me appreciate how lucky I am to have them, and it reminded me once again, that I should never let football problems affect the time I have with them.

By Sunday evening when we got home (with a lager in hand) I looked at what I could change for the replay. The game had changed – and its credit to Julian and Bomber who made the change - when Luke came on and we altered the shape. Ethan also tucked in well when we lost the ball and was a threat when we had it, so I had to try and maximise his involvement. With a couple more players being available for the replay, I felt we had a better chance. I needed to try and get my never give up mentality drummed into a few of the young lads as well. If ever there was a good example it had been our late equaliser, but it was not going to be easy. They needed to grasp that when teams got on top of us, we needed to scrap even harder. As I went to bed, I hoped and felt that the changes in personnel and formation would get us through. The best laid plans, eh? It could only happen to me...

I scored a goal, got my first competitive win as a manager and it was all wiped from the record books. The game was abandoned due to a serious injury in the 8th minute of added on injury time, with apparently forty seconds left to play. To cap it all, where in the hell did the Referee get nine minutes added time from anyway?

I spoke with Julian and Enda and we made four changes from the Saturday, two enforced and two tactical. We changed the shape as well, and for half an hour it worked as we shut Leverstock down quicker and made them play long which played into our hands (and mine in particular). We scored first, but then stopped pressing and they deservedly equalised - to be fair, they could have scored again in the fifteen minutes leading up to half time, but they didn't. The team talk was focussed on what we did right at the start, shutting them down early. We stressed that we had to stick to the plan. Five minutes into the second half I found myself in their box as a cross came in and this old fella looped a header neatly into the back of the net to give us the lead. It was great to score (even if I wasn't 100% sure what I was doing up there that early in the half), but deep down I think I knew it wouldn't be the winner, and so it proved. Five minutes later we should have extended the lead when Hani had a one on one, but the keeper got a touch and the ball went out for a corner, from that, I think it was Ethan's shot was cleared off the line. If either of those had gone in, well, who knows.

For 25 minutes we were severely under cosh. Levvy created chance after chance due to our inability to keep the ball. Our fitness levels weren't as good as they should have been with changes to the side and knocks and niggles. They equalised with about ten minutes to go and to be honest they did more than enough to win the game in the final minutes, but we rallied and showed a bit of bollox, then scored a late goal, Ethan again. Scrappy as hell but who cares, it counted. As the sides reset for Levvy to take the kick-off I asked the referee how long was left and he said: *"five minutes"*. More pressure, more defending, but, though we didn't get out of our half, they didn't get in our box either as the clock ran down. We kept them out in the corners, frustrating them and then their young left back, who had scored and had an assist, went down injured under no challenge, a yard from the touchline. The trainer came on and to be fair looked pretty concerned immediately, then the referee went over. After about fifteen or twenty minutes with their staff, our staff and a few others assessing the injury an ambulance was called, but they were told it could take up to three hours to arrive! The referee had no choice, he called the captains over and said that he was abandoning the match and he would leave it to the FA to decide the outcome. When he eventually called a halt to the game he had played eight minutes added time and said there were forty seconds to play. Open mouthed, I couldn't even comment, I was that gutted.

My instincts at time were to wonder if they were winning 3-2 would they have moved the player? After all, he was only just on the field and it was a leg injury, not his neck. I'm no medical expert, but with no obvious signs of broken or protruding bone surely you can move the person if it's done properly? (As it happens, the poor lad lay there till midnight when the club were informed that an ambulance wouldn't be coming. An absolute disgrace, the emergency services then spoke through on the phone how best to move him and he was moved to his parent's car. They drove him to Accident and Emergency themselves).

I mentioned in bar that if it was other way round and with that amount of time left I would have suggested that result should stand. And I mean that wholeheartedly. They had, had numerous chances to win both games and couldn't do it. If that was us I would have conceded defeat because it wasn't meant to be. They obviously didn't feel the same because as I left the Clubhouse a couple of their committee smirked and said: *"see you next week chaps"*. Tossers.

I felt incredibly flat the following day. I'd scored, we'd surely won and yet half a dozen suits in a Committee Room in London would decide if we had to do it all again. It felt like they could take a goal off us for something we were not involved in. How was I supposed to motivate my players for their first league match on the Saturday with that hanging over us? I couldn't even motivate myself. Thankfully, Julian took the lead at training on the Thursday and that helped lift my mood. What really grated was that we'd scored our third on ninety-one minutes and the ref said there was five to go. Seven minutes later the injury occurred and apparently there was still almost a minute left. I still don't see how that could have been right.

We got our answer on the Friday. The suits had decided that the match was to be replayed. I truly wasn't surprised, but I was devastated and angry. We'd need a siege mentality for the third attempt. Christ, it was pointed out that this was one of my longest runs in the FA Cup and we hadn't finished the first bloody game. I thought the decision was scandalous and I let a few people know so. The FA response said that because we equalised in injury time on Saturday who's to say that they wouldn't have on Tuesday? Bloody ridiculous! What if they had scored after 12 minutes then we equalised after 17 minutes. What then? Myself and Julian's first thoughts were identical, to throw the match. Why should we have to do it again? I suppose it was alright having a siege mentality if you knew your team, but I was still getting to know mine. I didn't know if they'd have the mental strength to overcome this. There was lot of 'fighting talk' on the players WhatsApp group but that was initial anger and soon quietened down. I had to focus, and I had to get my players to focus. We had a league game to contend with on the Saturday and that couldn't be overshadowed by yet another replay. Importantly I didn't want the side to go into the Tuesday game on the back of a defeat. I rang around a few people that I trusted and they all said pretty much the same. That I had to find a way from within to turn the anger and despondency into a positive, starting on Saturday and building it up to Tuesday. I had my challenge, but sadly, I had another challenge too; with a couple more injuries and un-availabilities, we were short of players for our first league game.

There were a few more debut's to be had, and the pre-match team talk started with a couple of paragraphs on what lay ahead, but how important that day's game was. It went down well and as we all left the dressing room, I felt as positive as I had before any of the matches. It certainly didn't seem that way in the first fifteen minutes however, as we started badly and could have been 2-0 down. Luckily, my old buddy Bomber in goal kept us in the game early doors. We eventually settled down and took control for the remainder of the half and went in 1-0 to the good. We doubled our lead in the second half before a shaky spell let St Margaretsbury pull one back, but we held on and saw the game out. Three games, still unbeaten and three points to boot!

Going into the replay, I talked about the never say die attitude and mental strength, but I knew with the players I had available, I wasn't really going to get it. I think it is a common thing these days, that footballers should just be #ballers and nothing else. What I mean by that, is they just want to go out on the pitch and play, winning is fair enough, but if they lose, so be it. It doesn't seem to hurt anymore. Well, it bloody hurts me.

We started badly again but showed some resilience when 2-0 down after half an hour to get back to 2-2 at half time. We stressed keeping things simple, keeping focussed and working for each other as we had the previous week, but it fell on deaf ears. We had a shot blocked by their keeper straight after the kick off and they broke forward and scored. All that was not right about us was summed up in that thirty seconds; too many bodies forward and then we didn't take a foul high up the pitch, a couple of missed tackles and we concede a goal. We dug in and equalised again but then we let them score a forth unopposed goal which knocked the stuffing out of us. With time running out, they got a fifth, but on the night, they were the better side, no matter whether the game should even have been played. I was frustrated, angry, gutted and out of the FA Cup again. I let it get to me and I refused to shake any of their players or their management's hands, which led to a few choice words and a bit of handbags. As a manager I should have acted with more sportsmanship, but my mind asked where was theirs in pushing for a replay? I was highly aggrieved, and it continued through until Wednesday unsurprisingly.

There were times over the following forty-eight hours that I contemplated jacking it in. Not just because of the result, but the behind the scenes stuff, even the little things, weren't right. The replay, our lack of money and warm up tops! No decent training balls! No effort to find money to help the lads get a tracksuit. No petrol money! Players not being available. I just felt everything was against me. It shouldn't have been like that, at even this level. Julian had managed clubs with no budget before, but even he hadn't experienced anything it.

Finally, I licked my wounds and began to prepare for the next game. I even managed to get a couple of players in from a level above to add to the squad. I chalked the whole episode up to experience and I rang the Levvy manager to apologise.

BAPTISM? I'D NEARLY DROWNED

The first forty-five minutes of my managerial career had been an absolute disaster from a footballing point of view. We couldn't keep the ball, we couldn't tackle and aside from that, we didn't do anything right. Positive words and a bit of tinkering at half time made little difference. A change midway through the half to personnel and formation slightly improved the overall performance and we snatched a draw from the jaws of defeat. Forget the fiasco of the FA Cup, or at least the surrounding fiasco and look at those performances: the first was poor, once again we snatched a late, late equaliser, then we battled well to get our noses in front in a tough replay only for the powers that be to snatch that one away. Perhaps I didn't realise enough that it wasn't only me that felt cheated, because the next performance was another downer. When we went behind it was obvious that heads and energy dropped, and we wouldn't get it back. It had been a hell of a couple of weeks.

At least in the weeks following there were some definite improvements, even though they were small things, improvements as to the amount of time we were under pressure in every game was a start. It even set us another challenge in that we had to stop conceding goals in those spells when we were under the cosh. I really hadn't expected my defensive nous to be tested that much, but in every game we either started slowly or lost our way, forced into frantic spells of do or die defending and invariably we'd concede one or two goals. Forgive me for stating the bleeding obvious, but that spell where concentration seemed to fail week in, week out made my job and to be fair, every player's job a bloody sight harder, because in this game we love there is one aim and it's to score more than the opposition. Giving them a couple of freebies is not part of the plan. It was particularly frustrating when in a couple of games, we'd gone two down then come alive and got back into the game drawing level, only then to falter and give away another goal. Maybe give away is a bit strong, but, just as in pre-season, we weren't making teams work hard enough for their goals against us. We were switching off, our concentration levels would drop, and our opponents would score, then we'd feel sorry for ourselves and let games slip by. On ability and even performance (in spells), we were more than capable of not losing and even winning most of the games that we had played in those first weeks.

Concentration wasn't the only issue either. Tactically we needed to improve as a management team, though it was not always helped by player availability. We tried two up top in the first game with two in central midfield and we were overrun. The centre of the park was far too open. Then we switched things to 4-3-3, using the full backs to overlap and guess what? We were still being overrun with three in the middle of the park. We realised quickly that we had two options: either to adapt our tactics to suit the players we had available or to adapt our squad and recruit players that would suit our preferred system. One thing obvious in every game was that we needed an enforcer to sit in the middle and break up the oppositions play, even to take one for the team every so often as the need arose, but despite a plethora of midfielders, none fitted the mould. It was a major problem, as teams were running at our back four at will. I knew because I was playing there. To be honest, even with me in the back line, the defence hadn't been great. Early additions should have strengthened the options, but we remained prone to the same lapses and errors. The pressure I had put on myself to have a solid back-line and to be a good, young attacking side was wearing us all down. The performances didn't reach the expected levels and it wasn't good enough. Sure, we could use the excuse that injuries and other un-availabilities had prevented us from fielding the preferred line up, (in the first seven or eight games there were at least two changes every match), but these were our players. We picked them, we coached them, we knew what we wanted but we were struggling to get there or find the answers. Two up front would occupy the opponents back line and work them harder, but that would only work if the two defended from the front, and the nine behind them did their share as well.

Then I got injured. Was it fate, football gods, my inner demons or just another kick in the nuts? Who knows, but it did give me a better perspective on things. In the afternoon before an evening game, I was kicking a ball around in the park with my boys, Aaron and Callum and I started getting spasms in my lower back. It's an old war wound, something I'd suffered on and off for a few years. Usually, they come, they go, and generally they aren't too bad, but this time the feeling was both more painful and more repetitive. It meant I was out of the side, watching from the side lines for a couple of games. It did at least give me a better view of what we needed to change.

That wasn't a good day all round to be honest; it was the same day that I heard Gordon Bartlett and Wealdstone had parted company after more than twenty-two years and he'd had a better start to the season than me. That gave me a strange feeling, almost like being alone I suppose, as my mentor was no longer 'just around the corner'. When I spoke to him later, I felt as though I was offering my condolences on someone's death, but we spoke for a bit and then I suggested that if he was at a loose end, I had a new twenty-two-year project at Edgware and he could help me out. He laughed. Perhaps he'd seen our results and didn't fancy the challenge, but at least from that laugh, I knew that he'd still be on the end of the phone, at least, as long as I had the job.

With a late call-up to cover for my injury, our squad of sixteen had five eighteen-year olds in it, and four started. It was a different line-up again, but we suffered the same problems; conceded an early goal, then equalised, then conceded another and equalised again. I was kicking every ball from the side-lines but could do nothing to help, then one lad got two daft bookings in the space of a few minutes before half time and was sent off. We were down to ten men and couldn't hang on for the final two minutes of the half, as we let in a third.

A calm head amongst all the chaos was needed and I thought I showed that quite well at half-time. Because we needed to chase the game I switched things about and we went 4-3-2. It worked as we began a second half onslaught and we had a great chance, as midway through the half the ref evened up the sides and ten minutes later sent another of their lads off. It was one-way traffic, but we could not find another goal. We hit the woodwork, their keeper made a couple of great saves and to cap it all, we missed a penalty. Eight or nine games into my management career, it felt like I'd suffered just about everything a whole season could throw at me, let alone less than half a dozen games.

YOUNG LIONS

Partly because we had no money and partly by choice, the squad had a higher than average level of young players. They were good enough in the main, if a bit raw in some cases, but I knew if we got the mix right, we'd get results and initially in small doses, so it proved. We had a blank Saturday, so I gave the squad the Thursday night off, arranging a friendly for the Saturday, away to Chalfont St Peter who had beaten us 2-6 in pre-season. We had named a squad but as usual when a side isn't winning or high on confidence, there were a couple of cry-offs and bearing in mind we had signed something like 27 players, on the morning of the game we had a revised squad of twelve outfield players, Taylor Montgomery, the young third choice goalkeeper and two youth players that I had never seen play before. Why did I bother? I gave up trying to decide who was genuine in telling me about their unavailability and who wasn't, and I was fuming as I was injured and desperate to play. My confidence and that of the players was already fragile and we'd arranged the game hoping to try a few things out in a match that didn't matter. Pre-game, I was left wondering how the hell we would feel if we took a beating from a superior team in a superior league (albeit in a friendly). I wondered why I had bothered, all the stress was adding even more grey hairs to my flowing locks.

What did I know. When we got there, I realised we didn't even have a left back, but I managed to cajole young Rio Beech into the three shirt and what a great move – he was outstanding. He'd been used in centre midfield and wide left and had been decent in both positions, but that day, he played left back like he had played there all his short life. In fact, with a bit of tweaking of the formation as well, the team were outstanding! It was by a country mile the best performance of my fledgling career. And we got a clean sheet, even without me. Chalfont had put out a strong side, though they did give a few of their squad run-outs, and perhaps they didn't put as much effort in with it being a friendly, but we took the 2-0 win and all the positives that came with it. The slight change in formation was to set up as 4-2-3-1. Dennis Marharjan was excellent with Luke Durnin, the two oldies providing experienced heads in the defensive midfield positions. That helped us protect the back four, keep possession and improve the supply to the forwards. For the first time, we'd gone ninety minutes without having a sustained spell where we were under pressure. My young full backs worked well pushing on, and the two youth players ran the ball well, especially young Mo Koroma, a natural winger, who ran the ball from well inside his own half all the way into their area, drew a foul and won us the penalty from which we scored our second. Alongside those two, the match finished with us having three eighteen-year-olds in defence and Taylor in goal; my six young lions had done us proud.

The dressing room after the game was buzzing, a happy place for a change, and for a change I had to settle things down and bring a few feet back to earth, all the time trying not to go overboard myself. I picked on a few things we did well and a few things we could have done better, and I explained to the lads that they had set the standard. They had to be good enough not to let it drop. An easy journey home and a quiet beer followed, content that for that weekend at least my demons and doubts would disappear. I hoped we could keep it up and it was only a few days before we would get the chance.

The friendly win started a little run of better performances (not completely reflected in the results) and a better mental state for me. Still injured I was on the side-lines, but with Julian there, we were able to stamp our style on the side and the young side were cutting down on mistakes and learning. Then my nemesis, an FA competition, this time, the Vase and the good news was, I still wasn't fit, so it couldn't be my fault if we lost. It was particularly good news for young Perry Aitchison at centre half, as he'd get another game under his belt to continue the development he'd shown thus far. We started well and pushed Risborough Rangers back into their own half for best part of half an hour, but we weren't clinical enough, then (old habits) we got slack again for the last part of the half. At half time, we tried to focus the boys (most of them really were boys, as well) and we started the second period as we had the first, this time scoring through young Mikkel James after an hour. Towards the end we got a second but again lost our way a little and let them back into the game with a goal and nearly a second. It was a nervy last ten minutes, but by then, I was more worried about getting enough drivers in the squad if we needed to go deep into Aylesbury for a Tuesday replay than the actual game. Thankfully we held on!

It meant a Tuesday league game against Welwyn, and Marksy. Nerves were killing me as they were a very experienced side with great firepower. We'd have to perform for ninety minutes and with nous way beyond the years in the side. I still wasn't available, so the young lions were to be put to the test. Another nervous start, a few do or die challenges and blocks kept the scores level, then we changed the shape slightly from the side-lines and grew into the game up to half time. We even took the lead after a decent spell in their box. If there was ever a time to keep a clean sheet this was it, but sadly it didn't happen. The second period started even, but Welwyn put us under more and more pressure. We defended in a strong breeze and heavy rain and even rode out ten successive corners at one point, but Welwyn scored twice in two minutes with about ten to go. I was disappointed, but pleased too, as we showed a bit of balls trying to get back on level terms with a couple of half chances in the last few minutes. It wasn't to be, but we were defeated not disheartened. I couldn't have been prouder of the young lions after such a fighting performance. We'd taken on a very experienced team with five eighteen-year-olds, a nineteen-year-old and three more in their early twenties in the squad, and more than given them a game.

GROWING UP

We were facing a tough run of games, and as always it seemed, we couldn't put out our best side. We played Oxhey Jets who were third after a better run of form, only to lose our most experienced centre-half (except for me), unavailable as he'd been approached to play for Hanwell Town in their FA Cup tie. It meant I got the start after a month out.

No changes though, the same frailties prevailed. After a good start in which Durnin scored a screamer to give us the lead, we conceded another poor goal for their equaliser. Our work rate had dropped and that was re-iterated at half time. A couple of quick yellows at the start of the second half saw Rio dismissed and it was backs to the wall for a while, as Oxhey took the initiative and the lead. That sparked us back into life and my resilient rovers created the best chances of the match, equalising in the last minute – a worldy from a Lolu free-kick. My delight at the equaliser was once again tempered by the concern that we had ability, skill, youth and a pattern of play, but we only seemed to be at our best when chasing a game. Still, we were getting plenty of chances to chase, because we kept giving away simple goals through individual mistakes. Not one individual, that I could have resolved, but it was all of us, as though we were taking turns. We were about a dozen games into the season and there weren't enough wins and no clean sheets, yet we'd been the better side in half the games and in patches in the others. Age was a factor – not me at forty-six, but lining up alongside three eighteen-year-olds? Christ! I've just realised that I was only seven or eight years younger than the three of them added together! I wanted a young side, but I wanted desperately to share some of my experience and knowledge with them as well. Lo and behold, in the first minute of the next game despite all my positivity and willingness to share, we went a goal behind to another mistake as the most experienced player (me) mishit a back pass and then clumsily took the forward out. I've made loads of errors like that in a career spanning over eleven hundred games but this one felt different and hurt a lot more. I'd preached in my team talk that we need as individuals to cut out our mistakes as it was costing us, then I did that. Foot in mouth. Up to the shin.

The penalty was scored and for a few minutes my head was all over the place. I knew I needed to get a grip as my young side needed me then than ever. I knew that if I showed that I'd lost it, or was giving up, it would be an easy way out for them. All the right thoughts and I knew as a fledgling manager with a young side I had to hide the anger at myself, but those few minutes were as hard as any in my playing career.

What normally happened when we conceded early? Yup, we did it again and quickly. Six minutes, two nil down and my inner thoughts were cutting through me like a knife through butter. If I hadn't gifted them the first, they wouldn't have got the second: I heaped the blame onto myself which made me feel even worse. I had to grow a pair and bloody quickly.

The referee gave them another leg-up with an unfair penalty award (not me this time) after half an hour. I looked around and a few heads were down, so I shouted, geed-up, cajoled, bawled out each in turn. We were against a side that could massacre us, and I wasn't prepared to let that happen. Thankfully, the boys around me rallied. Backs to the wall, a small spark became a fire and we took the game to them for the last fifteen of the half, scoring one and almost getting another in the last minute. At half time I held my hands up for my mistake, then tried to encourage more of that spirit from the end of the half. I looked around the dressing room and everyone was attentive, I knew then that they'd started to grow up a little, yet inside? I was talking the talk but the guilt and the pressure I was putting on myself was another matter. It was eating away at me, but I couldn't let the lads see.

Minutes into the second half, young Tom Rivett lost his cool with the referee and threw the ball away after a poor decision. Red mist no doubt, but also not in doubt was a second booking and once again resilient rovers would play the second half (or a large part thereof) with ten men. 4-3-2 was becoming a favourite formation, but against Hoddesdon? A tough ask. It proved much harder and with twenty to go, they scored a fourth. To be honest, despite the words and positivity about pride, keeping on the fight and such like coming out of my mouth, I thought we'd get murdered and I wanted, hoped and needed us to at least finish positively, going into Saturday's game in the FA Vase. Despite my inner misgivings, they didn't let me down, the boys stuck to their task and even got a goal back with a couple of minutes to go.

I went home and faced the first of a couple of sleepless nights as I dwelled on my early error. Still thinking as a player, the doubts started. Was I too old? Was it time to quit and concentrate on my new managerial career? Was I good enough for that even? People say that you never stop learning in football and I had to learn as fast as I was trying to teach my fledglings. My overall manner wasn't improved by the fact that we were unable to train on the Thursday as our youth team were on the pitch. Another thing that is so often taken for granted 'up the ladder' but we couldn't afford to pay to hire another pitch to train on. At least it was an opportunity to see the youth team play, and as it turned out, I was pleasantly surprised by the standard. I'd seen a couple of the boys previously in a friendly and they shone along with a couple of their team-mates, all of whom I thought could 'do a job' for me, so they were duly signed on first team forms. It brought the average age of the squad down even further but if I couldn't sign experience, I'd have to sign vitality, wouldn't I?

On the way home, I reflected on my week: Good spirit, my defensive mistake. Need experience, sign youths. It wasn't panning out quite as I expected. Then I got a call from Julian, my co-manager. He wouldn't be at the Vase match on Saturday as his wife had booked a surprise holiday for him! Enda was recovering from a knee injury and had been away for a while, and although he was getting to know the lads slowly, he'd been missing since almost the start of the season. Suddenly, I felt very alone.

Friday was a tough day. For once, I had more than enough players available and that meant a few had to be left out. Tommy Walsh, a new signing, Dennis Marharjan as the midfield was more than covered, Ben Gray and me. I made the decision and I was bloody fuming! The player in me always wants to be involved, now the manager in me had dropped me after one game back. How the hell did that work? I was gutted and spent the day at work swearing at myself. It was very surreal being gutted and angry at myself in equal measure and looking back it was perhaps the day when I knew the balance had started to tip. Not far, but perhaps a little bit: I was now more (well, at least as much) a manager than a player.

All that anguish was put aside mid-afternoon, when from having too many players, I suddenly lost both starting centre-halves. Dennis and I were back in the XI and Tommy and Ben were on the bench! Fair play to them all for taking my original decision so well and being ready and willing when the situation changed.

Friday night and Saturday morning were spent pondering the game. An FA competition and we were going into it with a centre-half pairing that was eighty-five years of age. Perhaps not ideal, but it was what it was. As it happened, we were fine as our opposition were particularly poor on the day, backing-up the pre-game scouting we had done on them. Three up at half time, I wanted us to push on and really put them to the sword as I felt we needed the confidence boost of a decent win and a clean sheet. We got a fourth but couldn't build on it, though we did keep a clean sheet, and we were in the hat for Mondays draw, even if I was a bit disappointed that we didn't get six or seven. I'd thought pre-game that when we got games like this where we were fully in control, we wouldn't know what to do. We only played at our best when we were chasing games and in games like this, young minds with little experience had so much time to think what to do with the ball that they often chose the wrong option. Acting on instinct we seemed a much more dangerous team. Still learning, I remember thinking then that the way forward would be to set the team up to counter attack, because we were less effective when in control of a game.

NO COACHES, NO PRESSURE

We finally got our first clean sheet in the league two weeks after the Vase game, then immediately regressed to lose to Cockfosters in a game we should have won comfortably. We were still a work in progress, and we were still suffering a lack of decent equipment and a lack of drivers to get the team to away games. Then, a couple of the Committee came up trumps. Tracksuits and Polo Shirts arrived for the squad, immediately accompanied by the two committee members agreeing to put in £20 per week each. It meant I could pay to top up an Oyster Card or two for those who travelled by train, and there'd be a bit of fuel money for the drivers. I also got given £650 from the money the club had won in the FA Vase which I decided we'd keep as a back-up or for a beer with the players at the end of the year. Things were looking up!

Not for long though, as we were down to bare bones for our next game and there was a problem brewing with Julian and Enda. There had been a bit of friction between a couple of the squad and Julian. Nothing major, but odd comments one way or another than I had picked up on. After a defeat on the Saturday, we had a longish midweek trip to Spelthorne in the County Cup, and lo and behold, with a few new injuries picked up on the Saturday, coupled with a few late pull-outs when they realised where we were going, the squad was thin. With six of the sixteen the previous Saturday unavailable, what I didn't need was to bring in a loan player on the Sunday only to have him recalled without playing on the Monday, as his parent club were short. I was down to fourteen when a couple of hours before kick-off, I lost Reon Thomas to a family emergency as well. It looked like a long night was in the offing. It didn't get any better, as ten minutes before kick-off, we only had a bare eleven as two of the lads from the youth team had been held up on route, only actually arriving five minutes before the start. It was going to be a very young side, playing against a team of men who were doing OK in their league and were certain to stamp their physicality on the game early on.

We got through the initial onslaught and came into the game as the first half progressed, and we were happy to go in 0-0 at half time. As usual, the team talk was effort, focus, concentration – and lo and behold, ten minutes into the second half we were two down and chasing the game. Our cunning plan! Once again, with hearts that belied their age the young side clawed themselves back into the match with a goal on about eighty minutes, then equalised (once again) with the last kick of the game even though it was to no avail as we lost 4-3 on penalties.

The day after, I got the news that both my joint manager and coach no longer wanted to continue in their respective roles. Enda (who had been brought to the club by Julian) broke the news to me. I didn't know him when he first came to the club, but I can't say a word against him, even though the news took me by surprise. He seemed to be enjoying doing what he was doing, but there it was. I'd said at the start of season to both that we would share workload and if none of us were pulling our weight we would let each other know. Enda said that he felt that maybe his input was not taken on board as much as it should have been, though he also said that it was nothing to do with me, the situation just wasn't right for him at that time, and he had a lot of work issues. On top of that, on a couple of occasions, Julian and I had a couple of niggles on the bench which perhaps made Enda feel awkward, possibly being stuck in the middle. When he spoke, I also wondered if he was so used to managing in his own right, he was finding it difficult having less responsibility. I'd stressed right at the beginning that the club wasn't the most professional off the field, but I was sure we could get it right on the park, yet Enda remarked on this as another reason for his decision. It was more of a surprise as he'd only recently bought some warm-up tops out of his own money for the lads because he was unimpressed with the club having none. He was a decent coach and a gentleman. I was sad to see him go.

As for Julian, during the Spelthorne game, he had, had a run in with one of our players and it wasn't the first time the two had clashed. From the bench, I'd had a slight niggle with him over kicking a ball back into play and with Enda looking on, it probably didn't help. It was just one of those things, nothing in it, nothing to cause a grudge and I just put it down to the heat of moment. Then, there was another exchange of words between Julian and the player in the lead up to the penalties. I intervened and told the player in no uncertain terms to shut up, which he did. After the game in the bar I pulled him aside and told him that he had no right to keep piping-up at Julian, even if he thought he was wrong, I said there was a time and a place. I knew from experience that it could and did happen, but I also felt that both sides sometimes had to take it on the chin and get on with things.

With all this in mind I then had to ring Julian and tell him about Enda. When I rang, unsurprisingly, Julian said Enda had already called and he said he was as gutted as I was. Then he said that he wasn't happy with certain things and that he was going to quit as well. Double whammy! We spoke about the player the night previous and I explained that I had pulled him aside, but it made no difference, Julian was adamant. He just re-iterated that he felt I shouldn't put up with that player's attitude and he said that in all the years he had been involved in the game... yada, yada, yada. On top of it all, he was having a hard time in his personal life and didn't need the hassle. That, I fully understood. We have spoken since and I can see where he was coming from on his personal life issues, he just needed to be fully devoted to his family at the time. As I look back now, it seems strange. We've always got on as we are similar, and we have had plenty of good times together. We both can be hotheads, and those things combined were perhaps both our strength and our weakness. For me, it was just a shame that our partnership, whatever the reasons, didn't last very long.

"Keep Calm and Carry On" is what the mug says. Well, this mug didn't exactly have any choice. When you are on your own, the challenges, or in our case, games, come thick and fast, and so it was. No training on Thursday but a match on the Saturday. I intended to leave myself out to manage from the side-lines as there was no-one else to do it, but with injuries and unavailability, I had no choice but play. Thankfully my old mate, occasional goalkeeper and coach, Bomber stepped in to the dug-out. It was the first time in my career, player or manager, that I actually hated football, never mind being in charge. Yep, think about that statement. I hated football, and it was at that moment, true.

As the Saturday approached, there were plenty of 'why me' thoughts and so much going on in my mind, not least preparing to tell the committee that my two assistants had walked. As it happened we had a brief meeting before the lads turned up, and I told them that both Julian and Enda had felt that the club being run shambolically was high up on their list of reasons to quit. The joint reaction was of shock, but it did seem to kick them into gear as they immediately set a few things in motion. It was a shame that we'd had to wait until then, but better late than never.

We played a couple of games with Bomber running things from the side-lines, then I left myself out, but where I added knowledge and a voice on the bench, we lost it on the field. To counter that a little, I called in another old mate, Mark Burgess who was coming to the end of his career but was another with a wealth of experience. He played at the back and controlled and encouraged the youngsters around him, for which I was very grateful. (Grateful enough that I kept him around for most of the season and he's signed on for this year too!). Then we had another blank Saturday which should have given me a chance to get my mind focused and to try and find a coach, assistant or both.

On the Friday I was put in touch with a coach who seemed very interested when we spoke. He agreed to come along to training the following week to put on a session, then we would discuss the way forward. Sorted (or so I thought). I still had a blank Saturday, so management was put to one side and I woke up knowing I didn't have the hassle of organising lifts or having to deal with late drop outs etc. I'd had the call, I was Fergus Moore, player, off to play for Belstone FC again in the Herts Senior League.

Joe Sheridan (the manager) and I have been mates for many years and I help him out when he's short and when I can. They were flying high in their league and unbeaten so were doing very well. For me, it was a complete change. No worries or issues except how far I would be able to clear the next header, and could I get the tackle in before the forward broke away! This was a cup-tie at Cuffley where I'd never played before, so it was also another tick on my non-league journey. After over eleven hundred senior games (which must be some kind of record in itself), the list of 'new grounds' also still increases every season. When Joe called me initially he was short but by the Saturday he wasn't, so I started on bench and found myself still in 'manager mode' as I started barking out instructions from the touchline. Once the game was safe, he wanted to give me a run-out, so I told him put me holding midfield. Yeh right, I had no intention of holding, I was going all out to score by whatever means, and I got my chance. We got a goal kick and was launched towards me on the halfway line, I nodded it on to Darren Turner who then played a one two with Butler, gaining ground to the edge of the eighteen-yard box on the angle. From my header, I've continued the run, and Turner laid the ball to me eight yards out but on my right shovel.

You've guessed. I managed to blaze it over the bar to roaring laughter from the Belstone lads, as they knew from my performance in that short spell that I wanted to score to show them what the dinosaur could do. It led to a fun night on social media as they weren't shy in coming forward. I got stick the whole night through and I loved it. For just those few minutes and with the banter in the evening it was great to be just a player again.

I don't generally like Mondays, and the one following that weekend release was no different. In fact, it was made worse by my prospective coach declining the offer. I was gutted. I suspect it boiled down to the fact that I couldn't offer him any money. Good coaches don't come cheap and in had been naive to think that I would get him for free, but he had made all the running, contacting me. Perhaps he was misinformed that Edgware had some finance, which couldn't be further from the truth. It left me totally deflated as I tried to get my mind focussed on another match the following day. Ringing some players and texting others to get the side organised wasn't helped by the whole back four from our previous match pulling out for a selection of reasons. It had been a tough couple of weeks, and the immediate future didn't look much brighter.

WINTER BLUES

November arrived with a blast of cold air and that did little to improve my mindset. We had another blank Saturday, but for once football wasn't on the agenda at all as I was babysitting. Probably not my forte, but a contribution to family life and a couple of brownie points in the bank as well. It gave me far too much time to contemplate my situation, or more accurately the 'lack of a coach' situation. I was finding it very difficult on my own, especially with injuries and unavailability meaning I was also playing. Burgo and Bomber were willing helpers and I was very grateful, but I found more and more that I needed help. It was starting to grate on me and get me down. No matter what I did, I felt that something conspired against me. I tried to sign three players, everything was agreed but I couldn't get hold of my Club Secretary to get the forms signed and I spent that day's babysitting trying to get a squad together for a game against table-toppers Berkhamsted on the Tuesday. Even with the three new lads I was still short. Trust me, it wasn't a good weekend, I'd had enough, and I very nearly threw in the towel. My thoughts were spinning round and the frustrations building as all I'd ever done was give it my all and I couldn't help but get angry and frustrated when the people around me didn't mirror that.

Another match out of the way and my head a little clearer, I was able to call in a favour for the Thursday training as my mate for many years, Frank O'Brien agreed to take a session for me. Frank is a full-time coach with Chelsea FC and it showed that night (and a couple of times since!) I watched an excellent session that the lads responded to very well and both they and I enjoyed it, even if it did prove one of the problems that I believed we had. The issue is that when there was only me shouting and bawling there is no variety and no opinion. With Frank coming in that night there were different styles and views and a more focussed session. Perhaps that's why he's at Chelsea and I'm at Off the Cuff United. That's not much to live up to for any coach I bring in then, eh!

On the field, it was same old, same old. Different players, same excuses, same mistakes and far too frequently giving the opposition an easy start, then we'd battle back into the game, get level and even get on top, then probably need a last-ditch tackle or save to see us through. It wasn't like that every week and we were improving both in results and performances. Perhaps I'd set the bar too high in my mind, but we weren't consistent enough. We would go one week where we'd struggle to hang on, then next game be a delight to watch, with a couple of reasonably comfortable wins. One particular week summed it up:

Tuesday; concede early v Biggleswade through a defensive error, battle well, equalise and should have gone on to win, but we ended up needing a last-ditch clearance off the line otherwise we'd have lost.

Saturday; cruise to a two-nil lead against Hadley. They get one back, but we step up and continue to dominate throughout, scoring a third, a Lolu hat-trick and a comfortable win.

Tuesday; pre-game we focus on all the good things from Saturday and then go a goal down after fifteen minutes. We stabilise the ship and don't concede a second which is a positive, then we create four excellent chances, two saved, two off the woodwork, as we play our best football of the season, only to lose concentration with five left before half time and we concede two more. A disappointing defeat and the first time in the season that we hadn't scored.

Another blank Saturday led up to the return against Berkhamsted. I asked all the lads to attend training on the Thursday to prepare for the game and expected them to be there. It was the first time I had asked having been quite easy going on attendance for training when 'other things' got in the way, but this was a big match and we needed the session. With another guest coach blowing me out about an hour before the session was due to start, I wasn't in the best of moods, and the dark clouds were circling when a few players were no-shows, having not let me know previously. Downright rude and disrespectful in my book and I let the player's WhatsApp group know my feelings. I knew what I expected, I knew what I wanted, I knew I'd watched Fabio fail trying, but I told them a no-show from now on would affect team selection. I knew that there would be times when that could be to the detriment of the team, but it was not fair on the ones who were there week in, week out. I hoped it wasn't an idle threat.

The few days in the lead up to the game were the worst of a bad spell and the worst it had ever been for me. All the doubts on my ability as a manager were to the fore and there was no-one I could bounce my ideas off. It was having a big impact on me. In the past when I've had doubts about anything, there's been someone close or involved that I could share with. In times of doubt I need that extra voice that might spark an idea that might have been overlooked. I felt very lonely as I was standing in the dugout and four or five days later, I didn't feel any better or reassured as to what the future may hold.

Matters were made worse throughout Sunday when pondering team selection. I queried Lolu's cautions and found out that not only was he suspended, so was Andrew Manitou. Top that with the injuries and the usual midweek drop-outs, and I was struggling for a bare 11. How the bloody hell could I have signed 45 players by November, yet was struggling to get eleven together to start a match? The issue of no-shows at training and my outburst on WhatsApp was still playing on my mind and I got it into my head that I would teach them a lesson by not playing them. Then I looked at the eleven I had. How could I consider not playing two out of the only eleven I had? It got to Sunday evening, seventy-two hours since training, seventy-two hours since I started thinking about my team and I had got nowhere fast.

Two days on the phone followed as I begged a couple and borrowed a couple and at 6:30 I had an eleven to start and a couple of subs including me. Then we were down one more as Perry, starting at centre-half failed a fitness test. It meant that the old dinosaur wouldn't be barking out instructions from the bench but from somewhere near the penalty box. At least, as long as the lungs held out.

Some things you cannot script in football and the result and all that led up to it fall firmly into that category. The match finished 2-2, a fantastic result as we were twice behind and managed to comeback and even though Berkhamsted created more chances, we could have nicked a winner right at the end and there were, for at least the next couple of days, a few plusses we could (and would) dwell on: Rio Beech, a young midfielder asked to do a job at left back, scored one of the best individual goals I have seen at any level. Picking up ball from our keeper he proceeded to beat three players from inside his own box and then unleashed an unstoppable shot from the edge of the area into the top corner. Young Stanley Arun, just turned 17, scored with his first touch in senior football seconds after coming on, I claim an inspired substitution. A forty and forty-five-year-old pairing at centre halves, didn't put a foot wrong all night and 'old' Stuey Blackburne, called in for his first appearance since the start of the season, gave a great hour up front. (I can't wait till we form a Vets team!) There were a few more I'm sure but they were the highlights. We dug deep, fought with passion and were concentrated and focussed for ninety minutes. All traits that I associate myself with and want from my team.

I summed it up in the dressing room after the game when I said that if I hadn't been so knackered, I'd probably have cried that night. Not out of emotion, just pure relief after what they put me through in trying to get a team out.

It gave me at least a short-lived spell of pleasure before the next match and for a while, any thoughts of jacking it in disappeared. Who knew for how long?

HAD WE PEAKED TOO SOON?

Actually, had we peaked at all? In the two weeks after the match with Berkhamsted the wall was metaphorically and physically hit. A win at Division Two Aston Clinton was followed by two gut-wrenching defeats in the league. It meant we had gained one point – albeit against the leaders – out of twelve and the problems were the same: Giving away early goals and no coach. With me on the side-lines we lacked a presence on the field. With me on the field, we lacked the nous to change things or spot errors from the side. In my mind, I was to blame, the self-doubt multiplying at an alarming rate going into each game, the next, our first league game at home for seven matches.

Pre-match I focussed on gift goals. We had been given a couple at Hadley, and they were the only two I could remember all season, yet we were giving one or two away every game. They get freebies, we had to work our nuts off for every goal we scored. There was no way we would win games if that continued, and what better place to stop the rot.

Yeh right. Fifteen minutes in and a set piece wasn't dealt with, then after half an hour a defensive error handed them another goal. Six minutes later, and we scored a worldy with a chest down and volley from the edge of the box. I let rip at half-time as I was fuming. It wasn't the same people, but the errors were spreading like wild fire. Then the inner demons; Why does it keep happening? Remember that it was me that made the mistake what seemed like a lifetime ago, should I have started to try and avoid the set piece frailties? Why didn't I have the answer? Not having an assistant reared its ever-uglier head again. Even when we did OK, I never really felt at ease, I suppose the good results just made it easier to muddle through, but now we were going through a bad patch I seemed to be putting myself under immense pressure to succeed and I never seemed not to be stressed. Even the Board lavishing praise on me about how I'd got the team playing well and how I was bringing on the youngsters was falling on deaf ears. To me, results were what mattered. Rightly or wrongly, I could not see another picture.

We'd set out our stall again, and coming from behind, we played the second half in Colney's half of the pitch. On the day, it wasn't enough as we couldn't score then to cap it all we gifted them another goal in the last minute. As the lads walked off I looked at Cain, our keeper. He hadn't had a shot to save in two games, yet we'd conceded six, and none were down to him.

Frank O'Brien came in again and did another training session for me, and fair play to the lads, with one or two exceptions they were all there. Was it enough to make a difference or had Frank become a bit of a talisman? I don't know, but what I do know was that in the last two games before Christmas we were almost everything I hoped we'd be. We played Hoddesdon and a little bit of me in my prime would have loved to play for them, as they are a team that no one particularly likes playing against because of the tactics you have to put up with on and off the pitch. We prepared well and won one-nil. A win, Cain saved a penalty and we kept a clean sheet. Behind early they couldn't bully my young side out of the game. Finally, the memory of the penalty I gave them after sixty seconds earlier in the season began to fade.

Still glowing after that result, the weather put paid to a couple of matches before we played a cup tie, midweek at home to Tring. Midweek usually meant drop-outs but on the back of the previous win, for the first time in my managerial career, I was able to field an unchanged side! Perhaps not so surprising was the reaction of the football gods to this news, as during the pre-match warm up Alfie Hills, our left back, pulled his groin, so I had to move Rio in there to cover bringing Steve Benavides into the wide attacking role. Well, sorry football gods, the disruption had no effect Steve ended up being the match winner, scoring the only goal of the night. It was an open and entertaining game and we perhaps hadn't bossed it like we had some previous encounters, but we deserved the win and our place in the league cup quarter finals. The laundry bills had been saved with two clean sheets and that gift, I was happy with.

Half a season gone, perhaps I was being a bit hard on myself compared to other people's opinions, but I wanted to turn the defeats into draws and the draws into the wins I felt some of our performances deserved. There was room for improvement, but coach-less (that was the first situation I wanted to improve), under the circumstances and with no previous experience, I was quite pleased. I'd given it one hundred percent as I always had as a player and I hoped I was setting an example the lads would follow, but I was sure there would still be a few bad days ahead. I hoped that I had the strength of mind and enough positive thoughts and memories in the bank to push on through them.

NEW YEAR'S RESOLUTIONS

We were on a roll! The last game of 2017 saw another clean sheet with a 2-0 home win v Wembley, though far from convincing, we did enough to ensure Christmas was a happy place! Even though we had kept a clean sheet, we had been fortunate, so for our cup quarter final that was the focus of the team talk. I also told the lads how big a chance it was to get to the final. Our form and a bit of luck continued in the first half as we created six chances, scoring two and though Risborough created three chances, they failed to test Cain in goal. Never was a team talk more obvious than the one at half time: *"Don't concede next goal, they aren't out of it yet, they've got nothing to lose"*.

Did my boys heed the warnings? Did they bollocks. From the restart, Risborough nicked one to claw their way back into the game and they got a second after ten minutes. On level terms again, we defended well and caused them a few problems, but they killed us with a winner in the last minute. I was fuming. Fuming at my players for letting themselves down, fuming at myself wondering what decisions I could have made to change things and most of all, I was gutted that the lads wouldn't get their cup final.

The journey home was quiet and reflective. It was a hard defeat for me to take because I was sure we'd progressed since the start of the season, yet we had made three mistakes, gifted three goals and I felt thoroughly deflated. After another sleepless night I rang a couple of my senior players, Burgo, Dennis and Bomber just to put my mind at rest. I needed to be told that I hadn't gone overboard in my rant at end of game and thankfully, they to a man said that I was right in what I had said; the team needed a sharp injection of reality having given away a 2-0 half-time lead with three silly and avoidable mistakes. As we finished up, I felt a little better but not much as I wasn't going to be at the next game (Mum's 70th birthday treat in Lanzarote), the old stagers I'd called would be in charge and I hoped would make my peace for me.

It's rare for me, I know, but sometimes, even I have to let the family take precedence over the game I love. If I hadn't made the trip with mum and Hayley I don't think I'd ever have been forgiven. Dads are a bit more independent, but mums are the ones you've got to look out for. As it happens, it was a lovely if short trip and it did help clear some of the clutter from my mind. With no kids there, it was a chance for some adult time with Hayley which we hadn't had for a while, limited of course to the periods when she wasn't partaking in here favourite hobby of sun-worshiping, that was.

I had left instructions with Director of Football, Dan Manzi, to name 'my' team and then to be assisted by Bomber and Burgo who was playing. They were also to be assisted by a new coach! Hector Varela was a mate of Dan's, who'd heard of our need and said he would like to come on board and help me out as a coach and assistant. It wasn't ideal that I wouldn't be there for his first appearance but at least Dan was around, and Hector would be able to build his own view of the side without any bias from me!

As usual when I'm away, I spent the afternoon on Twitter and making calls to Dan to get updates. The more the afternoon progressed, the more people around us in The Spinnaker in Lanzarote must have become engaged in my calls and the fortunes of Edgware Town FC. It wasn't a great afternoon for me, but it must have been so much worse for Hayley who was with me, taking the brunt of my frustration and anger and feeling the tension as the side took the lead but once again let it slip, though at least they held on for the draw. The result parked football for a couple of days and we enjoyed the break in the sun. More important, mum loved it and that was all that really mattered.

My midweek return saw a difficult build up to a difficult game. Once again, the problem of availability was key, as I had three goalkeepers on the books and none were available for the Wednesday, which I didn't find out until the Tuesday. Thankfully, James Duncan at Potters Bar Town loaned me his second choice 'keeper, a lad call Greg Marsh who was happy to help. It was a tough game against Crawley Green as we took an early lead but were pegged back, this time not conceding but scoring a second for a half-time lead. They came out all guns blazing at the start of the second period, but we held firm and after about fifteen minutes, caught them on the break to score a third and then got a fourth late on to seal a good win. What was more important was that Hector and I showed signs of a good partnership and understanding, a good chemistry, as we identified the same changes and tweaks several times in the match.

Our little run of results had lifted us to eighth in the table, and I felt relieved that Hector was now alongside to share a thought or two and some of the pressure as we looked ahead to another fixture against Leverstock Green. High flying, on a roll, our nemesis. This one, I really wanted to win.

Well, if there was a way to add sound to this page, you'd still hear the cheers. The boys were outstanding, a fantastic 3-1 victory. I'd said before the game that if ever there was a game to win, this would be it as Levy came across as arrogant in the way that they handled themselves the cup fiasco. A few of us had that stored in the memory banks. Equally, I hadn't behaved as I should have, and I'd apologised to my players and their manager afterwards. Looking back, right or wrong, it was a personal release from the pain of my first few weeks in management. My players at least could see the passion in me and I think they all excused me. If only I could inspire them and put that passion across as they learn at this level, we could go far.

We set our stall out – we, being Hector and I, the new dream team (what a start!) – to press them early then to soak up the inevitable pressure around half way as we didn't want to defend to deep, then to hit them on the counter-attack. It worked a treat as we stifled them going forwards, allowing them only a couple of opportunities (and they scored one) while we scored from each of our three attacks in the first half. The second half was more of the same without the goals and we banked a 3-1 win. Sweet, the boys made me extremely proud that day. I left hoping it would continue.

I could go on about hard luck, and make excuses, but the fact is we lost the next game against Leighton Town for all the same reasons as those before, mistakes. A tough game against a form side, but to take the lead then give it away and then to lose in the last minute had happened too often over the season. It wasn't one player, it was any of the players taking a turn at repeating previous errors. Something had to change.

Oh, did it change! The next two games were a bloody nightmare. We went to Welwyn short of a few players, but with a decent enough side, or so I thought. 4-0 down after half an hour, I had to make a change and brought young Perry off at centre half as he was having a torrid time against their forwards, bringing myself on. Looking for small positives here, we lost 5-2, so we actually won the last hour 2-1. Another positive was that at least we had taken a hiding from the title favourites rather than a team in and around us in mid-table. I'd also got 60 minutes under my belt and was in contention for a start on the Tuesday until that was called off because of the weather.

Onto Saturday and the day after my forty-sixth birthday. What a present! 1-6.

We were the one, Biggleswade were the six. Young, quick, organised, they looked like a side that had been together for a couple of seasons, but we still didn't deserve such a heavy defeat as despite their speed and pressure in the first half, we only went in one down at half-time.

At the start of the second half we tightened things up in the wide areas where they had beaten us with pace and following a great cross in, Hani should have pulled us level, but he skied the chance. Five minutes later we conceded a penalty and they doubled their lead. Heads dropped, and they doubled their lead again in the next five minutes despite the best efforts of Hector and I to gee everyone up and get their minds back on the game. It was game over, though Biggleswade didn't think so as they went on to get a couple more before we nicked a late consolation, which was no consolation at all. We'd been dicked, and we'd helped by giving away four of the five second half goals. It had been a tough spell, with three matches against sides in the top four and it showed the gap in the division between those fighting at the top of the table and us and the rest. In reality, in my first year, all I could hope to achieve was 'best of the rest'. I wasn't going to dwell on the result (for a change). The boys' confidence was low, but we'd had to make changes since the win over Leverstock, now, three tough games were behind us, and with players coming back it was onward and upward. Still fourteen games to play!

POSITIVE THOUGHTS

With pre-season included, I'd been in the job about eight months. Had it changed me? Well, I was more stressed and less at ease with my situation than I had been even a couple of months earlier. That was down to the recent run of bad form, not just in the results, but I also felt annoyed at my players and players around the non-league scene in general. They don't share the passion and desire that I do as a manager or did as a player. How was I meant to build a winning team or mentality when at the drop of a hat, players make themselves unavailable? Where was the dedication, the want to be part of a team and share in the drama that involves? I was having to make three or four changes every week purely because of non-availability, not injuries, suspensions and such like, it was ludicrous and reflected in the results. The players want to pick and choose when they make themselves available, yet they care enough to kop the hump when they are not picked after someone has stepped in for them and done well.

My outlook had changed. Early in my management career, and because of what I'd seen as a player, I accepted it. Now, it was really irking me, because with the side suffering a sticky patch, I wanted my best players available to try and put things right. I couldn't understand how some of them could just shrug their shoulders as if to say that's the way it is. I thought in twenty-five years as a player, I'd come across most excuses for not being around, and I thought I could tell who and when no-shows would happen, but almost every week, there was a new one to add to the list. Was it down to the fact that they don't get paid, however little? It was a factor, certainly, but overall, they, and I would say the majority, don't have a burning hunger and mentality to go out and strive to give it their all. It's frustrating to say the least, but it's something I've learnt from when looking at the squad now. It's not always about the best footballers, as attitude and character really do play a big part in the side.

I didn't rant and rave at the boys, because they were what I had and at the end of the day, I'd been responsible for signing them. I did need an outlet – just an opportunity for a novice manager to vent his dismay that he wasn't dealt a decent hand of cards to play with for the whole season, rather than just sometimes just trying to stay in the game. I knew that it was the same for many clubs as only one team could win the league, but I wanted more. I know that in the future when I am dealt a good hand I will use it wisely. Then the pressure will be to keep those not involved ready and willing at all times. Different situation, different pressure.

The situation with coaches and assistants hadn't helped for sure. I looked at myself and looked more closely at the people around me. There are people who I now realise I couldn't work with. Absolutely nothing against Julian, Enda and Hector, as I enjoyed working alongside all three, but I didn't really know them when we started out, and I think that had been to our collective disadvantage at times. I look back at some of the partnerships I've played under and I get jealous. Look around me: Gary Mac and Freddie Hyatt at Hendon (before they moved on), previously Steve Newing and Del Deanus at Enfield, both great friendships before they worked together. I know they can talk for hours after a game on what has gone on and how they will make things better etc. I think this makes a hell'uva difference and we collectively haven't had that insight. I know it's never too late to start new friendships, and many managerial partnerships can work and be successful that way, but it had made the early stages that much harder, learning each other as much as the game.

Maybe it is just what would suit me? I know (and perhaps reading between the lines, so do you), I have always felt lonely in the job, believing on occasion that if I'd let my true feelings come out, they might not have wanted to hang around! What I mean by that is that it takes me a while to switch off from a defeat and to get my emotions back on track. They may not want or need that mental space, nor understand why I do. It means that sometimes comments have been misdirected and misconstrued. No intent, it's just the way it is. If I had gone into management with a person who knew me and thought like me, perhaps I wouldn't have got my self-doubt issues on top of trying to handle theirs. I suppose logistics and finance are the reason why I didn't have that person, and maybe my relationship with Hector will continue to build. I don't know, but it is something I feel I'll need if I am going to continue.

On the field, my objectives changed during the season as well. At the start I was literally praying for pre-season to fast forward and to get to the nitty gritty of the league to see what it was like and how I would cope. Then, once I got the early games under my belt, I started to enjoy the job, setting personal targets and objectives in my own mind. The first was to be more successful position wise than my predecessor, and five points from the last eleven games would achieve that. It's not a grudge, but I do feel Fabio even now, for all his success back coaching at Hendon since he moved on, I think we could have achieved more with him in charge, had he just asked me for a little more help, rather than thinking I was trying to undermine him.

Midway through the season, I was desperate for the boys to reach the cup final, but we threw that away, losing a two-goal lead in the quarter final. I genuinely wanted the boys to do it as they deserved it. A young bunch that had been literally thrown together, it would have been great for them to get to a cup final even at our level, for all that it brings. It would have given us a great platform to go forward, but it was not to be.

As we passed the two-thirds mark in the season and the first target was within reach, I moved it up a notch. I wanted to finish in the top seven and with a plus goal difference. At the start of the season, I'd have thought that was a big ask, but with a challenging run-in in front of us, I believed we had a chance. It may not sound a lot but considering it was my first job, first season and I had spent much of it on my own, I would have to be really happy with that. When we suffered a couple of heavy defeats we were in tenth and I said we were top of the shit league. Everyone below us had a negative goal difference and everyone ahead of us had a positive. We weren't in the same league as the top six (though we're good enough on our day to upset one or two, home or away), seventh would make us best of the rest. I'd take that for year one.

Aside from matches, I tried to make the club a more enjoyable place to be around. Team-spirit hadn't really been as good as I'd have liked, perhaps because the players are both younger and different to those in my early playing days, and perhaps I should have concentrated more on that, but for most of the season, getting a bloody team out, match to match, was hard enough.

I wanted the squad to have theme days and to fine players for non-participation. I wanted to have players rules, and fine them for turning up late, dodgy clobber, forgetting boots and such like, but getting 50p or a pound of some of these boys would have driven me to distraction. They're weren't paid after all, but those odd pennies and pounds soon add up and normally get used to pay for a night-out which everyone can enjoy. It adds to the banter, too, but not here. Not then, anyway.

I look at me now and compare what I see to what I think I was at the start of the season, and to what I wanted to be. Had I changed? Maybe it would be better for the players to answer, but I know my mood changed over the periods where we suffered a bad run. I can't be happy to lose, but it's tough not letting emotions show – I know if I had, it would have brought down some of the players as well and then things would have worsened, so perhaps my management style developed. I can't wear my heart on my sleeve as I did as a player. Win or lose, I must be a bit more on an even keel. If it's good enjoy, congratulate, motivate and push on. If it's bad, cajole, look for positives and perhaps most of all, believe myself and convince others that I can make it better. With Hector around it's better because he is mister positive. He'll always put his arms around someone and tell them nicely, while my inclination is sometimes to raise the roof and the decibel level. Good cop, bad cop, I suppose, but I will always try and be honest with the boys and I believe I have maintained that so far. Whenever questioned about why they have been left out I have always told them the truth and that will never change.

I know I started on about commitment, but you know what I have realised and respect? Every one of my players had always given me 100% on the pitch. It's just actually getting them on the pitch that is sometimes difficult! A couple will progress up the non-league ladder and go on to better things. Hopefully they will say that I have given them some guidance and help on their way. You cannot even now understand how I will feel if any of this young group can make a career in the game, even at the top of the non-league ladder. Proud wouldn't cover it.

I'm grateful to them all too, and to Dan and Anthony Manzi who gave me the chance. Management has given me a new understanding and outlook on how to deal with the younger generations, and I hope it helps me pass on my knowledge, in turn helping them on the road to eventual success. One thing I can show but cannot give however is the mental strength and that they will need if they are to achieve their full potential.

THE RUN-IN

After the three defeats We tried to lift the atmosphere pointing out that we had had good spells in each game, even though we were lacking a few regulars, that sort of thing. We arranged another friendly to give a few fringe players game time and that was worthwhile, with a good turn-out and positive attitude. We thought we were set fair to end the run and get back to winning ways.

Once again two or three late cry-offs disrupted our plans. We got to the ground at 1:30 and we were another player short, as one hadn't made his designated lift; Apparently, he'd broken his phone on the Friday, had no numbers, didn't know how to get in touch, couldn't arrange his lift, hadn't told anyone, didn't even ring the club etc. etc. All of which I found out on the following Monday. On top of that, one lad had played a half on the Wednesday (the friendly) and because we had cancelled Thursday training, he went out for a kick about with his mates and turned his ankle. That was two out of the starting XI. Positive Ferg, positive.

The game (at St Margaretsbury) summed up the season: We were decent in patches on a quagmire of a pitch which I loved, but it took a late equaliser to get us something out of the game. We – including the old dinosaur at the back – defended well, and we kept fighting to get back into the game. It was positive in that respect and something I really wanted to build on as I didn't want the season to fall away. I wasn't ready to let all the hard work go to waste.

Others seemed less keen, as I realised that out of five centre halves at the club, three were unavailable for the next home game against Biggleswade United. Worse still, they were with me, the most experienced players in the squad. It was an uphill battle and the first half ended with us only one down. Hector felt he had seen a weakness we could exploit so we made a change at half time and brought on Mikkel and we totally bossed the second half. He caused them all sorts of problems, backing up my message that he seemed to have more impact off the bench. If only he'd do it from the start when he got the chance.

Sod's law, we bossed the game but couldn't score till the last ten or so, a Petty free-kick, then with five to go we switched off and conceded a second when we lost possession. Biggleswade were in amongst us in the league placings, so they gained the advantage. We let it slip when a draw at least would have been a fair result.

Even keel? Calmer me? Good cop, bad cop? The air was turned blue, totally out of frustration. I even had to apologise for my rant in a WhatsApp message to the players later that evening. The boys had done so well to respond to our first half performance and had thrown it away late on.

It seemed that no matter who we played, they were on a bit of a roll, and so it proved as we went to bottom of the table Stotfold, who had just won 4-2 at Tring. I know as a player that when you are at the bottom, a result like that can start a mini revival, so the pre-match team talk focussed on that; keep it tight, don't let them get a sniff early on, that sort of thing. Apart from a shaky opening five minutes when they threw everything at us (as expected), we grew into the game and took full control and were two (Petty) goals up at the break. My priority was to win the game, but I also wanted the clean sheet, but as we went out for part two I knew we had to focus hard, as we'd been in similar situations before and let a lead slip. With confidence a bit fragile I didn't want that to happen again. Ten minutes. We were comfortable and in control then we let them pull one back with their only meaningful attack of the game. Thankfully, we didn't let it disrupt us and we regained our composure, then scored with about fifteen to go, seeing the game out from there.

There were some good performances, and Hector's influence again, as he'd helped get Tyrone Mullholand and Christian Londones on board, both well known by Hector from his time at Hadley Wood. I said I'd give him a big input into the side, especially when I was called upon to play, and it was starting to work well, these two lads were both very comfortable on the ball and made a decent impact. That lad Tyrone has a big future in the game, I'm sure, as I was given him a lift to the station after the game he couldn't believe that I was forty-six, and in his words: *"Still doing bits!"*. Good lad.

Tuesday was a day of rest after the three points gained, then boom! Down came the snow. Even with a 3G pitch, the temperature stayed well below freezing, so the pitch remained frozen and was unplayable. Not quite *all-weather* then. Luckily the temperature rose a little as the weekend approached and that helped to thaw the surface, then groundsman Tom with the help of a few hardy souls got the snow cleared so our match could be played.

We hadn't trained all week, and suffered the usual couple of drop-outs, so I had to switch a few things about versus a Harpenden side well placed in fourth and who look to get the ball forward as quick as possible and play in the final third.

We were on our game right out of the starting blocks and Luke showed great feet (for a big lad) slotting home after about seven minutes. We were pinned back for the rest of the half, but we were solid and didn't really look like conceding. The second half started in the same way, out we came, all guns blazing though Harpenden got an early chance which Greg Marsh saved. From his clearance, we went straight up the other end and Lolu finished well for 2-0, but within a minute, they had pulled one back. No clean sheet (again) and it was game on. They piled on the pressure, but we held firm at the back and even created a few good chances on the break. Finally, we managed to get a clincher and make the game safe in the last few minutes when substitute Steve Benavides scored to give us a great win. We had shown real fighting spirit and took our chances on the break. They perhaps were aggrieved not to have gotten anything out of the game but that had happened to us often enough, so it was nice that the boot was on the other foot. A very tired but happy boss was left to reflect a great victory, whilst consuming a few celebratory lagers. You know what? I love a winning weekend!

A couple of wins and another game approaching. No drop-outs and a couple of players returning gave me the sort of headache every manager wants, that of too many players. One dead leg and a couple of pairs of tired legs saw two changes made, and goal scoring substitute Steve Benavides was one who got a start as we faced Tring on our own pitch.

We'd played them previously and the game was a bit cat and mouse as we won 1-0. This time they started better than us, but for ten minutes, couldn't score. Then all hell broke loose as we hit them for five in thirty-five minutes. We had totally blitzed them. We passed short and long, pressed high and were clinical, a word I've used all season, finally we were clinical in spades. We probably used up a whole season of clinical in that one half!

Now, you may have noticed, I can talk a bit, but what the bloody hell was I supposed to say at half-time? I don't think even as a player I was ever involved in a team that is five-zip up at the break. All I could think of was: *"Well done"* but I did add that the '0' was important: I didn't want the game to turn into a farce where they scored a couple then we get one and it ended up 6-3 or 7-4. I wanted a clean sheet.

For eighty-five minutes we continued to look good, if less clinical in the second half then bugger me, five to go and we conceded. Maybe I should leave a few lines blank here and you can fill in what you think I might have thought and said at that time;

....

....

....

....

Three wins on the bounce, but we'd done that before. I wanted four. Target one, achieved. We had a point more at this stage than the whole of the previous season. Target three, just. We were in seventh place. The goal difference was almost there, and we had eight games remaining. Though it meant very little, six of those were against teams below us in the table. I knew we had to take each game individually and that wasn't too difficult as each presented its own unique challenges with hardly any of my players able to commit to two games in a row.

WIN LOSE OR DRAW

The good times, and after three wins on the bounce is a good example, were good, but I knew also that I had to work harder to see the positives when we lost. Accepting that defeat doesn't always mean failure and is not always a time for despair can be a challenge. Not on the outside, but again, in my mind, which can lead me down a rocky path. Sure, there is always an immediate reaction, but I had to learn that sometimes, I should look again when the dust had settled. You can learn more from defeat than victory, as victory is glazed over by relief and you don't always see the full picture. I had to analyse our defeats a little more, to see a truer reflection of what had happened, however I still find it hard to accept it happens to everyone. I am learning that it is how you react that matters most.

My players too, react differently. Each is motivated by different things, but each needed to be motivated to turn up and give their all. It was and still is the key attribute needed to be successful, either as an individual or as part of a team. I had that driving force in my career as a player and I had to utilise it more often to fight of those inner demons as a manager. I also had to try and instil it in a young side.

Motivational speech over. A truly dreadful performance was to stop us getting the elusive four wins a row. Hoddesdon again, a team in transition, having to rely on their reserves and youth team players as there was a mass exodus from the first team when the manager resigned. They were on a bad run of defeats, while we on a run of wins were favourites for the game. Could we cope with that? The answer was a big fat no.

I mentioned pre-game that the two previous meetings were history and that no two games were the same. Hoddesdon weren't going to be thinking that we had just beaten a team 5-1, so we shouldn't go thinking that we would be playing a team which had been on a bad run. It didn't work. As the game started I could see *were* taking that approach and Hoddesdon were on their game. We looked to be getting even more anxious thinking we should be winning as the half progressed, while they gave us no respect and grew in confidence as we didn't trouble them. Half time came and went with a team talk based around: *"Don't panic"*. I told the lads to play their game and it would come. We only had to panic if we were one down with five to go, and then...

Mystic Ferg. Five to go and their right winger broke down the flank, I closed him as he hit the cross... straight into my arm from about a yard. My arm was raised, and the referee gave a penalty. Greg saved the kick but couldn't keep the rebound out. One down, five to go, panic ensued. We huffed and puffed to no avail and the black cloud that loomed after every defeat was well and truly above my head this time. We'd only needed one player to step up and be a match winner, but it seemed everyone had decided to have the same off day.

I apologised afterwards but reiterated that in these last few games there were going to be games where we had to dictate and be in control. In most matches, we had chased the game, or they had been nip and tuck, and we knew how to play that way. We had to learn very quickly how to play on the front foot, how to dictate games when teams were weaker than us. I had spent the season telling players: *"Stop the cross"* but I bloody wished I hadn't stopped that one, as there was no-one in the box anyway. I didn't say that out loud, did I? They were becoming my bogey team, so it's a good job I'm not superstitious, eh!

You hear of a run of bad luck, but to be honest I don't think I had ever really suffered one. Or at least, I didn't. Our next game was another 'should win' against Holmer Green who were second from bottom. Collectively the previous game we had been poor, but I had to keep faith with the XI (no cry-offs permitting), it was at our place and it could be a game to get ourselves back on track. For forty-four minutes we were played off the park and we were losing 1-2. Then, Petty missed an opportunity to 'take one for the team' with a foul on halfway, as they broke forward and it left me exposed. It's normally a split-second thing, I'd block the runner, hold my hands up and take the booking. The problem was that I had a couple of seconds to think and my body position instead of being upright was sort of lowering. Contact made, we both crumpled to the floor, their players surrounding the referee baying for all sorts. I really thought nothing of it, it was a booking that I had received a hundred times before. The referee shoed their players away and consulted his assistant. The same one I'd been having a bit of banter with, about his silver boots and his tight shorts. He obviously lacked a sense of humour as following their chat, the referee sent me off.

Half time was a bit surreal as I tried to build the lads up and get them re-focussed on the game and I hoped, push on for a win. All I really wanted to do was shout and curse about the sending off and what lead up to it. What made it worse was that for the first time all season, I had no centre half cover on the field or on the bench. On came Martin Flannery, a holding midfielder, to play alongside George. I'd sacrificed two of three midfielders to go 4-3-2 and chase the game.

The second half started and within about ten minutes, we were level and had them reeling! In fact, they were on the back foot for the remainder of the game aside from a couple of breaks, then we had (and failed to take) a gilt-edge chance at the death to win it. It had been very strange, as I wasn't allowed on bench for the second period, so I bellowed out my instructions from the stand all of five feet from the dug-out. I had to get used to that, as a three-game ban was on the cards!

The changes had worked even though we only got a draw, but I'd upset Luke and Tyronne at half-time with the changes, so I had to apologise to them. It was probably made easier as we had got a point back from a losing position, but it was a tough call all round. I know I wouldn't have been happy either. I drove home, hoping that bad luck really didn't come in threes.

After another break for bad weather followed by a decent friendly draw with landlords, Hendon, we were off to Wembley. Don't get too excited – it was Vale Farm, home of Wembley FC and a place I like going to for the nostalgia value. It's a ground and team that I have come up against almost every season of my career and without fail, a visit brings up memories of previous encounters, but they haven't always been successful.

A few changes in personnel meant a 4-1-3-2 formation and that just showed that for forty-five minutes, we couldn't adapt. It was only thanks to Alfie Bonfield in goal that we were only one down. It meant another tough call at half time as I had to change the shape and give us some width. After discussing it with Hector we pulled Luke (again) and Mikkel, bringing on Ethan who was back from university and Christian Londones and we switched Lolu through the centre. We instantly looked more comfortable but without threatening until Alfie gave us a lifeline with another fine save. Almost straight after, we went up the other end and Lolu equalised. It became a very open game and it was obvious next goal would win. And so, it proved as Lolu scored his second to seal a win for us. We needed that win and you could see the relief in both the players and management, but on entering the bar, Lolu told me to me look at my phone. I saw a message that Luke Durnin had left our WhatsApp group. I'd seen him leave the ground as soon as he was changed after the substitution, but I didn't pay much attention as we had a game to win. Once again, I'd apologised for making the changes and Mikkel came out and sat on the bench for the second half. Chalk and cheese attitudes again. I tried to call Luke on the way home but to no avail, though to be fair he did eventually get back to me. I explained to him that I felt I'd played him in a system that should have suited him with legs in and around him in midfield. Even by Luke's own admission he isn't the fittest and I also mentioned that I wanted to make things up to him somewhat for being taken off in the previous game. It was supposed to be his chance to prove me wrong as was the most technically gifted player in the squad by a mile, but if he didn't get the ball or was chasing for it, we had to change tactics. He insisted that it was personal and not tactical, so I asked why he thought it was personal when he was, beside me, our longest serving player. He said: *"It felt muggy"*, he felt I was mugging him off, but I tried to explain again that it was purely tactical. The conversation petered out as I told him he needed to be mentally stronger to cope with these situations and he said he needed time out to think about what he was going to do.

I have been in similar situations before and I hoped that in time, he would see that he wasn't mugged off as he thought. He may even realise that in that forty-five minutes, he was the poorest of a poor bunch. We had to change it. I hoped that time would be that great healer.

It really was getting to the last few games, all coming thick and fast as we made up for previous postponements. It was difficult keeping everyone focused as we had nothing to play for other than disrupting others' plans. It showed versus Hadley at home, as we were flat all round, lost 1-0, and without really making a chance in the game. Two games the following week meant a chance for everyone to be involved at least once and that was how we set out our stall, those not involved on the Tuesday would play on the Thursday. The match against London Tigers, a fixture reversed and played at our ground as theirs was unfit, was the first in a while where we started well and took an early lead. That signalled a real end to end tussle until we nicked another goal just before half time. Looking to build on our lead in the second half, we managed to concede one from a shot from about forty yards which moved and deceived Alfie in goal, but rather than sitting back, we continued to play until the last minute. With me having palpitations on the line, Tigers broke forward and Alfie produced an excellent save to protect our lead and the win. A win but once again the clean sheet eluded us, but it meant fifty points in the bank with four to play. What we didn't know was that the weather would turn again overnight and Thursday's match would be postponed. It meant three games, all away in the following week to look forward to, and a few players a bit miffed that they'd missed out on the Tuesday and now couldn't play on the Thursday. Suddenly, the weather was my bloody fault as well.

Three games in a week started away to Biggleswade on a balmy Tuesday evening, a match played at Langford FC. They had dicked us at home and I didn't want a repeat. For thirty-five minutes we were fine then we conceded and looked poor. Second half we should have had a penalty that may have put us level, but it wasn't given. We also conceded another to lose 2-0. That should have been the end of it. I had learned my lesson and wasn't going to seek out the referee to question why we didn't get a decision that could have changed the game. Then as I was towards the dressing room, there he was. I bit my lip.

No, I didn't. I veered towards the referee and his assistant. I wasn't shouting or gesticulating but I raised a point or two. I felt I was met with a smug arrogance in response to a simple question and I got a bit of red mist I suppose. I kept walking and apparently, he sent me off. My back was turned, but I heard a word or two, the last of which was: "Off". I really didn't hear the rest. Twenty yards. That was all I had to walk. If 'd kept going it would have taken no more than five seconds. I didn't, I collected another three-game ban, two of which would be held over to the following season.

I did regret it, but although the referee and his assistants deserved respect, sometimes it does have to be a two-way street. I'm not the only passionate player or manager around, but rarely does that seem to be considered when what seems to be an unjust decision is made and the cards start flying. I chalked it up as a lesson learned, but it wasn't my last of the week. The Thursday saw a much-changed side as we played Holmer Green in the most lack-lustre match of the season. In the first half we were on top but failed to create a meaningful chance then in the second half we were completely off the pace. I was playing and was growing increasingly frustrated by the poor performance, yelling at whoever was in my sights as I tried to fire my players up. Then, with ten to go I conceded a silly free kick in a not too dangerous position. The kick was played in and Ryan Carruthers misjudged the flight, sending his header straight into our net. He's shown a great attitude most of the year and didn't deserve, shall we say, the feedback I gave him as the ball flew in. He hadn't meant it and to be fair, nor had I. It was just an outpouring of frustration and a little anger at myself. Fair play to him at the Presentation Evening, we had a good laugh about it in front of the lads as they took the piss out of me really for being Mr Angry. I'm sure I was channelling Georgie Talbot! A massive rant and rave at the time, but when it's all calmed down we have a good laugh. I tip my hat to Ryan for getting on with it and ignoring my stupid misplaced comments. And RIP George.

We didn't have time to dwell on it as we had another game on the Saturday, away to Tring Athletic, managed by Ian Richardson. The former Watford winger is someone I've got to know over the years and has become a friend. He is also just about the only manager in the league I can say that about funnily enough. I was wary that Tring might be a wounded animal after the awesome display we'd put in against them previously, even though that was a performance level that we had got nowhere near since. Rotation and unavailability's meant Myself, Burgo and Dennis all started to up the average age and typical of us, we didn't get out of the traps until we were one behind, but we got back on level terms before half time and then dictated the second half without threatening, while Greg Marsh in goal kept us in the game. The only other positive of note was that we drew and gained another point.

Clean sheet syndrome was still in full flow. I thought then that if we are to improve in future season, the first thing is that we must start keeping clean sheets. There's a running joke in the dressing room that if you could bet on us at this level, you would be quids in every week on the 'both teams to score' coupon. In all seriousness, we don't defend that badly, but we always seem to suffer the ultimate punishment for any error. We need to learn to love to defend as a unit and we need everyone to be the someone who puts their body in the way of the ball, having that desire to stop the ball at whatever cost. I used to know a bloke who would do that...

As we had played three games in five days and we had nothing to play for in our final match, Hector and I decided to give the lads the midweek off and we told the whole squad to report for the last game of the season at home v Berkhamsted. Especially as we had the Presentation Evening planned for that night. I wanted everyone there as I wanted to thank them all for their efforts during season. It meant three or four wouldn't get a game which seemed a bit harsh, but it was the first time I'd asked players not involved to attend. If they did, that was great but if not, I couldn't really hold it against them. On to matchday and what happened? Out of squad of twenty-one, I only had sixteen available.

I had everyone in the dressing room for my last team talk of the season, and I thanked the players for giving me their all throughout. I said I'd hoped that they had enjoyed the season and learnt a bit along the way. I also said we had a game to play and I wanted to go out on a high. Berkhamsted needed a point to guarantee their promotion and it was our perfect moment to wee on their parade. My mentality, right or wrong is, if you can't get success yourself try and stop others enjoying it, especially on your patch. It was a motto we had at Uxbridge as a perennial mid-table side. We used to love the opportunity!

True to form, the lads took the team talk to heart and went out fired up. Fired up enough to go three down in fifteen minutes, and if Bomber in goal hadn't been on his game it could have been six by half time. The half time team talk was damage imitation, not wanting to leave a sour taste etc. Trying to be positive I said they were vulnerable at the back and we should try and get at them. Don't be kidded here. This dressing room was like any other. The players weren't looking down as they were full of guilt, taking a moment on their own to re-focus ready for the second half. They were just like any other dressing room: Don't make eye contact then you don't get bawled out, they were thinking of their evening ahead, having a beer with their mates, looking forward to seeing their girlfriends, booking holidays, all that sort of thing. In truth I doubt many would even remember what I said by the time they were back on the field.

Ten minutes into the second half, we brought on Mikkel, and within minutes he got at the vulnerable defence and pulled one back. Twenty-five to go and we brought on Tyronne. Ten minutes later he put in a great cross for Dan Pett to score. Game on for the last fifteen minutes of the season!

Berko manage to hang on and get the points needed to secure promotion after a second half that was almost an epitaph for our year: Full of energy and a never say die spirit but just not quite good enough. We had to chase the game and it became mentally and physically exhausting doing it week in, week out.

Fair play to my 'Young Lions' though. With a little more steel and aggression mixed with the attributes they already have, they will only improve. As a manager, I couldn't ask anymore from my players, many who had just completed their first season at senior level. I was grateful, and I tipped my hat to each and every one that played a part, big or small in the foetal stage of my management career. The players to their credit had to hang around in the bar as Berko celebrated their promotion (which was a little grating), but it also may have given one or two an insight to what success for them may mean in the future. It delayed our presentations a bit, but hey, we'd have done the same if the positions had been reversed.

One big regret of the season had been not being able to get players to bond socially. This is a different generation of players, not all like a drink or to socialise after game. Maybe those player's fines would have given us a night out and a bit more bonding, but honestly, it was hard enough managing the side. Next year maybe. An example was that presentation evening. The committee very kindly put up a tab for the lads to have a few drinks over the evening. I went to bar about an hour and a half after the presentations and the tab was still going. It wasn't the amount in the tab that kept it going it was that most of the lads weren't drinking... not even Lucozade (other sport drinks are available). I thought back to my Yeading, Uxbridge, Wealdstone and Hemel days. That tab would have been destroyed in minutes, and by the way, Bomber and I weren't 'in the round' that night.

The presentations started with Dan and Anthony saying a few words, then I took over. I could hardly speak as my throat was hoarse, but I had a speech prepared and duly carried on with it despite some heckling, from Bomber in the main. I thanked everyone involved and told them that I'd given everything I could. I also said that I'd made mistakes along the way and, just like in my career and this book, if I'd upset anyone, I hoped they would accept my apologies. I went back over a few highlights and a few stats, especially on the young players that I'd got into the side, which I'm proud of, and my first Managers Speech was concluded by reminding players of the two points I had stressed every game; take a high foul and stop the cross, both things I'd been penalised for as the season reached its end!

My two goals were to better the previous season's finish and I wanted the players that played for me to enjoy it. I had achieved my first goal and I left it to those same players to decide if I had achieved the second.

Dan Pett. My skipper in midfield deservedly got Players Player of Year and Supporters Player of the Year, Omalolu Omabolu (Lolu) won Top Goal scorer and Managers Player of the Year having come from nowhere in preseason and Rio Beech won Young Player of the Year in a season where I had played him in nearly every position bar goalie. Not once had he complained. I thought that wrapped up the awards on the night, until Dan and Anthony called me back, to present me with the David Allbone Award, named after a long-time supporter. It was a merit award, presented to the 'Clubman', someone who in their eyes had done a great deal for the club over the year. It was the first time that the award had been presented and I remain extremely proud to have received it.

Our season done, a few knocks and a few kicks and a few lessons learned, but I left that night looking forward to the summer. I'd watch a few games and am extremely jealous as I write this on the day my old club, my local club, Boreham Wood go to Wembley for a chance to play in the football league. Unbelievable! I wish nothing but Good Luck to my pal Luke Garrard the manager, and Chairman Danny Hunter, who has played a massive part in taking the club from Division One North (level eight of the pyramid) when I was there, to a match just ninety minutes from the Football League. A remarkable achievement all round. Perhaps a fitting reminder that teams always do better without me!

(As it happened, Boreham Wood missed out on the day. Maybe next year).

EPILOGUE

Nothing can prepare you for management at this level. Higher up it may be easier and hopefully I will find out in time. At least at the level above you are not worrying about kit being delivered on time, getting players signed on, pumping up balls and making sure you have enough etc. Basically, the infrastructure is better, and you are able to concentrate on just managing the club on pitch, not constantly worrying about off field stuff. My remit to both Julian and Enda was to make sure we got things right on the pitch and hopefully things off the pitch would look after themselves. I pre-warned them that for whatever reason things were not right behind the scenes at Edgware, so I didn't tell any lies. The people are genuine nice people and are all volunteers so do it all for the love of the club, and they would be the first to admit that they are first supporters of club and second Committee members, which in itself is admirable. The club wouldn't exist without these people. What I have also told them, and they accept, is that they need someone on board with experience what's needed to progress. Wheels are in motion, I believe...

As the season went on without Julian and Enda, myself and Hector saw it through, though I was on my own for about three months. People in the game found it hard to believe that I'd done it on my own at this level for that period of time, but what else could I do? Resign? As you've read, I did think about it a few times over the course of the season. For me, the times when we lost were the hardest and not having anyone to bounce off made things very lonely, and me isolated. Small fry in comparison to what happens in the world day to day, but when I'm in that mode nothing hurts more in life than a defeat. My only cure is a victory and just as easily, that would turn my whole world around. It's something I must learn from, not so much the winning because to be honest that was more relief than jubilation, but I have to leave the defeat at the ground sometimes. I can look for positives and address the issues when I get the squad back together, but I can't let it eat away at me, or take away the faith I should have in myself. I know I'll lose matches no matter how good or successful we are, I just need to accept that as part of the game and do what I can to ensure those defeats get further and further apart!

In the main, in my first season, I've been delighted and, in some cases, proud that my team has given their all, even in defeat. It's all I could ask of them. Only on a couple of occasions did they feel the wrath, and then I think even they knew it was the right time. I'm not one to go ballistic for any reason however passionate I am. With the current genre of players, you can't rant and rave all the time, so you must be positive. It's how I try to be. If things maybe are not right at half-time and I think it's best not to rant, I'd set them a challenge for the second half to try and keep things positive, for example, if we had zero shots in the first half, I would set the ultimate challenge of trying to have at least one in the second. It's a little bit tongue in cheek but I hope it's a positive way of trying to get something out of them without blowing my top.

The way the season has gone could work out well for me as I look ahead. It's only been one season, but I feel I've experienced about twenty years' worth of problems. When I recently rang Gordon Bartlett for a chat and to update him on how things were progressing for me, he mentioned that the issues that I'd encountered over the season had only happened to him over the course of his twenty-five years as a manager. Perhaps it'll get easier from here on, but I know there is a lot to learn and I have more pitfalls to overcome on the rollercoaster journey of player management. That word, player will keep me going... for now. I don't know who wrote this originally and it appears in several places online, but I think it remains a sound piece of advice to any player and competitor, especially on those 'down' days:

"One day you won't be an athlete anymore.
You won't have those long bus rides with your teammates.
You won't have those bruises all over your body.
You won't have that routine you do before every game.
Your teammates will become distant and your laughs will become limited.
Eventually, the one thing you looked forward to, will come to an end.
The one thing you relied on to relieve your stress and allow you to escape
from your problems won't always be there.
One, day, you won't be an athlete, you'll just have the memories of one..."

Everything that you have read really happened over the last almost thirty years in my career. I may have left out or changed a name or two to protect the innocent (guilty, mainly), but it happened. I, Fergus Moore was there, and I've enjoyed it all. I've played in front of a couple of thousand and I've played (and managed) in front of one man and his dog (more often).

And sometimes the dog was busy...

DRAMATIS PERSONAE

You'll have noticed that several my former teammates, Managers and current players appear in the text of this book, but there are many others that deserve a mention. Every one of them is a great lad and has earned their right to be catalogued, and to take their place among the characters that make up the non-league game, my career and for a long time yet to come I hope, my memories. Please doff your cap as I briefly introduce in no particular order:

Ken Batten	An Edgware man through and through. Part of the club it seems forever, and now Club President. It's great to see his beaming smile on a match day. Just a football loving man who doesn't get involved with the political in-fighting that you can get at clubs. Even when going through bad times Ken has always backed players and never once have I heard him say a bad word against any player. He absolutely loves Edgware Town FC and football would be a much greater place if the game was full of Ken Battens. A true gentleman too.
Dan Pett	My skipper. He has got an everlasting engine and loves a goal from midfield. I could not have asked more from him as a captain and a person, not a bawler on pitch but the ultimate lead by example skipper. An inspired choice of captain and he gets me and knows what I want. He oozes class!
Omalolu Omabolu (Lolu)	Top goal scorer and Managers Player of the Year. Lolu came from nowhere in preseason and would be our talisman for the season. His goals were vital to us and without them we would have been in trouble. A character, he only just beat me to the most yellow cards of season award!
Rio Beech	Young Player of the Year. I played Rio in every position bar goalie this year and not once had he complained. I say that because he literally does not talk. He is so shy it's unbelievable. You would have thought if you were on the pitch you would open your mouth to receive a pass... not our Rio. Kicked all over the pitch at times, but just dusts himself down and gets on with the game.
Sam Styles	Far too good looking to be a keeper. Very agile great technique with his kicks but he's a bit OCD – takes him ages to get ready, taping up all his fingers, strapping this and that. Twenty minutes to get his kit on and another twenty to warm up... And he can come off the pitch with his bloody kit pristine. He's one for the superstitions, his own water bottle, the same routine, kit perfectly laid out.
Alfie Bonfield	Son of Bomber, another keeper who's done well. Not as big as his dad but

he can get around the box, another with good technique and it was great to see Bomber as proud as punch watching Alfie when he made his full debut.

Mark Blackburne (Bazza)	I've played with the three brothers, Mark, Robbie and Stuart, all now in their 30's and all part of my Dad's army in the league. Mark is a great lad who laughs at himself but takes everything in good heart. I just wish he'd turn up a bit more often. Right up there for nonsense value.
Olu Quadri	One of the only survivors when Rochey and Fab moved to Edgware. Plays right back but also has a game in midfield, he's a dead ringer for Patrick Truman from EastEnders which got him a nick-name. Good legs and if he can get his head right, he'll be OK. Always smiling too.
Nick Turner	Joined us from Northwood and still lets us know he was doing us a favour as he'd come from a higher level. He's played at the back and turned into a bit of a goal scoring machine, twenty games, fifteen or so at RB scored seven or eight. Unusually well-educated for a NL player and a nice guy, his experience helps too.
Mayo Balogun	You get a bit wary when players are turn-ups, but he's a strong lad with a good tackle, he got into the side for his chance and did well, made the spot his own. He's very strongly supported by his mum on the side-lines, but fair play, she cheers on the team, not just her son!
Glen Parry	Played at a higher level and with me at Hemel years ago, was out of the game for a while and has managed as well. Made a comeback to help us out a couple of years ago and he stuck. Never bloody trained, never there every week, he gave Rochey someone else to bounce an idea off...
Craig McKay (Gio)	A great lad with bags of ability that fell out of love with the game. Only 29 or 30, he trains like a sixty-year-old which might explain why he's down here with us. He and I have got a bit of a sixth sense thing going on, so we get on well on and off the field except when he's tipping winners. He's also happy to wind anyone up on or off the field at any time.
Richard Morton (Morts)	A former Wealdstone team mate who has dodgy knees, but was a goal scoring midfielder, strong in the air, richest player in the squad, we called him Sir Morton, always in Switzerland or somewhere on business. 100% player, scored vital goals as well. Not as mobile as he once was.
Bilal Butt (Bilzy)	International England Futsal player. When he's got the right head on he can be unbelievable, tall, elegant silky skilful always wants the ball. A powerful runner and a great knack of right place right time, quick feet and loves a curled shot. Problem is he expects to play all the time, but he never trains. Passionate about his goals, never thinks he's had a good game if he hasn't scored.

230

Lee Inch (Inchy)	Inchy, by name and size. Been around for ages It seems got described as a great squad player and took offence – it wasn't meant like that! Good on the ball, had great banter with Gio which was fun for all around, just a bright bubbly character good to keep the spirits up. Got torn a new arsehole at left back by James Brophy in a friendly against Belstone and he had nightmares about that for weeks. James went on to sign for Swindon Town, so no surprise there.
Luke Durnin	He's half my bloody age. I was playing before he was born. A decent player but he sulks like a big kid if things don't go his way. He could make a step up, but he needs to believe it. And he needs to wake up a bit in the car. He's always got a cold or the flu. He had the flu so long the Physio kept a chest rub and a nasal spray in the box for him.
Paul Marks (Marksie)	My best mate in the team, we've known each other years, older (30+) but fresh faced, out of the tackles he would time seven so well, taking the ball, the man everything, tenacious, all action player and like me always wants to play and win. Gees everyone up too. He's a horrible opponent as he's always in your face niggling, but off the pitch, great. Can't drink soup on a night out. Two coronas and he's all over the place... Great mate. Till he left. Bastard. Just re-signed for the 18-19 season. Not a bastard anymore.
Jack Cook (Cookie)	Age? about 12 (it's all relative, isn't it?) Apparently, this boy is at university to continue his education. F**k knows how. He doesn't strike me as very intelligent at all. Maybe his parents should stop wasting their money, I reckon it's a lost cause trying to give this lad brains, but on a football pitch, top notch. He's filled in at almost every position and he's capable in all of them. 6'3" tall and about three stone wet, the butt of many jokes, we miss him when he's not around.
Vince Rispoli (Steady Eddie)	Vince is a left back that I've known for longer than most people play the game! He's the only guy I know who can do pre-season in four layers of training gear and still not lose weight. Like a lot of non-league players, on a cold wet Tuesday night after an away game, he does seem to have shares in the local Mackie D's which probably doesn't help.
Dennis Marharjan	In some teams you get the star player who can do what he likes and get away with it. We've got Dennis. Next in line in seniority at thirty-six (I think), they obviously think more of him than me because he's never played ninety minutes in his life. He disappears so often on the hour you can set a bloody clock by him. Decent lad and adds flair to the side when he's around, but he thinks we only play on Saturdays. Constantly reminds us that he scored the Edgware goal that appeared on the BBC.
Ben Hammond	Ben is a modern-day mix of Del Boy, Rodney and Stig of the Dump. Every club has someone who is forever trying to scam the next quid from

231

someone, somewhere. Trouble is, with Rodney's brains behind the scheme, I doubt even Del Boy would fall for most of them. Loves a T-shirt and (nearly) Adidas trainers, but he's a great wide man on the pitch. Loves to tell us about when he was a pro under Barry Fry, which probably took its toll on previous managers who may have released him just to get some peace and quiet!

Lasalle Simon	Broke into the Cockfosters side from the stiffs. He's a midfield enforcer and when you realise that outside the game he's a well-respected and successful Cage Fighter, believe me I wouldn't be taking the p*ss too often. In one game he really did say to an opponent *"I have to warn you by law to stop now as I will hurt you"*. I nearly wet myself, but he'd given fair warning to cover himself. And he can play.
Stuart Blackburne (Stuey)	Another that has played at a higher level and probably still could if he got his arse into gear and sorted out his work-life. He's not the biggest centre forward but leaps like a salmon, often causing centre halves to have nightmares, but you always hope he doesn't have time to think on the ball.
Darren Bonfield (Bomber)	A real gentle giant, if he had possessed an appetite for the game like he does a beer he would have been up for the Ballon d'Or. He just lacked that little bit of nastiness in his earlier days that could have got him higher up the ladder. Being the person that he is I don't think he regrets much, he's just enjoyed what he achieved. He can sometimes be seen still between the sticks for me at Edgware but can always be seen with me at the bar! He's my only drinking pal at the club in this generation of Lucozade guzzlers!
Emond Protain	What a handful as a forward and he made his name as a full back! Could leap like salmon and was mustard attacking the ball. Scored bundles of goals and his hold up play was top notch.
Lee Walker (Walks)	Doesn't give a damn. A real talent in the art of influencing people! None more so than at my wedding when he instigated LAMBY and others at his table to stop the video camera from rolling hence missing important parts of the reception! In many years' service to the game I think I can genuinely say that he is a "one off". You meet with so many varied characters, but Walks has just got his own unique way. I remember him randomly during a home Wealdstone game at the White Lion carrying out a spice girls survey. He asked every fan in earshot who their favourite Spice Girl was!
Steve Newing	A good friend to this day, but far too busy for my liking. Never knew a bloke with so much hatred for a club (Wealdstone) but when the opportunity arose to earn a few shillings to be part of Gordon Bartlett's coaching team, he couldn't get there quick enough! A legend at Edgware and rightly so for the games he played, and the goals he scored for them.

Gordon Bartlett **(Gaffer)**	How is he out of work after more than 22 years at Wealdstone! Shows what a cruel game it can be. My football father over the years, he gets me, and many don't. He never held my passion against me, he knew it was real and saw the fire in my belly. Privileged to be his friend all these years even though we've had our ups and downs, another true gentleman and someone who almost single handedly put Wealdstone back on the footballing map...
Paul Sweales **(Swealsy)**	An absolute diamond, sadly, taken away from us with cancer a few years ago but fondly remembered by all. The nicest funniest guy you ever come across off the pitch but on it he was a changed man. Early in my non-league career at Yeading, he would often be seen within minutes of games finishing, leaving without showering. When we asked him once why he was going so quickly, he responded: *"I offered out their goalkeeper during the game, he's a f*cking big lump and I ain't hanging around to see if he takes me up on my offer"*. Typical Swealsy! RIP mate!
Joe Gadstone	We clicked straight away when he took over from Colin Lee at Brentford in my 2nd year of YTS. He believed in me as a player and could see something in me, if only I could have had that much confidence in myself! He helped me get a full-time job when I left Brentford due to his contacts outside the game. A lovely man who made me a better player and person in the short time I worked with him.
Paul Lamb **(Lamby)**	Lamby came to Wealdstone later than Walks but two became three as we clicked straight away. The dynamics were that Walks would get Lamby to side with him and proceed to try and hammer me with insults and jibes. Lamby loved this and between the three of us it worked well on and off the field. We shared great times often going up to Lamby's home town of Northampton and carrying on our booze filled banter much to the bemusement of the locals. He's a tough cookie who has battled through personal and family tragedies, but he always pulls through and gives his life to his boy Harry. I will be forever grateful again to have shared not only a football friendship with Lamby but a forever friendship outside of football.
George Talbot **(Talby)**	George was a manager who has had a profound effect on my whole life. George would be like your favourite uncle, an outstanding character and totally off his rocker as a manager and person. What other manager do you know that tried to injure you in training? What other do you know wants to give you and your mates a good hiding? Talby! Underneath the tough exterior George had a wonderful heart, a bit like me he let his emotions run away with him sometimes but when he realised, he'd see the funny side and he always laughed it off. Even after I left Uxbridge I used to go on their end of season trips to Blackpool such was the need to be back in Talby's company as he would keep the whole group (and others who wanted to join in) entertained with his antics, which normally

consisted of getting on a microphone and telling a few jokes at my expense followed by his version of Frankie Bennett's San Francisco. When he passed away after a fight with illness I was devastated. I like many others at his funeral took comfort from the fact that we had had the pleasure of knowing him and that helped with our pain. A truly special man who will always be in my heart♡ PS we share the same birthday does that mean we share the same traits?

Michael Roche (Rochey)	My regular booze binging partner back in the day who became my manager. I never saw management in the guy, but he did a fantastic job at Cockfosters and Edgware. We were all mates in team, but he managed us well and we kept on winning. We had our occasional bust ups, but he was one who could see past the tantrums and see my value to team and youngsters breaking through. It was a shame that personal reasons took him away from the game as I could do with him now as I look to get the winning formula he had...
Gerry Crawford	A relative latecomer to our Uxbridge gang but nonetheless he became an integral part of us not only on pitch but more importantly off it. A very intelligent man which is something you cannot often say in non-league, a father figure, he always had words of wisdom even if sometimes us mere thickos couldn't understand! He was a calming influence on and off pitch, because if we were getting a bit boisterous or loud on an Uxbridge night out Gerry would be the one to tell us to calm down. I'd have loved to see him play in his prime.
Troy Birch and Lee Hanratty	Mentioned together as they were inseparable in the Uxbridge days. The Terrible Twins, always up to harmless mischief, generally made worse by the barrel loads of beer that was being drunk. These two were childhood pals who basically never grew up. Tours with them in tow were always going to be messy, but they were fabulous characters who added to the lives of those around them. I haven't mentioned their footballing ability (both decent), their social abilities were Premier League status!
Sean Dawson	The smallest goalkeeper I played with but probably up there with one of the best. He'd played millions of games before I got to Uxbridge and a million after so a true club stalwart in every sense, he's also a top-class bloke who also loved a beer or three. The back-pass rule was probably the end of his career – his shot stopping wasn't in doubt, but kicking wasn't his game. We would avoid passing back to Sean at all costs when the rule came in, much to his dismay, but to his teammates, it was their way to wind him up. That we did, and good fun was had! Another great one to have in your touring team!
Paul McCluskey (Macca)	Whichever route I may have had back into the professional game from non-league was ended the minute this man arrived at Uxbridge FC. I knew

him a little as both our fathers were publicans. He signed for Uxbridge, we got chatting and that was it. He didn't drive so I was to be his chauffeur for the next however many years. My one drink after games went out the window as I was made to wait by Macca as he finished his 5th or 6th pint. He's a very persuasive type and after leaving Uxbridge and getting back nearer to home, our nights would carry on till the early hours. After a win, a Sunday lunchtime session would be called for as well. How wives Hayley and Donna ever put up with us, I don't know. He's local so our families still see a lot of each other and he is someone I still confide in. My footballing big brother.

Gary Downes (Downsey)	The best goal scoring centre half I've played with, who would score 8-10 goals a season from set pieces and could also score from the spot. My hero as he looked after me on me pitch (without the bully boy antics of Macca). He was a great leader, but he also loved a beer, though his humour was much drier than everyone else's. It was normally me that would be the butt of his jokes because I was the youngest out of that bunch, and probably the likeliest to have a nibble back at one of his remarks. A genuine and honest guy who still looks out for me and is always trying to get the old Uxbridge boys back together for a social. Another that has become a lifetime friend who I will always look up to.
Steve Bircham (Powders)	A greatly underestimated player in our successful Wealdstone team but he was plagued by back injuries. Never had a problem though carrying his wage packet... He loved a beer and a gamble and was truly one of the lads and a damned good player with it. He made us tick with his range of passing and set piece deliveries, if only he could have stayed fit or kept out of the bookies!
Bryan Hammett	A proven goal scorer at whatever level he played. We played at various clubs together and Bryan would always be a good mixer and bring his humour to the party. A hard-working centre forward with a passion for the game, he also had a zero-tolerance level to any stick that was given to him either by fans or players. Bryan would not think twice to voice back his opinion to others who had voiced theirs to him! A quality I liked in him and which he showed on the pitch. He's one of those who as soon as the game had finished would put the ball away and not talk about it, (unlike me). Numerous times he would tell me to bugger off as I tried to right the wrongs of the game just gone. It fell on deaf ears as far as Bryan was concerned!
Paul McKay (Macca)	The little quiet lad from Burnley. What a gifted player in many different positions and the unsung hero of that Wealdstone era. A shy unassuming lad, but once out of his shell he was always great to be around. So calm, nothing ever phased him either on or off field and he would team up with Walker, Lamb et al to take p*ss out of me, but when it deflected back onto him, he would join in just as enthusiastically. He wasn't much of a

drinker to be fair and when we took him to Blackpool on one tour it definitely took its toll on him... A great mixer and someone who loved Wealdstone and what it was about. We both had access to good old fax machines while we were at work in those days, and he was a great artist who would draw caricatures of the players at Wealdstone at the time - they were hilarious! He was a very funny guy who added great dynamics to that team!

Chris Walton (Walts)	The little magician! He was perhaps (apart from me) one of Gordon's best signings who joined in the twilight of his career but proved an asset to the team for longer than many thought. He was composed on the ball and scored a few important goals as well as being very fit (for his age). He brought, along with his good pal Roy Marshall, the experience factor. Walts was a great example to all us young lads and the only bad thing I could say against him was he had a bloody annoying squeaky voice when he was shouting. I teamed up with him again when he became coach at Hemel. One thing you may not know was that he liked a sneaky beer or five, even though he portrayed himself as a do-gooder.
Roy Marshall	Another astute signing by Gordon as Roy had played at a higher level, mainly at Hayes FC. I forget what I said about Roy when I presented him with his Player of the Year trophy after we won the league, but it must have been something like he's a man mountain and a legend. The quiet assassin, he wouldn't talk about nailing someone, he would just do it, and normally got away with it. He was formidable that season and I learnt a lot from him. He was a lovely fella as well who I got along with and we made a great combination.
Simon Garner (Garns)	Wow, what a bloke! Can't speak highly enough of this fella! Came to Wealdstone and mesmerised both players and fans with his skill and his appetite for the game. Surprisingly, he hadn't won a title in the pro game, so he was just as delighted as anyone when we won the league. He's a very humble person who also liked being one of the lads, another who amused himself by trying to give me loads of stick. How can I forget him leaving his false teeth on my bed when we twinned up in a room in Northampton on a team jolly? A master; Mr Garner I tip my hat to you!
Dominic Sterling	The guy who ended my first spell at Wealdstone! He was quicker than me, he was just as good in air, he was left footed, aggressive, tough tackling... I couldn't really argue with that could I? I played my part in his progression as I was his babysitter at left wing back. He took to the position like a duck to water and that was me done! In a way I didn't mind because he was a lovely kid who went onto play at a higher level, and deservedly so.
Brian Jones (Jonah)	Madcap! He has got a screw loose (probably more than one) somewhere. A nutjob! These descriptions don't do him justice. We played in a Legends

236

match for Wealdstone v Watford and he even started a fight in that, but what a player. He had bags and bags of skill to go along with all the verbals. I don't think I have ever seen in all my time, a player takes the amount of beatings he did on the pitch. Did he learn his lesson? Did he heck! He more than earned his place in Wealdstone folklore, even though he only played there for a few seasons. A unique mercurial character and someone who I enjoyed immensely being around!

Martin Carter (Carts)	A quiet unassuming lad unless you met up with him in Watford on a Friday or Saturday night. He could and would play anywhere equally well. A real unsung hero to many at Wealdstone as he went about his business. Another great signing at the time, and another that got the club and still pops down to support them!
Richard McDonagh	A funny little sod! It took a while to get used to his humour, but he certainly is a great character. A nasty little bugger at times on the pitch but he had a touch of class as well. His fiery temperament probably cost him a longer career at the 'Stones as he would always have a bite back at the fans, but you know what, he probably doesn't regret a thing!
Dave Boggins (Boggy)	What a man! He's probably the most misunderstood man in non-league football. Basically, a Chairman who supports his club (Hemel Hempstead Town) fanatically, so he lets his heart rule his head more often than not. He has a better back up team now than when I was at the club, so it pleases me to see him and Hemel do well. He's always up for a laugh and we certainly had loads of them. Apart from his silly hats and dodgy clobber he is a fantastic bloke.
Tony Kelly	My type of player. An out and out winner. As tough as they come and sometimes, (ok more often than not), he stepped over the line of competitiveness. I would have loved to have played in a team with him in his prime and he loved a beer as well. A perfect fit. I don't think he was suited to management as he would want to be on pitch sorting things out and probably seeking retribution for every foul. Beneath his tough exterior, he was a soft cookie really!
Frank O'Brien	I first met Frank when he coached my brothers under 11 team in about 1980, since then we joined forces at Wealdstone but then Frank went big time! He got a job coaching at Chelsea School of Excellence and within a year or so became full time and still is to this day. For someone who always wanted to shy away from the limelight he is seen forever on Facebook now showing off who he has coached or coached with at a UEFA course of some sort, but I'm very grateful that he was willing to help me out taking a few sessions last year at Edgware and they were absolutely terrific. I genuinely appreciate his friendship and guidance and the fact that he will go out of his way to help me. I need it!

Josh Price	A reoccurring feature here but not only a very gifted footballer but also very funny. He had a great midfielder's knack of scoring goals, some very spectacular and he was always at the heart of all the banter which was often borderline abuse. There was never a dull moment in his company!
Lee Thomas and Marcelle Bruce	I've put them together because they are another two that were inseparable, they even married sisters, and so spent a lot of time together. Playing alongside them was perhaps the best defensive trio I played in. We kept clean sheets for fun the year we won the title with Hemel. It was made even more amazing as these two would always be at the Friday Club establishments around town. We complimented each other on the pitch perfectly, Marce sweeping up with his electric pace, me giving us balance on left side with a bit of aerial prowess and Lee (Tiggy) with his magnificent reading of the game. A big fella, he wasn't bad with his feet for a big man. I didn't really appreciate it at the time, but if you don't mind me saying so myself, we were awesome!!
Jermaine Beckford (Becks)	At least he can say he had the pleasure of making his senior debut alongside me...or should that be me saying that about him? He made his debut versus Staines for Wealdstone and you could see his talent then! He's also a lovely kid who climbed the football ladder and scored goals wherever he played, when he remembered his boots! Fair play to him.
Andy Carter (Carts)	I persuaded Carts to join Wealdstone from Edgware and what a stalwart he turned out to be! As goalkeepers go, he wasn't the biggest, but he had a voice like a foghorn! Many a night, I would go to bed with the sound of *"SQUEEEEEEEEEZZZZZZEEEEEEEE"* ringing in my ears! A great organiser of a defence and a phenomenal shot stopper, he was my travel buddy for a couple of years and I shared many a laugh with him. Surprisingly really, as he is a Welshman.
Marvin Morgan (Starvin)	Marv broke into the Wealdstone team as a sixteen-year-old, during my second spell at the club. He was a very skinny, gangly, cumbersome teenager at first, but had a tremendous work rate. He developed into a very good striker but was not exactly prolific, then he got his chance at a higher level and blossomed for a few seasons. He's a great lad who I have a lot of time for. I think he always respected me, as I was forever in his ear lending him advice. He worked hard for his opportunity and indeed, now has a very successful clothing business on the go!
Mick Swaysland	On his day Mickie was unplayable. On other days you wouldn't even know he was playing. He's too nice a bloke to be ruthless but he has scored goals whatever level he played at. A very quiet unassuming fella, on the field, goals win games and he certainly won a few for us at Wealdstone. I linked up with him again at Hemel and guess what...he scored goals. More recently, I played against him for Edgware – he scored.

Tony Smith	Tony played a part in our Championship winning team at Wealdstone as a very skilful midfield player who chipped in with a few goals as well. Another who played with a smile on his face, generally a happy go lucky chap, nothing seemed to faze him. I always thought that song was made for him: *"Don't worry be happy"*
Ian Waugh	A major lynchpin for the 'Stones as we progressed through the divisions. His recovery pace was second to none, which was just as well as he needed it a lot! Waughy thought he was a bit of a #baller, so tried to play a bit at times and got caught in possession. His lightning pace was then needed to get him out of the s@@t! He complimented me well as I had aerial prowess, was left sided and had no pace. Once he realised he was there just to defend, he was at times impossible to get past. Very stubborn and outspoken at times, he couldn't be taken seriously with his outbursts as he was too articulate. It was usually a case of *"yeah whatever"* and we got on with it.
Fred Cummings	Fred is by far the best coach I've had in non-league. A no nonsense military style, his training sessions weren't for everyone, but they worked for me. He's never wanted to manage so he felt he could say it how it was. ...and he does. I've shared many a pint with him over the years as I rate his opinions very highly and he is still not shy of telling me how it is, which I respect and benefit from. Cheers Fred, you are a diamond.
Steve Toms	Another great character from the Uxbridge days, I still find it amazing how he managed to fit his massive head into many a small changing room! One of the most limited centre backs / centre midfielders I have ever played with, but he made up for it with his pure aggression and determination. He was a bit of a jack the lad round the Watford area, but we always brought him down to earth, continuously slaughtering him about his ability, then he'd respond with a goal or a great display. A big character in every sense of the word who you would want in the trenches with you, Tomsy excelled in the bar with his larger than life personality and another I'm delighted to say remains a friend today.
Leo Morris (LFM)	Gordon's right hand man for most of his career, it's no surprise that he's in charge of the bar facilities at Wealdstone. Proper 'old skool', Leo loves a beer and a fag. He went about his job quietly and loyally as GB's assistant, yet we players could have a beer with Leo and tell him what we thought, knowing that it wouldn't go any further unless it was a necessity for the team. He's a great bloke and always fantastic company when I pop over to the 'Stones now as an opponent or just as a fan.
Paul Rumens Mr Wealdstone!	Paul filled various positions at Wealdstone, but I still call him Mr Chairman. That was his role when I first went there as a player. That first season he put no pressure at all on us as players announcing to the press *"Wealdstone will walk the league!"* Knowing him, he'll say the same thing

now as his passion for the club cannot be underestimated. He was a major reason the club survived its nomadic years, continuing to raise money through the hard times. A bloody good job well done, he's a kind-hearted man who bleeds Wealdstone and he probably saw that it me too, he remains one of many friends forever at Wealdstone FC.

Paul Fruin (Fingers)

Legend! Enough said! Unless you're 'in the know' at Wealdstone FC you won't appreciate how much this man does for the club. To try and sum it up in a few paragraphs would be unfair, so in case I've never said it before, I will say *"Thank You"* to Fingers, not just from me but on behalf of every player and fan of any club that has ever set foot in the various Wealdstone grounds. Thanks for making the facilities top notch and for always giving us a warm welcome. Magnificent.

Gilly (Mark Gill, but no-one calls him Mark!)

Another of the Uxbridge 'old skool'! Gilly would agree that he was one of the laziest players in the history of non-league, but then he'd point you at his 'goals scored'. For someone who had no pace and no right foot, he scored loads of goals from his goal-hanging left-wing position. He definitely knew where the goal was, the flicked-on near-post header from a corner was a particular speciality! Off the field, how he came back alive from some of the Blackpool trips is amazing too. He seemed to be semi-conscious from the first Champagne & Brandy mix at 8am on the train from Euston, but 'World Cup Gilly' always survived till the end...

Neil Twelfree) (The Tradesman)

I will be forever indebted to this man for making me a National Sunday Cup winner with the Duke of York Northampton. He never managed a Saturday side, but I think he would have been a great success if he had. He knew everybody in the Northants area and was quite ruthless, focused on what he wanted to achieve, winning the FA Sunday cup. He managed, coached and knew how to mix it socially and that helped him know and judge players – he could see I was a bag of pooh in that dramatic semi-final win, but he knew I'd be OK for the final. That gave me my greatest day and I hope I helped give him that same feeling.

James Duncan

We never played with each other at Wealdstone but that's where I got to know him. As I continued to live the dream, JD forged himself a career in coaching and has now progressed into management. Without his help, I may not have seen my first season through, he loaned me players but most of all, he was one of the few always there to listen to my moans and groans (and offer me advice!) He has done a magnificent job so early in his managerial career and I'd be stupid if I didn't listen to his words of wisdom – he also takes whatever stick I dish out to him as he knows it's only my jealousy and bitterness shining through. Hopefully in time, I'll get to his level and I won't have to beg as much...

Lee Chappell

Cheeky chappie is our Lee! He took a lot of unwarranted stick in his Wealdstone career but deserves a mention as he is one of very few players who in recent times has played more games for Wealdstone than I. He occasionally let's his exuberance run away with him, but all credit to him for the level of football he has played over a ten-year period. Now I get to hear his dulcet tones again as he's just signed for Hendon.

Dave Ryan (Rhino)	A real gentle giant and a more than decent player for the 'Stones, though I only ever played against him! He was an instrumental part of their promotion season and the play-off with Dulwich Hamlet which saw them rise to the Ryman Premier Division. (More success after I'd left!) I'll always remember him for the stick I gave him when he was marking me and I scored on my return for Hemel at the White Lion ground. He took it well and didn't hold it against me, as I ran a commentary of the goal throughout the night in the Change of Hart afterwards!
Robin Tucker (Tucks)	Tucks was another of the Milton Keynes / Northampton crew that was encouraged to ply their trade by Chairman Paul Rumens at Wealdstone. He got one or two to sign and they had a mate....you know the rest. Tucks was quite simply too nice to be a centre half, a genuine lovely fella and another who could only give 110% every game. He scored the goal that stopped Stones being relegated at Salisbury, a 1-4 defeat but the 1 meant they survived by about 0.3 of a goal. A great clubman as well.
James Gray	We briefly had a spell as teammates at Wealdstone and he is now our landlord's manager. He was a no-nonsense centre half who occasionally played centre forward as well. I'll always remember him coming up to me in his first session at Wealdstone and saying that I was the person he was told that he should be like. It was a nice compliment and Jimmy went on to show the commitment and desire that I always had, so in a way he achieved that goal. I think we have a mutual respect and I hope that that will help in the relationship with Hendon!
John Lawford	A great goal scorer at whatever level in his prime, it's just a shame that I wasn't around to see it. We shared a spell at Hemel together and became good friends, though by then he was a poacher as a striker as he certainly didn't like running. Like Swaysie, the stats say goals win games and he certainly won a few with the amount of goals he got.
Chris Moore	A gem discovered by George Talbot at Uxbridge (after I left), he went on to have great success in the pro game with Brentford and Dagenham. I first met him when I was invited to join an Uxbridge 'Blackpool trip' even though I was at Wealdstone. I soon saw that he had the Uxbridge mentality of partying hard. Chris is another who is now taking his first steps as a manager at Hanwell Town, and I'm sure our paths will cross over a post-match beer soon!
Wayne Carter	Joint assistant manager with Chris Moore at Hanwell Town. When I was an apprentice at Brentford, Wayne's mum ran the canteen where all of

us YTS boys were given lunch. We'd see him running around, causing mayhem as a 7 or 8-year-old. He went on to play at Wealdstone and Uxbridge and also Northwood where I played alongside him. He's another typical Uxbridge character who enjoyed the after match more than pre-match, but he is a great bloke to be with. Except against us, I'm sure he'll do well in management!

Ashley Bayes (Bayzo)	They say goalkeepers are mad and I can vouch for that with Bayzo. He's another from my Brentford YTS days, though he's gone up the footballing ladder as I have slipped down the snake into the lower leagues. He played professionally for Torquay, Exeter and Leyton Orient amongst others, then Stevenage and Grays most notably in non-league. He is an absolute nutter whose enthusiasm for football is beyond belief. He came down from Lincoln with no fashion sense and he couldn't dance. Now, he's the best dressed in the business and no one can beat his moves to any Madness tune! A fans favourite at every club as his desire and passion spreads like wild fire, he's an unbelievably infectious character still living the dream as AFC Wimbledon goalkeeping coach and doing a fantastic job!!
Andy Driscoll	A long-time friend from schoolboy football who was also YTS at Brentford, Andy is another bubbly character who broke into the first team at the Bees at an early age. Unfortunately, he suffered a couple of knee injuries that soon curtailed his professional career. At the time he was a bit of a rarity as he wasn't a lover of alcohol, but he used to join in on team nights out, often with hilarious results as you can imagine. I will leave it there....
Luke Garrard	Doing an amazing job at National League side Borehamwood as manager. Luke is a clean-cut type that I tried to lead into mischievous ways, but it never worked. I gave him lifts when we teamed up for a short period at Northwood before he joined AFC Wimbledon. I thought he'd cut short his career, finishing as a player quite early, but he obviously knew what he was doing embarking on his managerial career. I like Luke a lot and take a lot of pride in the great job he is doing at my local club. Who knows what would have happened if I had managed to lead him astray in those early years...
Danny Hunter	The Chairman of Boreham Wood, who had a dream to get his club noticed and boy has he done it, a terrific example of making a small club big. I played there when they were ICIS Division One, and just last season they were one game away from being a football league club. To be successful you have to be ruthless and make decisions that people don't like: Danny has had to make them to get his club where they are today, but what you can't argue with is the stature of the club and infrastructure that he has built. I always pass on my congratulations and best wishes to Danny when I see him Boreham Wood games.